Supporting Students with School Attendance Challenges

For some students, school is not a place of growth and opportunity—it is a source of overwhelming anxiety and distress. Behind every empty desk lies a complex story of a child who often feels unseen, unheard, and disconnected from the school community. This illuminating book reveals the hidden world of school-avoidant students through an attachment-theory lens. These are not simply "truant" children making defiant choices—they are young people whose emotional dysregulation has led them to withdraw as a survival strategy. Drawing from extensive research and real-life cases, this volume offers deep insights into the psychology of school avoidance, providing practical strategies that honor student autonomy and self-determination, along with inspiring stories of successful reengagement and healing. Whether you are a concerned parent, dedicated educator, or school mental health professional, this guide provides a roadmap for reconnection. By understanding the true nature of school avoidance, we can build the supportive environments these students need to return to learning with dignity and hope.

Monica L. Mandell, PhD, LMSW, is a bilingual social worker with extensive experience working with students and their families to develop individualized educational plans (IEPs) that address both academic and social needs. Her dissertation focused on understanding how school personnel view and interact with school-avoidant students. As part of her research, she developed a scale to assist school personnel in identifying quiet students who may be at risk for school avoidance. She is currently an adjunct faculty member at the Wurzweiler School of Social Work at Yeshiva University, where she teaches MSW and doctoral students. Additionally, Dr. Mandell runs MLM Advocacy, which helps students access special education services, mental health support, and a full circle of holistic services. She also works with a nonprofit organization to support school-avoidant students and assist families in obtaining IEPs. She is a member of the International School Avoidance Network (INSA) and has presented on using attachment theory when helping school-avoidant students, as well as on attendance policy.

Also Available from Routledge Eye on Education

www.routledge.com/k-12

Challenging Common Myths of Teaching
Practical Strategies to Transform Learners
Thomas R. Rosebrough

How to Have Difficult Conversations as an Educational Leader
Self-Reflections and Strategies for Success
Patty Corum

From Empathy to Action
Empowering K–6 Students to Create Change Through Reading, Writing, and Research
Chris Hass, Katie Kelly, Lester Laminack

Handbook of Mental Wellness Strategies for Educators
Research-Based Best Practices
Ken Badley, Genie Kim, Iriel Jaroslavsky Rindlisbacher

Supporting Students with School Attendance Challenges
A Collaborative Guide for Educators, Families and Therapists
Monica L. Mandell

Supporting Students with School Attendance Challenges

A Collaborative Guide for Educators, Families and Therapists

Monica L. Mandell

Routledge
Taylor & Francis Group
NEW YORK AND LONDON

Designed cover image: Getty

First published 2026
by Routledge
605 Third Avenue, New York, NY 10158

and by Routledge
4 Park Square, Milton Park, Abingdon, Oxon, OX14 4RN

Routledge is an imprint of the Taylor & Francis Group, an informa business

ISBN: 978-1-041-22215-6 (hbk)
ISBN: 978-1-041-22216-3 (pbk)
ISBN: 978-1-003-73122-1 (ebk)

DOI: 10.4324/9781003731221

Typeset in Optima
by Apex CoVantage, LLC

Contents

Acknowledgments

The idea for this book began in 2011 when I met a student who refused to attend school. He did not give a reason for not attending school but did state that he preferred to play video games. I remember sitting at a table filled with school district members and the students' parents and wondering how we, as a team, were going to get him back to school because he absolutely refused to attend. I was confounded as to how to help because there was so little information about what a school-avoidant student was and how to best reengage a school-avoidant student back to their school community. This sparked curiosity about the relational aspect (or lack therof) of a school-avoidant student, propelling me toward a Ph.D. in social work. My dissertation focused on better understanding the relational aspect of school avoidance using attachment theory as my theoretical framework. I defended in 2022 at the Wurzweiler School of Social Work and have been continuously curious about how a dysregulated attachment impacts decision-making and establishing and maintaining functioning relationships both familial and social.

My journey from my PhD to this book was helped along by an editor, Ian M. Rogers, who answered an email about helping me with writing an article based on my dissertation. My trust in Ian was instantaneous as he is thoughtful about his editing, always asking questions to ensure that my voice is not lost in the words that I write. One day, I asked him about this crazy idea of writing a book on school avoidance and he jumped at the idea. From the beginning, Ian has been and continues to be the most encouraging editor, and my gratitude is immense. I also want to thank the editorial team at Francis and Taylor who incredibly decided to take this book over the finish line! Truly an honor to work with all of you!

This book could not have been written without the research from my colleagues at the International Network for School Avoidance. INSA, based in the Netherlands, is an international organization dedicated to researching and understanding the purpose of school avoidance. They are at the forefront of evidence-based research analyzing school avoidance as a multifactorial concern.

To my family, whose love is boundless and is never avoidant.

To my family: first to my own children, Zachary, his wife Tricia, Sammy, his girlfriend Virginia and Danny, whose constant support, laughter and love kept me sane while I wrote about these student stories. To my grandson, Dylan, who knew enough to sleep at least an hour and a half during nap time so that I could both babysit and write a few chapters. My mother Molly Nozyce, my sister, Susan Nozyce Schwartz, my brother-in-law, Joel Schwartz and my niece Rachel and nephew Jeremy for their encouragement and excitement about this book! And, from the other side, my father, Maximo Nozyce, who I know has been guiding me along this journey.

Although last on this dedication, but never least, my husband Mitchell, whose support never wavered. His cheerleading and pride in this accomplishment is more than I could have asked for. This book is in fact my husband's idea, as he knew these stories were powerful and needed to be told. He listened over countless days, meals, and vacations about these stories and how these students' motivations were unique. Mitchell, my love for you is beyond measure and I am not sure that a thank you is enough, but it is a good place to start and so I thank you with all my heart.

Client Acknowledgments

KL: Dr. Monica L. Mandell combines her deep clinical knowledge and human-centered approach to illuminate the complexities of school avoidance. Her writing bridges research and practice, offering readers a roadmap grounded in empathy, insight, and achievable solutions. With clarity and compassion, she helps readers understand the emotional, behavioral, and systemic factors that contribute to avoidance. Dr. Monica L. Mandell reminds us that progress is possible when understanding meets action, and that every child deserves the opportunity to feel safe, capable, and connected at school. Her calm, reassuring personality is evident in the pages of her writing, empowering families and schools to navigate challenges with confidence and clarity. This book is both a guide and an inspiration for those committed to helping students reengage and thrive.

DR: Without Monica's help, my son would never be where he is today. She played a pivotal role advocating for him so that he could get into the right program to meet his educational needs.

1 The Complex Layers of School Avoidance

This book is about five students who are school-avoidant. They do not live near one another, and they are not friends. Their decision to stop attending school was neither sudden nor due to an abrupt change. Rather, it was a slow, steady walk toward a decision that could have significantly impacted their futures. Alejandro, Brandon, Sandra, Nathan, and Ivan are five students who are school-avoidant, and each of them faces unique challenges that have significantly impacted their educational journeys. Although for different reasons, these five students felt isolated from the school community and believed they had to disconnect and disengage. This was not an act of defiance but a protective measure—an emotional shield against their intense anxiety about participating in school life. Ultimately, this led to a dysregulated attachment to their school, its staff, and their peers.

While each of these students is school-avoidant due to their insecure and disorganized attachment to the school community, they each have their own unique stories and reasons for their decisions. Starting in eighth grade, Alejandro began to slowly and quietly withdraw from his school community after the sudden deportation of his father, which left him feeling unsafe about leaving home. Because Alejandro's mother worked an early morning shift at a local fast-food restaurant, she would return home after he had left for school. This meant that if Alejandro attended school, he would not know if his mother arrived home safely. Thus, he would remain awake, in his bed, until he heard her come into the house. He would then fall asleep, missing the school bus and the school day.

Brandon felt that it was more important to protect his mother from an abusive father than to attend school. Although he cited an argument with a friend as the reason for his absence from the school community, the truth was that Brandon was deeply committed to ensuring his mother's safety, making daily school attendance impossible. Given that Brandon's family had experienced domestic abuse, Brandon's commitment to ensuring his mother's safety was a manifestation of his intense attachment to her; thus, attending school was not possible for him.

DOI: 10.4324/9781003731221-1

Sandra was finishing up fifth grade when schools shut down due to COVID-19 federal mandates. As a fifth grader, Sandra thoroughly enjoyed attending school and was an active participant in all school-related activities and social events with peers and friends. However, as school closures and remote learning stretched into the spring of 2020, Sandra became more and more anxious and scared about returning to a school environment on the first day of sixth grade in September. Her anxiety became so intense that her once-healthy attachment to the school environment was now marked by emotional insecurities and dysregulation. She needed a smaller, more supportive school setting where she could better manage her feelings with the help of staff who intimately understood her emotional needs.

Nathan had a complicated relationship with his school community, leading to a disorganized attachment that he could never rely on for gaining academic skills. Multiple suspensions from elementary to high school caused him to lose significant time, making it easier for Nathan to avoid school altogether rather than risk being suspended again for a minor infraction. In the classroom, Nathan had trouble understanding content and classroom direction. He was not easily soothed, required constant redirection, and was easily frustrated. Despite attempts by school personnel to teach him coping skills, his inability to regulate his emotions led to numerous suspensions, shifting the focus to his maladaptive behaviors rather than understanding their underlying causes.

Last is Ivan, who felt that he was not provided a voice in how he wanted to be educated or which school he wanted to attend. Ivan felt marginalized, overshadowed by school officials, and denied the opportunity for self-determination and autonomy, leaving him disconnected and unsupported. His story reflects the conflict between school officials' obligations to ensure that Ivan attended school—where he could reconnect with the school community, maintain academic rigor, and build friendships with peers—and the extent to which they should have granted Ivan autonomy. Ultimately, Ivan's experience underscores the tension and challenges schools face in balancing administrative responsibility with a student's right to self-determination.

Accordingly, this book aims to examine how students' feelings of isolation, disconnection, and lack of attachment can contribute to a decision to avoid school. School avoidance can be understood through the lens of attachment theory, which conceptualizes attachment as the emotional bond that helps children feel secure during times of anxiety.[1] Attachment theory suggests that early relationships with caregivers shape an individual's ability to form secure relationships and adapt to social environments. The same concept can be applied to students and their relationship with a school community. When students exhibit school avoidance, it can often be traced back to feeling that they have an insecure attachment within the school community and do not feel emotionally safe to take academic and social risks.

Thus, students' inability to regulate their attachment to the school community prevents them from maintaining a stable relationship with the school community. Intense feelings of anxiety may lead to insecure and disorganized attachments, causing a student to avoid school at all costs.[2] And, ultimately, students like Alejandro, Brandon, Sandra, Nathan, and Ivan feel that no one can provide a safety net for their emotional distress. As a result, they believe that staying attached to the school community only exacerbates their anxiety rather than serving as an emotional bond that protects them from their feelings of anxiety.

The Importance of a School Community

Understanding school avoidance within the context of attachment theory is crucial because it helps to identify the underlying emotional and relational issues that contribute to a student's avoidance behavior. However, to better understand school-avoidant students and their fragile connection and insecure attachment to the school community, it is important to also view school avoidance as a reflection of feeling isolated within a boisterous school environment. The need to belong, and to feel accepted, respected, included, and supported is a fundamental aspect of the school experience,[3] as it promotes better academic functioning and maintains emotional well-being.

A school community offers more than just an opportunity to learn new facts based on previously acquired knowledge: it also provides a space where students can experience a sense of belonging, feel valued, and have the opportunity to both succeed and fail with the support of the community. Members feel that they are important because they experience a shared emotional connection, as well as opportunities to engage in collaborative, experiential learning.[4] In a school community, students function as a social group, and how inclusive or exclusive this group is depends on how well a teacher and school community design and maintain communal activities in which all can share and contribute.[5]

At the same time, a school community is also defined as a community where achievement and mastery are the goals, and where there is a reward for compliance and a punishment for disobedience. The focus on individual success does not easily align with building and maintaining a sense of community or fostering a belief in shared experiences. If a sense of relatedness is absent in a school community, a student's emotional well-being will not be well supported, leading to diminished motivation to attend school or maintain an attachment to the school community. Thus, even though a school community promotes inclusion, some students feel lonely and isolated, even within a supportive environment. This is known as *social exclusion*, which is defined as the absence of intimate and meaningful relationships with others.[6] Social exclusion reflects a lonelier school experience that can lead to social problems, poor academic functioning, decreased feelings of resilience, and poor self-esteem. Students who feel lonely and socially excluded will be at risk for both internalizing and externalizing behaviors that will significantly impact their relationship with the school community, leading to disengagement and eventual detachment from the school community.

A school community plays an important role in other factors such as attitude and motivation to attend school, a commitment to following rules, feeling that the school is a safe place both physically and emotionally, and trust that the student has a voice that will be respected and validated by both staff and peers.[7] Accordingly, a school community represents social bonding between the student and the school. If students perceive their bond with the school to be weak or not available, they are more likely to view absence as a preferable option to the consequences of discipline, poor academic achievement, or losing access to social connections with friends and peers at school.[8]

For many students, the school community provides a positive relationship in which the student is encouraged and supported within all spheres of the school experience. However, for a subset of students, a boisterous and active school community feels overwhelming and can be difficult to manage. These students begin to disengage from a school experience that includes learning, teachers, and peers because they doubt the responsiveness of the school community during their times of emotional crisis and need. As a result, school-avoidant students will utilize a variety of strategies to deactivate their attachment to a school community. For school-avoidant students, the act of detaching themselves is a self-protective measure against feelings of stress and anxiety.[9] These students can easily go unnoticed in a busy, interactive school environment, with their absence only becoming a concern when daily attendance is compromised.

Why Is Attendance Important?

Daily school attendance is the foundation upon which a student's future success is built. Even missing just one or two days a month can significantly impact learning outcomes, as consistent attendance is essential for academic achievement, developing social skills, and nurturing soft skills such as teamwork, persistence, and problem-solving resilience.[10] Missing school due to nonattendance can lead to various detrimental outcomes, including mental health concerns like anxiety and depression, as well as an increased risk of dropping out.[11] Other concerns such as influenza, strep, gastroenteritis, fractures, asthma, diabetes, chronic fatigue, chronic pain, or obesity can also affect daily school attendance.[12] Although it is expected for students to be absent when sick, absences can quickly add up, leading to chronic absenteeism. If a student has multiple health concerns that are untreated or unrecognized, or the student lacks access to medical care, the student may feel too sick to attend school, causing interrupted learning and chronic absence.[13]

No matter the reason, students who miss school days receive fewer hours of instruction and miss valuable opportunities for interactions with teachers and peers in school-related activities. This can lead to poor academic and socioemotional outcomes later in life.[14] Simply put, teachers cannot effectively teach students who are absent, as making up missed lessons and assignments in a fast-paced school environment is nearly impossible. Even one day of missed instructional time widens the gap between what has been learned and what has not, making it increasingly difficult for students to catch up.[15] In other words, every school day, every classroom learning opportunity, and every chance to socially engage with peers is vitally important and has a significant impact on students' future success.

The importance of daily school attendance begins in the early elementary school years when children are learning and incorporating foundational basic social and academic skills and developing critical thinking methods. Starting in kindergarten, students who are chronically absent will not have daily learning experiences and will thereby have fewer approaches to learning organizational skills, a decreased ability to work independently, less eagerness to learn, and an increase in internalized behaviors such as disengagement and feeling isolated and anxious.[16] If the absences continue throughout elementary school, this increases the likelihood that a student will become disengaged and school-avoidant.

By third grade, if daily attendance was inconsistent starting in kindergarten, this can result in lower competency levels in math, reading, and general knowledge skills, and may require additional support to catch up. In other words, inconsistent attendance can result in sporadic participation in school, which can lead to difficulties in developing the skills needed to perform tasks effectively. This inconsistency may result in struggles with academic performance, social interactions, or other areas requiring proficiency, as students miss essential opportunities for learning and growth. Moreover, it becomes more difficult and costlier to help these students,[17] which exacerbates the problem as these students move up through the grades. By the time the student enters high school, there may be a long history of chronic absenteeism with limited time to catch up. This results in persistently lower academic achievement, increasing the risk of school failure and potentially leading to school avoidance.

This decline in academic performance diminishes the student's desire to stay connected to the school community. When students perceive that the school cannot meet their needs or provide adequate support, they become detached, leading to feelings of insecurity and disorganization in their attachment to the school community.

How Is Attendance Defined?

Daily attendance is the foundation for a student's successful completion and graduation from high school. According to the U.S. Department of Education, every grade level in the nation's 16,800 school districts faces challenges with students who are chronically absent or truant. In the 2020–2021 school year, the number of students who were chronically absent or truant nearly doubled from 8 million students in the 2017–2018 school year to 14.7 million students nationwide.[18] Thus, from the 2018–2019 school year to the 2021–2022 school year, in every state, chronic absenteeism and truancy rose from 14.8% in the 2018–2019 school year and skyrocketed to 28.3% in the 2021–2022 school year.[19] These alarming trends underscore the importance of daily attendance, as student success depends on consistent, active engagement with their school community.

Attendance is tracked across various types of schools within the U.S. educational system, including public, private, and charter schools, as well as alternative educational programs like career and technical education and homeschooling. All of these programs exist within a decentralized system in which the provision of education is considered to be the primary responsibility of each state.[20] Each state has school districts that operate within residential boundaries that are administered and financed by both the local communities via property and school taxes as well as by their respective state department of education. Although school districts have considerable local control, they must comply with federal and state laws, along with local policies and procedures concerning the recording and reporting of attendance and absenteeism data.

All school districts nationwide define attendance as the number of students who attend school each day. Attendance is taken either once a day, or by class periods for older students. School districts also take average daily attendance as the total number of student attendance days divided by the number of instructional days during a specified time period for funding purposes. Broadly, attendance is made up of student behaviors, policies, procedures, and protocols that count the number of students who attend using a database system such as Power School, Infinite Campus, or RaWee to track days present or absent from school.[21]

Continued absence from daily school attendance can generally be understood within three broad categories. The first category includes students who may not attend school due to illness, family responsibilities, lack of steady housing, family instability, or because they are involved in the criminal justice system. The second category includes students who do not feel safe at school due to bullying or unsafe conditions. Furthermore, the third category includes students who have been suspended and miss school for the duration of the suspension or who have been expelled from the school community.

Federal Laws Regarding Attendance

In 2013, under the guidance of the Office of Civil Rights, federal law began to require all state educational departments and schools serving kindergarten to twelfth grade to report the percentage of students who were chronically absent, as well as other types of absences such as excused absences, unexcused absences, and absences due to disciplinary actions.[22] In 2015, the No Child Left Behind Act was reauthorized and renamed the Every Student Succeeds Act (ESSA), a federal educational policy that requires each state to develop rigorous plans aimed at closing achievement gaps, increasing equity, and improving both the quality and outcomes of education for all students. The ESSA also specifically requires states to report chronic absenteeism and truancy rates, and districts can use federal dollars on training programs to help reduce the problem. This was the first time that the Department of Education began to address and provide additional funding for a longstanding attendance problem in all school districts.

Alongside the ESSA, there are also compulsory education laws in all 50 states and Washington, D.C. Compulsory education is a series of state legislative mandates for attendance in a public school or authorized alternative school program for students within a certain age range for specific periods of time within a school year. Compulsory education also includes admission and exit ages, the length of a school year, enrollment requirements, waivers and exceptions, alternative educational programs, and enforcement and truancy provisions. Compulsory education varies by state, as does the age range: for example, Alabama's compulsory education ranges from ages 5 to 17, Arizona's from 5 to 21, Connecticut's from 5 to 21, and Florida's from 6 to 16. Enforcement of compulsory attendance laws occurs through local school attendance officers, school superintendents, law enforcement, and/or local juvenile courts.

Noncompliance with compulsory education laws places responsibility on the parent or guardian, who may face penalties if a child fails to meet attendance requirements. These penalties can include investigation, mediation, misdemeanor charges, and even imprisonment for up to one month. States vary as to whether truancy is treated as a criminal or civil offense, leading to differing enforcement practices across states, and the sample of state policies on punishment for noncompliance below highlights the variation in penalty determinations across states. There is no federal law mandating uniformity in punishment for noncompliance, with each state independently deciding the legal consequences, the duration of penalties, and any associated punitive damages.

For example, in New York State, truancy itself is not considered a crime, but it is taken seriously under the state's compulsory education laws. In New York State, children are mandated to be in school between the ages of 6 and 16. Parents can face legal consequences if they fail to ensure that their children attend school, and may be fined or even jailed if they do not comply with the law, while students who are habitually truant may be subject to school disciplinary actions or intervention programs. A more specific, stricter example is in Indiana, where parents can be charged with Failure to Ensure School Attendance (a Class B Misdemeanor that includes 180 days in jail and a $1,000 fine) or Neglect of a Dependent (a Level 6 felony that includes three years in jail and a $10,000 fine). In Alabama, state law requires parents to provide a valid excuse for the absence, and when a student has five unexcused absences in a school year, the parent or guardian must attend a school conference and participate in an early warning program with juvenile court. If the parent or guardian does not comply and the student has seven unexcused absences, the school will file a complaint in court against the parent or child, and unless the parent or guardian can offer proof for the absences, they will be fined up to $100 dollars and possibly up to 90 days of hard labor. As a final example, in California, absence from school three times in a year and/or being late or away from school counts as an absence. The state has a complex process for addressing truancy that can start with notifying parents about legal rights, having the student attend weekend makeup classes, and meeting with the school to develop a plan for improving attendance. If the student's absences persist, the student may attend a truancy mediation program with community service. Parents can be found guilty with fines and possible jail time for misdemeanor charges for up to a year.

Although every state constitution includes a legal definition for compulsory attendance laws, there is no federal mandate for school attendance, as this is prohibited by the 10th Amendment of the U.S. Constitution. The Tenth Amendment reserves powers not delegated to the federal government, nor prohibited to the states, for the states or the people. The federal government may only intervene in educational matters if it serves the national interest or aligns with the U.S. Constitution. As a result, the provision of education is a state right, and the right to an education is enshrined in each state's constitution.

Consequently, each state, through its department of education, grants local school districts the authority to define chronic absenteeism, truancy, lawful/unlawful absences, habitual truancy, and excused/unexcused absences in their school manuals. There are exceptions and exemptions to the attendance requirements, such as if the student is attending home school because the family prefers homeschooling over attending a public school, or if a student is receiving certified private tutoring because the student is an athlete or performer, is unable to benefit from school because of disabilities such as being wheelchair bound, or if the school is too far from the student's home.

While comparisons of all 50 states' definitions for chronic absenteeism, truancy, lawful/unlawful absence, habitual truancy, and excused/unexcused absence is beyond the scope of this book, a few are highlighted here, as they represent different geographic areas of the United States and can provide an understanding of the similarities and differences in each state. For example, in New York State, where I live, the New York State Department of education defines chronic absences (which includes truancy, lawful/unlawful absence, habitual truant, and excused/unexcused absence) as missing 10% of school days within one academic year for any reason. However, this is different in Illinois, as the state department of education defines truancy as a student who is absent without valid cause for 5% or more of the previous 180 days and allows for nonattendance due to illness, religious observance, or family emergency. There is no definition for students who are chronically absent.

The ESSA mandates that states collect and report data on chronic absenteeism, truancy, lawful/unlawful absences, habitual truancy, and excused/unexcused absences, while compulsory education laws are designed to enforce daily attendance. Although the intent of these policies is to ensure regular attendance, the result is that both ESSA and compulsory education laws can criminalize students who do not attend school consistently. While there is a known correlation between attendance and achievement, neither ESSA nor compulsory education laws address the potential underlying causes of absenteeism. Factors such as family economic status, race, the need for a student to care for a family member, poverty, lack of affordable housing, limited access to health care, housing instability, and homelessness all contribute to chronic absenteeism.[23] When these and other factors are not considered, punitive measures can further alienate students, deepening their disengagement and making it even harder for them to reconnect with the school community.

The History of Chronic Absenteeism and Truancy in the United States

The history of compulsory education in the United States reflects the English Poor Laws promulgated in 1601, which required that destitute youth receive vocational training in schools.[24] In the United States, the first compulsory education law was enacted in 1642 by the Massachusetts Bay Colony, which transformed the provision of education from a moral imperative to a legal imperative. The law required that supervisors, known as selectmen, were charged with ensuring that parents did not neglect their obligations and were to report to the court any offenses committed by the parent if they neglected their parental duty toward educating their children. This education law was the first attempt at codifying moral and social values, as the law aimed both to train children for labor purposes while at the same time maintaining Puritan religious values.[25] Additionally, these laws became the framework for establishing systematic educational standards that required parental supervision.

By the 1800s, the social landscape of the nation began to change very quickly due to industrialization and increased immigration, which led to bigger and more crowded cities and straining Puritan values. To help integrate the immigrants into American society as well as to embrace American ideals and values, the idea for a common school became vitally important, as it would intertwine Puritan/Christian values with democratic values, thereby teaching immigrants how to be patriotic and productive American citizens. From 1852 to 1918, compulsory school attendance was enacted in all states, although there was little uniformity from state to state for the enforceability of these laws, and parents took their children out of school when needed at home.

As the nineteenth century rolled into the twentieth century, there was a movement to reform child labor laws to ensure compliance with compulsory education. However, due to the lack of uniformity in the implementation of child labor laws and compulsory education throughout the nation,[26] many reformers believed it was time for Congressional action. However, pushing reforms and legislation through Congress became difficult, as it was felt by Congress that this was a violation of state rights and therefore unconstitutional.[27] As Congress debated, children were moving between states for jobs in factories or mines and ignoring state law for compulsory education. With increasing public support for curtailing child labor laws so that children could attend school in their hometowns, a law was passed in 1916 using the Commerce Clause of the constitution. The Commerce Clause provided the federal government with a loophole, as it gave Congress the authority to regulate commerce between states or with foreign nations. Upon passage, states could no longer export children to other states for employment, which then paved the way for the development of a systematic regulation for school attendance.

By the beginning of the twentieth century, school attendance was a legal requirement in every state, which allowed schools to hire truant officers with legal power to ensure attendance via the newly enacted passage of the child labor regulations. Moreover, state aid became tied with daily attendance records, which recorded how many students attended on a daily basis, how many parents and children were held legally liable for nonattendance, and how many students were sent to correctional institutions for failure to attend school.[28] Schools also grew in size and complexity, becoming more administrative and bureaucratic, and there was a shift in educational thought that public institutions such as schools were superior in teaching children social and individual development compared to their families. In fact, advocates of compulsory school laws stated that poor and immigrant families could not teach American values that would promote success for future endeavors, with school being the only vehicle for instilling and teaching these values. Compulsory school attendance was also based on the idea that students who did not attend school were truant, and the ones most in need of training.[29] Thus, truant students were seen as most in need of an effective policy that would enforce attendance through legal means, ensuring they stayed off the streets and avoided deviant behavior.

Over the decades and into the twenty-first century, compulsory education policy has remained in place and is enforced at the state and local levels. Although school districts are federally mandated to report absences, daily attendance data only reveals who is not attending school, without offering insights into why a student is absent. As is often the case, the policy regarding daily attendance does not address the diverse needs of students. Attendance policies remain punitive, and fail to consider the emotional needs of school-avoidant students. If a student does not feel supported, validated, or understood by the school community, it can lead to disengagement and school avoidance, leaving the student unheard and unsupported. Thus, to best address attendance policies, attendance policies should not criminalize or legally hold parents or students liable for nonattendance, but rather explore and address the underlying factors that may be contributing to absenteeism.

Punitive Attendance Policies Significantly Affect Attachment to the School Community

Understanding how attendance is defined and the legal framework that school districts use to ensure daily school attendance helps to better reveal how punitive attendance policies alienate and discourage a school-avoidant student from feeling attached to a school community. If their absence has been defined as breaking the law, then there is little reason for school-avoidant students to trust the school community to care for their needs.

Alejandro, Brandon, Sandra, Nathan, and Ivan are illustrative of how ill-equipped school districts are to help school-avoidant students return to a school community, especially when their attachment has been fractured and their lack of daily attendance was defined within a legal definition of attendance. These students should be viewed within the context of attachment theory, and are representative of the many students who are school avoidant because their feelings of attachment to a school community are disorganized and insecure.

This book will use these five students as examples of students whose attachment to a school community has been broken due to intense feelings of anxiety that ultimately compromise their bond with the school community. Each student's challenge will have its own chapter, detailing how that student's attachment was influenced and how it impacted his or her school journey and the outcome, such as referral to an out-of-district placement and the use of mental health providers to address feelings of anxiety. Subsequently, the final chapter will provide methods for how to best address and meet the needs of school-avoidant students, as well as focusing on attendance. Parents, teachers, and other school personnel, school administrators, outside service providers, and most importantly, students could benefit from the toolbox that will be discussed in the final chapter. Overall, the purpose of this book is to highlight school avoidance as a significant concern for students whose attachment is tenuous, and thereby potentially impacting their future success.

Notes

1 John Bowlby, "Grief and Mourning in Infancy and Early Childhood," *Psychoanalytic Study of the Child* 15 (1969).
2 Kelly-Ann Allen et al., "What Schools Need to Know About Fostering School Belonging: A Meta-Analysis," *Educational Psychology Review* 30, no. 1 (2018); David Heyne, "Developments in Classification, Identification, and Intervention for School Refusal and Other Attendance Problems: Introduction to the Special Series," *Cognitive and Behavioral Practice* 26, no. 1 (2019); Christopher A. Kearney and Anne Marie Albano, "The Functional Profiles of School Refusal Behavior. Diagnostic Aspects," *Behavior Modification* 28, no. 1 (2004).
3 Gökmen Arslan, "School Belongingness, Well-Being, and Mental Health among Adolescents: Exploring the Role of Loneliness," *Australian Journal of Psychology* 73, no. 1 (2021).
4 Karen F. Osterman, "Students' Need for Belonging in the School Community," *Review of Educational Research* 70, no. 3 (2000).
5 Arslan, "School Belongingness"; Osterman, "Students' Need for Belonging."
6 Arslan, "School Belongingness."
7 Heather P. Libbey, "Measuring Student Relationships to School: Attachment, Bonding, Connectedness, and Engagement," *Journal of School Health* 74, no. 7 (2004).

8 Gil Keppens and Bram Spruyt, "The Development of Persistent Truant Behaviour: An Exploratory Analysis of Adolescents' Perspectives," *Educational Research* 59, no. 3 (2017).
9 Heike A. Winterheld, "Hiding Feelings for Whose Sake? Attachment Avoidance, Relationship Connectedness, Protective Buffering Intentions," *Emotion* 17, no. 6 (2017).
10 Christopher A. Kearney and Patricia Graczyk, "A Response to Intervention Model to Promote School Attendance and Decrease School Absenteeism," *Child & Youth Care Forum* 43, no. 1 (2014).
11 Allen et al., "What Schools Need to Know"; Heyne, "Developments in Classification"; Kristen N. Sobba, "Correlates and Buffers of School Avoidance: A Review of School Avoidance Literature and Applying Social Capital as a Potential Safeguard," *International Journal of Adolescence & Youth* 24, no. 3 (2018).
12 Mandy A. Allison et al., "The Link between School Attendance and Good Health," *Pediatrics* 143, no. 2 (2019).
13 Allison et al., "School Attendance and Good Health."
14 Gil Keppens, "School Absenteeism and Academic Achievement: Does the Timing of the Absence Matter?" *Learning and Instruction* 86 (2023).
15 Jamie Mahoney, "Daily, Monthly, Yearly Attendance Data Charts: Improved Attendance Equals Improved Achievement Scores," *Children & Schools* 37, no. 2 (2015).
16 Jennifer Freeman et al., "Research-Supported Practices for Improving Attendance in High Schools: A Review of the Literature," *Educational Research and Evaluation* 24, no. 8 (2018).
17 Hedy N. Chang and Mariajosé Romero, "Present, Engaged, and Accounted for: The Critical Importance of Addressing Chronic Absence in the Early Grades," Report, National Center for Children in Poverty, September 2008; Freeman et al., "Research-Supported Practices."
18 Attendance Works, https://www.attendanceworks.org.
19 Fabiola Cineas, "Why So Many Kids Are Still Missing School," *Vox*, January 9, 2024, https://www.vox.com/2024/1/9/23904542/chronic-absenteeism-school-attendance.
20 Patricia A. Graczyk et al., "Searching for Consistency in Attendance Data Recording, Reporting, and Utilization in the USA," *Orbis scholae* 16, no. 2 (2022).
21 Carolyn Gentle-Genitty, James Taylor, and Corinne Renguette, "A Change in the Frame: From Absenteeism to Attendance," *Frontiers in Education* 4, no. 161 (2020).
22 Graczyk et al., "Searching for Consistency."
23 Augustina Reyes, "Compulsory School Attendance: The New American Crime," *Education Sciences* 10, no. 3 (2020).
24 Michael B. Katz, *In the Shadow of the Poorhouse: A Social History of Welfare in America* (New York: Basic Books, 1996).
25 Katz, *In the Shadow of the Poorhouse*.
26 Michael Schuman, "History of Child Labor in the United States—Part 2: The Reform Movement," *Monthly Labor Review*, Bureau of Labor Statistics, January 2017, https://doi.org/10.21916/mlr.2017.2.
27 Schuman, "History of Child Labor."
28 Katz, *In the Shadow of the Poorhouse*.
29 Reyes, "Compulsory School Attendance."

Reference List

Allen, Kelly-Ann, Margaret L. Kern, Dianne Vella-Brodrick, John Hattie, and Lea E. Waters. "What Schools Need to Know about Fostering School Belonging: A Meta-Analysis." *Educational Psychology Review* 30, no. 1 (2018): 1–34.

Allison, Mandy A., Elliot Attisha, Marc Lerner et al. "The Link between School Attendance and Good Health." *Pediatrics* 143, no. 2 (2019).

Arslan, Gökmen. "School Belongingness, Well-Being, and Mental Health among Adolescents: Exploring the Role of Loneliness." *Australian Journal of Psychology* 73, no. 1 (2021): 70–80.

Attendance Works. https://www.attendanceworks.org

Bowlby, John. "Grief and Mourning in Infancy and Early Childhood." *Psychoanalytic Study of the Child* 15 (1969): 9–52.

Chang, Hedy N., and Mariajosé Romero. "Present, Engaged, and Accounted for: The Critical Importance of Addressing Chronic Absence in the Early Grades." Report. National Center for Children in Poverty, September 2008.

Cineas, Fabiola. "Why So Many Kids Are Still Missing School." *Vox*, January 9, 2024. https://www.vox.com/2024/1/9/23904542/chronic-absenteeism-school-attendance

Freeman, Jennifer, Sarah Wilkinson, Jennifer Kowitt, Angus Kittelman, and Brigid K. Flannery. "Research-Supported Practices for Improving Attendance in High Schools: A Review of the Literature." *Educational Research and Evaluation* 24, no. 8 (2018): 481–503.

Gentle-Genitty, Carolyn, James Taylor, and Corinne Renguette. "A Change in the Frame: From Absenteeism to Attendance." *Frontiers in Education* 4, no. 161 (2020).

Graczyk, Patricia A., Carolyn Gentle-Genitty, Amber Humm Patnode, and Sara E. Moulton. "Searching for Consistency in Attendance Data Recording, Reporting, and Utilization in the USA." *Orbis scholae* 16, no. 2 (2022): 75–103.

Heyne, David. "Developments in Classification, Identification, and Intervention for School Refusal and Other Attendance Problems: Introduction to the Special Series." *Cognitive and Behavioral Practice* 26, no. 1 (2019): 1–7.

Katz, Michael B. *In the Shadow of the Poorhouse: A Social History of Welfare in America*. New York: Basic Books, 1996.

Kearney, Christopher A., and Anne Marie Albano. "The Functional Profiles of School Refusal Behavior. Diagnostic Aspects." *Behavior Modification* 28, no. 1 (2004): 147–161.

Kearney, Christopher A., and Patricia Graczyk. "A Response to Intervention Model to Promote School Attendance and Decrease School Absenteeism." *Child & Youth Care Forum* 43, no. 1 (2014): 1–25.

Keppens, Gil. "School Absenteeism and Academic Achievement: Does the Timing of the Absence Matter?" *Learning and Instruction* 86 (2023).

Keppens, Gil, and Bram Spruyt. "The Development of Persistent Truant Behaviour: An Exploratory Analysis of Adolescents' Perspectives." *Educational Research* 59, no. 3 (2017): 353–370.

Libbey, Heather P. "Measuring Student Relationships to School: Attachment, Bonding, Connectedness, and Engagement." *Journal of School Health* 74, no. 7 (2004): 274–283.

Mahoney, Jamie. "Daily, Monthly, Yearly Attendance Data Charts: Improved Attendance Equals Improved Achievement Scores." *Children & Schools* 37, no. 2 (2015): 125–128.

Osterman, Karen F. "Students' Need for Belonging in the School Community." *Review of Educational Research* 70, no. 3 (2000): 323–367.
Schuman, Michael. "History of Child Labor in the United States—Part 2: The Reform Movement." *Monthly Labor Review*. Bureau of Labor Statistics, January 2017. https://doi.org/10.21916/mlr.2017.2.
Sobba, Kristen N. "Correlates and Buffers of School Avoidance: A Review of School Avoidance Literature and Applying Social Capital as a Potential Safeguard." *International Journal of Adolescence & Youth* 24, no. 3 (2018): 380–394.
Reyes, Augustina. "Compulsory School Attendance: The New American Crime." *Education Sciences* 10, no. 3 (2020): 75.
Winterheld, Heike A. "Hiding Feelings for Whose Sake? Attachment Avoidance, Relationship Connectedness, Protective Buffering Intentions." *Emotion* 17, no. 6 (2017): 965–980.

2 Wrapping a Student in Care

In 2019, Alejandro was an eighth grader at a middle school in a large suburban school district in the northeastern United States. The district had 1,500 students split between two middle schools, and each was composed of a racially diverse population, with African American, White, Asian, and mixed race making up just under half of the student body and Hispanic students making up more than half. Nearly half of the student population was also economically disadvantaged, and just under a quarter were English Language Learners. Each school had music and arts, sports, and academic class offerings, PTA, and family-centric services. Both middle schools took pride in their commitment to educating the varied population that walked the halls in preparing them for high school. Fitting into this system was Alejandro, whose profile fit neatly within all three categories: Hispanic, economically disadvantaged, and an English Language Learner.

Alejandro and his family were part of a tight-knit Mexican community, as his parents were originally from Mexico. Alejandro, who was born in the United States, was bilingual, speaking English and Spanish with his friends and Spanish at home. His family included his father, his mother, and two older sisters who attended school in the same district. Both parents worked, but his mother worked part time, which enabled her to be home at three p.m. when Alejandro returned home from school so that dinner could be family time. Alejandro's father coached his soccer team; both of them loved the game, and they would watch televised soccer matches and discuss strategy. Alejandro's family was typical in that both parents worked while the children attended school, played with friends, and participated in family activities.

Alejandro had no problems at school or within the school community and felt secure in his attachments, which provided him with a sense of safety. He had no problems with daily attendance, as he enjoyed learning and being an active participant in school. His friends had been the same since kindergarten, and he would advance from grade to grade with his

DOI: 10.4324/9781003731221-2

friends in each class. Although he was an average student, he was also studious and quiet, and liked being in the classroom. He enjoyed participating in school-wide events and playing soccer for the middle school modified soccer team. His teachers had no complaints about either his attendance or participation. Then, he entered eighth grade.

For Alejandro, eighth grade was a pivotal year, not because he was about to start high school, but because it began a slow slide toward a major decision that could have a significant impact on his life. That slow slide had begun a year earlier, when Alejandro's father was arrested after failing to pay a speeding ticket he had received a few months earlier. He was stopped, again for speeding, and when the police checked his record, they realized that he had failed to pay. Alejandro's father was arrested, and very quickly deported back to Mexico and told that he could never return to the United States. Alejandro and his father were forced to say good-bye to one another via the telephone, with no indication of when they could see each other again. It took only a few minutes to completely alter Alejandro's feeling that he was safely cocooned in the family system.

After his father's deportation, Alejandro began to feel a sense of dread, and worried that when he got home from school every day that his mother would be gone too. In the meantime, his mother had to switch from part-time to full-time work, and, with her limited English, she could only find a job with a local McDonald's that had hours that did not match Alejandro's school day. Alejandro would go to school without seeing his mother in the morning and would often return to find her sleeping. Dinner was prepared earlier in the day, and everyone ate when they felt hungry. What was once a well-defined family system now became individual members living separate lives, and as the youngest member, Alejandro felt increasingly alone as his attachment to his family system weakened and no longer seemed to provide feelings of safety.

By eighth grade, nearly a year after his father was deported, Alejandro had become withdrawn, with little to no participation in school activities. Given his quiet nature, he began to disappear from the school community. At first, he would skip a few classes or not show up at school at all, but by the middle of the school year, school officials became concerned at his chronic absenteeism and truancy, and referred him for initial consideration for special education. Although his mother did not understand why the school requested the initial evaluations, she signed the consent forms allowing the district to evaluate Alejandro and determine his eligibility. At no time did any school official ask Alejandro why he was not attending school on a daily basis; the assumption was that he felt anxious, and therefore required special education. He was found to be eligible, and classified with emotional disturbance during the initial meeting with the committee on special education. He was taken out of his general education classroom and placed in a specialized class with only eight other students, all of whom had significant mental health concerns.

By the ninth grade, the autumn before school closed due to the COVID-19 pandemic, Alejandro began school in his new classroom, but was even quieter than before. His hair often covered his eyes, and he had gained weight. Then, a few weeks into the New Year, he stopped attending school. He remained home, in his bedroom off of the main hallway, across from the kitchen. No sunshine made it through his blinds, and he would lie in bed staring at his phone with his dog at his side. He was able to hear when his mother got home, and when she did, he would then fall asleep. At first, his mother did not notice that Alejandro was staying in his room all day, but, after a few days, the school began calling about his absences and she realized what was happening. That was when the daily ritual of begging and pleading for Alejandro to attend school began—but it was to no avail, as Alejandro refused to leave his bedroom and would not tell his mother why he was not attending school.

Alejandro's decision to disengage and disconnect from his school community was reflective of his intense need to control his feelings of extreme distress. At first, the slide toward self-isolation began with truancy and chronic absence until he finally made the decision to no longer attend school, as he believed his bedroom offered a safer haven from the outside world, where he felt alone and unsafe. Understanding the distinctions in the definitions of *school avoidance, truancy*, and *chronic absenteeism* is very important, as each term has a unique definition. To provide effective support, everyone who supports students such as school principals, school nurses, school social workers, school psychologists, teachers, individual therapists, parents, and the students themselves would benefit from knowing which definition best describes the student. When all members of the team understand the differences between school avoidance, truancy, and chronic absenteeism, it can pave the way for tailored interventions and compassionate support systems that can ultimately guide students like Alejandro toward a path of healing, empowerment, and a return to the classroom.

School Absenteeism Defined as School Avoidance, Truancy, and Chronic Absenteeism

Overall, school absenteeism is an umbrella term that describes all attempts by a student to either skip classes or not attend school for many reasons. In general, students who refuse to attend school are a heterogeneous group of students in gender, income, and racial make-up. School absenteeism can be considered a pernicious problem due to its complex and multilayered set of concerns that encompasses the student, caregivers, family, peers, and school community. Additionally, school absenteeism also includes partial or full-day absences, skipped classes, tardiness, and any behavioral concern that might interfere with daily attendance. There is no one type of student who can be easily identified as school-avoidant. Triggers, as listed, can fit any student profile. Thus, given the nuanced nature of school absenteeism, it is crucial to understand the distinctions between school avoidance, truancy, and chronic absenteeism. This clarity helps identify the most effective support strategies for students struggling with school refusal behaviors.

A *school-avoidant* student is defined as a student who refuses to attend school.[1] Kearney defined a school-avoidant student as a student who is missing large amounts of school time because of internalizing and externalizing behaviors and emotions, noting that school avoidance can also be defined as students who skip classes, habitually arrive late, present with somatic complaints, or have feelings of dread about attending school.[2] In general, a school-avoidant student seeks to avoid aversive social or evaluative situations and will attempt to avoid or escape a school setting.[3]

Refusing to engage with the school community represents a student's final recourse, and consequently, a student might refrain from school avoidance due to its extreme nature, and instead opt for less severe forms of disengagement such as *truancy* or *chronic absenteeism*. While both truancy and chronic absenteeism encompass unexcused absences, their definitions are distinct and precise: *truancy* is defined as frequent, unexcused, or prolonged absence from school,[4] as either a student or parent's decision to miss parts or all of a school day for which the school district did not provide a legitimate excuse for the absence.[5] *Chronic absenteeism*, meanwhile, is defined as missing at least 10% or nearly one month of instructional time in a school year, which may or may not be the result of a mental health issue.[6]

Truancy and chronic absenteeism involve frequent absences, with the student eventually returning to the school community. Although school avoidance is similar in that school-avoidant students are frequently absent, school avoidance entails complete withdrawal, both physically and emotionally, from the school community. While there is overlap between the three terms, understanding why school avoidance becomes the final recourse for a student necessitates understanding the functions it serves for the student. These functions are characterized in four ways: (1) avoiding negative stimulation, (2) escaping aversive social or evaluative situations, (3) gaining attention from a significant other, and (4) pursuing tangible reinforcers outside of school.[7] The four functions stem from internalizing and externalizing behaviors that significantly hinder a student's ability to attend school. Each function serves to maintain the maladaptive behavior or behaviors, and students may engage in school avoidance to fulfill one or more of these functions. No single function is inherently more significant than the others.

The first two functions, which are defined as avoiding negative stimulation and escaping aversive social or evaluative situations, highlight the student's need to diminish emotional arousal that was triggered by the urge to avoid or escape either the negative stimulation (such as a test) or aversive social or evaluative situations. In younger students, the school refusal often revolves around transitions from either being away from home or transitions throughout the school day from class to art, gym, or lunch, while in older students it involves the desire to not participate in evaluations or peer-related activities. The third and fourth functions of gaining attention and pursuing tangible reinforcers outside of school suggest that the student perceives a preferable alternative outside of the school environment. The preferable alternative to attending school is often linked to complex or problematic family dynamics or a desire to ensure the family's safety by staying at home.

Irrespective of whether a student is school-avoidant, truant, or chronically absent, frequent and prolonged absences inevitably lead to a decline in academic performance, peer relationships, and social connections within the school community. While there is overlap among these categories, the key distinction lies in the underlying purpose of the avoidance. Specifically, a school-avoidant student's behavior often reflects internalizing or externalizing challenges that significantly hinder their ability to attend school regularly. This fragile relationship with school can be understood as stemming from a dysregulated and insecure attachment, which amplifies feelings of anxiety. These dynamics underscore the importance of addressing the emotional and relational needs of school-avoidant students to foster a sense of safety, connection, and belonging within the school environment.

Psychodynamic Framework

School avoidance represents an umbrella term that encompasses multiple stressors experienced by school-avoidant students. These stressors can include, but are not limited to, chronic absences, declining academic performances, medical problems, family conflict, trauma, and social isolation. These multifaceted stressors can lead to internalizing and/or externalizing behaviors such as general and social anxiety, depression, fear, fatigue, somatic complaints, tantrums, running away, and employing maladaptive behaviors either in the classroom or at home. Additionally, inconsistent daily attendance that extends over a period of one to two years may indicate a student's decision to stop attending school. Frequent and unexcused absences, particularly on important school days, can act as signals that a student is grappling with overwhelming emotions. Other factors such as school safety, bullying in any form, cultural or family needs, neuropsychiatric disorders, or academic and social pressures can also be factors in the decision to avoid school.[8] Any of these signals can indicate that a student is experiencing feelings of loneliness and isolation.

Thus, a school-avoidant student's limited ability to regulate and maintain emotional stability results in a fractured relationship with the school community, a fragile connection that reflects extreme and heightened feelings of anxiety. When school-avoidant students feel intense anxiety, their emotional response is to protect themselves from the perceived threat, which is the school environment. By avoiding, escaping, or fleeing from the perceived danger, school-avoidant students believe they have control over their anxiety so long as they remain away from the threat. Clearly, feeling anxious is a normal part of our daily lives, as it provides motivation toward being prepared for challenging times; however, for some individuals, such as school-avoidant students, these feelings of anxiety are so intense that they exceed the individual's ability to effectively manage them.

The *Diagnostic and Statistical Manual of Mental Disorders Fifth Edition* (*DSM-5*)[9] defines anxiety as excessive worry and apprehensive expectations occurring more days than not for at least six months about various activities such as work or school performance. To be diagnosed with anxiety, a person must also experience avoidance behaviors that interfere with daily activities. School-avoidant students who are feeling overly anxious will worry about many things that make them feel uncomfortable. They experience a feeling of apprehension about future events that have not yet occurred or may not occur. These feelings of anxiety and worry are intense and disruptive in that they impact sleep patterns and concentration, which can lead to somatic complaints and irritability.

It is not uncommon for a diagnosis of anxiety to also impact a school-avoidant student's mood, which can often lead to depression. According to the *DSM-5*, depression is characterized by a persistent depressed mood, feelings of sadness or hopelessness, and a loss of interest or pleasure in almost all activities.[10] A school-avoidant student experiencing depression may also exhibit irritability, feelings of worthlessness, difficulty concentrating, and indecisiveness, along with physical symptoms such as sleep disturbances and changes in weight. Anxiety and depressive disorders are among the most prevalent mood disorders and are often comorbid, with one condition frequently co-occurring with the other. Anxiety typically emerges during preadolescence and early adolescence, while depression commonly appears during adolescence.[11] Recognizing and addressing anxiety and/or depression early on can be crucial in preventing the development of either mood disorder.

School avoidance can also be defined within a similar context of alienation. Alienation refers to disengagement from the school community because a student has developed negative attitudes toward the school community. Alienation is the student's perception of feeling powerless, that an education will not provide meaning toward the possibility of a future, estrangement from the values of the school community, and self-isolation.[12] Alienation reflects a mismatch between the student and three domains of a school community: learning, teachers, and peer interactions. In the first domain of learning, school-avoidant students may become unmotivated to attend classroom instruction if they feel disinterested or bored. In the second domain, teachers, a teacher is viewed as both a mentor and an authority figure; if a school-avoidant student has a negative relationship with the teacher or perceives the teacher to be unfair, disrespectful, or disengaged, the school-avoidant student will feel emotionally unsafe in the classroom and seek ways to avoid either the classroom experience or the teacher. In the third domain of peer interactions, if school-avoidant students have repeated negative experiences with a peer group or have difficulty finding ways to connect socially, they will avoid social interactions or connections. A school-avoidant student does not have to feel alienated from all three domains, as alienation from even one domain can strongly impact a decision to remain at school.

Indeed, school avoidance can be understood within the framework provided by the *DSM-5* classification for anxiety and depression or as a sense of alienation from the school community. For school personnel and families, a framework can help define a school-avoidant student, particularly one who exhibits heightened feelings of anxiety, depression, or alienation. This framework includes five specific criteria: (1) the student maintains less than 80% attendance for two consecutive school weeks; (2) there is a diagnosis of anxiety and/or depression present; (3) there is parental verification of the student's whereabouts on days marked absent from school; (4) there is the absence of a diagnosis of conduct disorder; and (5) parents commit to collaborating with a team to facilitate the child's return to a school environment.

Finally, school-avoidant students can also be understood within the parameters of learning disabilities, as they often experience co-occurring challenges beyond school refusal itself. These learning disabilities may include neurodevelopmental conditions such as ADD, ADHD, autism spectrum disorder, and learning disabilities involving processing, memory, reading, math, or language. In addition, emotional and trauma-related diagnoses such as separation anxiety and post-traumatic stress disorder can further complicate a student's relationship with school. Each of these diagnoses may create difficulty for any student in a classroom; however, for school-avoidant students, it not only impedes and disrupts the learning process but also contributes to a feeling of confusion and difficulty comprehending academic content. These struggles often pose a challenge for school staff, who may focus primarily on academic understanding while overlooking the underlying emotional function of the avoidance. At the same time, the school-avoidant student experiences heightened anxiety related to academic success, which can intensify feelings of insecurity and self-doubt. As a result, school-avoidant students with co-occurring neurodevelopmental diagnoses may not respond effectively to classroom interventions. School-avoidant students may compare their academic performance or social connections with that of their peers, which can negatively impact the school-avoidant student's self-esteem. Finally, when information sharing between home and school is limited or absent, both sides struggle to reach consensus on decisions regarding the school-avoidant student. This lack of collaboration often leads to fragmentation between home and school systems, resulting in increased stress for students and their families.

Using the *DSM-5* framework to identify and understand anxiety and depression helps to create a shared foundation and diagnostic language for collaboration among teachers, school psychologists, school social workers, nurses, administrators, students, families, and outside providers. With an action plan in place—or the ability to collaboratively design one—this team can offer multiple reentry pathways for the school-avoidant student to reconnect with the school community.

Ultimately, school avoidance is a nuanced issue. Recognizing the signs and implementing a thoughtful, collaborative plan enables parents, schools, and outside service providers to support school-avoidant students in the most compassionate and effective way.

Wrapping a School-Avoidant Student in Care

It is clear that school avoidance is a multifactorial problem, one that is marked by physical and emotional disengagement often driven by feelings of fear of failure, frustration, or denial. Supporting school-avoidant students involves fostering self-determination and emphasizing the significance of human relationships to reengage them with their school community. It requires a commitment from the school-avoidant student, parents, the school community, and outside service providers to work together toward a resolution. However, helping a school-avoidant student return to a school community can be difficult because school communities, outside mental health professionals, and parents have different perspectives about best methods, leading to a disconnected and fragmented set of expectations for the school-avoidant student.[13] Helping to unite the school community, outside mental health professionals, and the family system will provide a unified approach that considers the emotional needs of the school-avoidant student, a multisystem approach known as wraparound service provision.

Wraparound services consider students within their environment, recognizing and validating students' complex emotional and behavioral needs.[14] Wraparound is not a service or set of services; rather, it is a process that is collaborative and culturally responsive. The wraparound process focuses on the design, implementation, and coordination of support networks between the school-avoidant student, families, the school community, and mental health professionals.[15] Developing tailored and targeted supports and interventions will envelope the student in wraparound services that are practical, realistic, and, most importantly, reflect the needs of the student.

Using wraparound services helps to create an atmosphere of collegiality and shared responsibility to target the specific area of need for school-avoidant students. The integration of different systems emphasizes a strength-based set of interventions that are committed to blending all perspectives to achieve consensus on desired outcomes.[16] An effective wraparound team thinks outside of the box to address the unique needs for each individual student. Although school-avoidant students represent a tiny fraction of a school population, they require a significant amount of time and resources to address their needs.

School communities have also begun to recognize that school-avoidant students have chronic and debilitating emotional needs that require a support system that is supportive rather than punitive. A successful team approach using wraparound services uses knowledge and skills from a variety of people that can include school administration, community-based organizations, the department of social services, school staff, parents, teachers, and outside providers such as therapists. This collaborative method provides opportunities and methods for obtaining resources and coordinating services toward helping students access academic and social support that will allow them to learn and succeed.

Thus, a school community, in collaboration with parents and outside mental health providers and other key players, can effectively facilitate the wraparound process because a school community can provide the structure and daily routine of a school day; offer a wide range of student support services such academic remediation, counseling, and daily check-ins with a trusted staff member; provide special education services via the provision of an Individualized Educational Plan; integrate different learning opportunities; and provide positive school interactions.[17]

Alejandro is an example of a student who received all of these services via a wraparound process. The process was initiated by his mother, who felt alone and uninformed about what to do given that Alejandro was refusing to leave the house to attend school. A meeting with the school team was immediately arranged to review his Individual Educational Plan (IEP). This team included Alejandro's guidance counselor, the school social worker, the school psychologist, teachers from both Alejandro's home school as well as his new school placement, Alejandro's mother, Alejandro himself, and his educational advocate. As a team, they collaborated to create opportunities to obtain resources and coordinate services to help Alejandro get back to school.

As a result, Alejandro was able to return to the daily structure and routine of a school day, and he was provided with student support services that included daily individual and group therapy and academic remediation to help him obtain high school credits. Most importantly, Alejandro felt supported due to the positive nature of the wraparound process and the development of services that most reflected his mental health and academic needs. Thus, the wraparound process offers all participants the opportunity to collaborate using positive, strengths-based interventions that consider the specific needs of the school-avoidant student, the family system, and the school community.

Other Types of Interventions

An effective set of interventions to assist school-avoidant students back into school communities depends on the age of the student. Younger students are better able to develop strategies of resiliency compared with older students, who may be experiencing deeper and more intense psychological deficits. The severity of the student's avoidance will influence how effective treatment planning can be. Since the goal is a return to a school community, a variety of different assessments that include behavioral and evaluative assessments are recommended to determine how to best assist the student.

Examples of behavioral and evaluative assessments include structured diagnostic interviews, behavioral checklists, and observations to better understand the function for the avoidance. Diagnostic assessments include those that assess for anxiety as well as other internalizing or externalizing disorders. Examples of scales that have been administered to measure levels of anxiety of school-avoidant students including the Children's Depression Inventory, the Fear Survey Schedule for Children—Revised, the Revised Children's Manifest Anxiety Scale, the Social Anxiety Scale for Children—Revised, the Behavior Assessment System for Children (BASC), and the State-Trait Anxiety Inventory for Children, while parental assessments include the Child-Behavior Checklist and the School Refusal Assessment Scale—Parent. The School Refusal Assessment Scale can measure the function or maintenance of the four different variables of avoidant behavior.[18] Along with this scale, there is the Screen for Child Anxiety Related Emotional Disorders (SCARED), with a subscale for school phobia and the Reasons of School Non-Attendance Scale, which was developed to assess functional types of reasons underlying school nonattendance. The School Refusal Evaluation Scale (SCREEN) can also measure and assess school avoidance.[19] All of the aforementioned scales measure anxiety or depression and focus on the anxiety that may lead to fear or avoidance of the school community. However, they do not measure the student's perceptions, or the feelings of the attachment between the school community and the school-avoidant student.

Initially, parents are often the first to recognize that their student is no longer attending school. In the school community, it is the school social worker, school psychologists, or teacher who can identify a student who is more than chronically absent or truant. No matter who recognizes that the student is school-avoidant, however, a diverse range of approaches is necessary to effectively provide support. Implementing various intervention methods allows for the development of a collaborative plan aimed at assisting school-avoidant students in reintegrating into the school community.

To develop a successful intervention requires an understanding of how to provide therapeutic management of either anxiety or depression alone or as a comorbid diagnosis. Providing in-school or out-of-school therapy and counseling will provide school-avoidant students with strategies to manage their intense feelings of either anxiety or depression. Therapeutic approaches can also include the family system to better address communication and problem-solving needs. Additionally, collaboration and interaction from both school and family is vital in initiating and maintaining a strong support system where daily communication between all members allows for flexibility in thought and purpose. This collaborative approach also allows for referrals to outside agencies and referral to the committee on special education to help develop a plan of action. This collaborative approach helps to determine the nature of the avoidance by compiling data on when and how often the avoidance occurs. It also allows for a better understanding of the reasons for the avoidance and developing a resolution that is reflective of the student's needs, both academically and emotionally.

Targeted intervention can also include developing or maintaining a dedicated attendance team to identify emerging patterns of absences.[20] Various members of a school community can participate, ranging from school principals, school nurses, related service providers, teachers, and lunch attendants—anyone who may have knowledge about problems or concerns. Other members of the team should include outside service providers, thus creating a network of individuals who can provide assistance from medical, mental health, and legal perspectives. Ultimately, the purpose of the team is to identify the warning signs and what would trigger either assessments or referrals to the community early on.[21] Signs that an attendance team might look for include daily attendance taken by a teacher, frequent requests to leave the classroom, visits to the school nurse, remaining quiet in the classroom, or avoiding peer or teacher contact. School-based screening, observations, and monitoring the number and frequency of somatic complaints are other indicators that can lead to identifying risk factors. Other signs might include how a student manages feelings of stress or responds to difficult situations; a history of bullying or difficulties in learning or retaining what is learned in the classroom can also be indicators toward avoidance.

However, ensuring that a school-avoidant student feels safe in the school community is, perhaps, the most important targeted intervention. Forming positive, trusted relationships with adults and peers allows a school-avoidant student to feel safe in a school community and overcome feelings of social isolation. Having a sense of social connectedness or social capital[22] provides school-avoidant students with reciprocal social relationships in which they can trust the community to take care of their needs.[23] This allows for the creation of a sense of psychological safety,[24] which enables school-avoidant students to regulate their feelings of anxiety when overwhelmed and find calmness to be able to return to the classroom.

There are many ways the school community can provide support to school-avoidant students and their families: educating school staff on the early signs of school-avoidance behaviors, working with the family and the attendance monitor on flexible attendance and immediate feedback, providing academic support and a safe place where a school-avoidant student can go when feeling stressed or overly anxious, modifying academic expectations, and increasing participation in group activities, all of which can go a long way in helping a school-avoidant student return to a school community.

Ultimately, respecting the feelings of school-avoidant students as well as ensuring that their feelings matter are vitally important in helping them return to school.[25] Using a multidisciplinary approach with school personnel, family, the student, and outside providers is essential in opening lines of communication. A team-based collaborative coordination that includes school, home, and community-based agencies should be included when developing a plan to help the student toward reentry, even if the student will be placed in another school setting. School options, partial hospitalization, and out-of-district options should be both therapeutic and academic to help the school-avoidant student develop and internalize strategies toward emotional regulation as well as credit recovery.

Alejandro's Return to School

The lengthy process to get Alejandro back into a school community began with acknowledging his feelings about school. He had been spending an increasing amount of time alone, in his small bedroom, and was anxious, irritable, not sleeping well, and complaining of somatic issues. As a result, his feelings of depression and anxiety remained elevated. Alejandro also had a large number of unexcused absences that stretched over a two-year period, and helping him return to a school community required a team approach that included Alejandro, his mother, outside therapeutic service providers, and the committee on special education. This team began to address Alejandro's specific emotional and educational needs, and together they created a safe, planned reentry that included Alejandro being given out-of-district placement at a school that understood the specific needs of school-avoidant students. Alejandro was provided with intense therapy, maintained a flexible schedule, and was allowed to determine which days he would or would not attend school. He was never penalized for nonattendance, but was expected to keep up with his schoolwork via online Zoom sessions. The school worked closely with Alejandro's mother, who remained engaged and invested in Alejandro's success.

Two years after his new placement, Alejandro successfully graduated from high school, with a diploma and an acceptance letter to a local university where he intended to pursue a degree in nursing. His road back to school was filled with bumps, but with a determined team that wrapped and enveloped him with multiple services, Alejandro found that he could feel safe in school and take pride in his accomplishments.

Notes

1 Jo Magne Ingul et al., "Emerging School Refusal: A School-Based Framework for Identifying Early Signs and Risk Factors," *Cognitive and Behavioral Practice*, 26 no. 1 (2019).
2 Christopher A. Kearney, "Forms and Functions of School Refusal Behavior in Youth: An Empirical Analysis of Absenteeism Severity," *Journal of Child Psychology & Psychiatry* 48, no. 1 (2007).
3 Christopher A. Kearney and Anne Marie Albano, "The Functional Profiles of School Refusal Behavior. Diagnostic Aspects," *Behavior Modification* 28, no. 1 (2004).
4 Trude Havik et al., "School Factors Associated with School Refusal- and Truancy-Related Reasons for School Non-Attendance," *Social Psychology of Education* 18, no. 2 (2015).
5 Gil Keppens and Bram Spruyt, "The Development of Persistent Truant Behaviour: An Exploratory Analysis of Adolescents' Perspectives," *Educational Research* 59, no. 3 (2017).
6 Attendance Works, https://www.attendanceworks.org; U.S. Department of Education, Office for Civil Rights, "2015–16 Civil Rights Data Collection: A First Look," Report, 2018.
7 Christopher A. Kearney and Wendy K. Silverman, "A Preliminary Analysis of a Functional Model of Assessment and Treatment for School Refusal Behavior," *Behavior Modification* 14, no. 3 (1990).
8 Nannette Lingenfelter and Sheila Hartung, "School Refusal Behavior," *NASN School Nurse* 30, no. 5 (2015); Mary Wimmer, "School Refusal," *Principal Leadership* 8, no. 8 (2008).
9 American Psychiatric Association, *Diagnostic and Statistical Manual of Mental Disorders: DSM-5-TR* (5th ed., text revision) (Washington, DC: American Psychiatric Association Publishing, 2022).

10 American Psychiatric Association, *DSM-5-TR*.
11 Ned H. Kalin, "The Critical Relationship between Anxiety and Depression," *American Journal of Psychiatry* 177, no. 5 (2020).
12 Tina Hascher and Andreas Hadjar, "School Alienation: Theoretical Approaches and Educational Research," *Educational Research* 60, no. 2 (2018).
13 Lucille Eber and C. Michael Nelson, "School-Based Wraparound Planning: Integrating Services for Students with Emotional and Behavioral Needs," *American Journal of Orthopsychiatry* 67, no. 3 (1997); Lucille Eber et al., "Wraparound and Positive Behavioral Interventions and Supports in the Schools," *Journal of Emotional and Behavioral Disorders* 10, no. 3 (2002); Rondy Yu et al., "Integrating Supports for Students with Wraparound," *Contemporary School Psychology* 26 (2020).
14 Eber and Nelson, "School-Based Wraparound Planning."
15 Eber et al., "Wraparound and Positive Behavioral Interventions"; Yu et al., "Integrating Supports."
16 Eber et al., "Wraparound and Positive Behavioral Interventions."
17 Yu et al., "Integrating Supports."
18 Kearney, "Forms and Functions."
19 Marie Gallé-Tessonneau and Kamel Gana, "Development and Validation of the School Refusal Evaluation Scale for Adolescents," *Journal of Pediatric Psychology* 44, no. 2, (2019).
20 Ingul et al., "Emerging School Refusal."
21 Ingul et al., "Emerging School Refusal."
22 Kristen N. Sobba, "Correlates and Buffers of School Avoidance: A Review of School Avoidance Literature and Applying Social Capital as a Potential Safeguard," *International Journal of Adolescence & Youth* 24, no. 3 (2018).
23 Cathleen Halligan and Sarah Cryer, "Emotionally Based School Avoidance (EBSA): Students' Views of What Works in a Specialist Setting," *Continuity in Education* 3, no. 1 (2022); Sobba, "Correlates and Buffers."
24 Halligan and Cryer, "Emotionally Based School Avoidance."
25 Mohamed Mohamed Elsherbiny, "Using a Preventive Social Work Program for Reducing School Refusal." *Children & Schools* 39, no. 2 (2017).

Reference List

American Psychiatric Association. *Diagnostic and Statistical Manual of Mental Disorders: DSM-5-TR* (5th ed., text revision). Washington, DC: American Psychiatric Association Publishing, 2022.

Attendance Works. https://www.attendanceworks.org.

Eber, Lucille, and C. Michael Nelson. "School-based Wraparound Planning: Integrating Services for Students with Emotional and Behavioral Needs." *American Journal of Orthopsychiatry* 67, no. 3 (1997): 385–395.

Eber, Lucille, George Sugai, Carl R. Smith, and Terrance M. Scott. "Wraparound and Positive Behavioral Interventions and Supports in the Schools." *Journal of Emotional and Behavioral Disorders* 10, no. 3 (2002): 171–180.

Elsherbiny, Mohamed Mohamed. "Using a Preventive Social Work Program for Reducing School Refusal." *Children & Schools* 39, no. 2 (2017): 81–88.

Gallé-Tessonneau, Marie, and Kamel Gana. "Development and Validation of the School Refusal Evaluation Scale for Adolescents." *Journal of Pediatric Psychology* 44, no. 2 (2019): 153–163.

Halligan, Cathleen, and Sarah Cryer. "Emotionally Based School Avoidance (EBSA): Students' Views of What Works in a Specialist Setting." *Continuity in Education* 3, no. 1 (2022): 13–24.
Hascher, Tina, and Andreas Hadjar. "School Alienation: Theoretical Approaches and Educational Research." *Educational Research* 60, no. 2 (2018): 171–188.
Havik, Trude, Edvin Bru, and Sigrun Ertesvåg. "School Factors Associated with School Refusal- and Truancy-Related Reasons for School Non-Attendance." *Social Psychology of Education* 18, no. 2 (2015): 221–240.
Ingul, Jo Magne, Trude Havik, and David Heyne. "Emerging School Refusal: A School-Based Framework for Identifying Early Signs and Risk Factors." *Cognitive and Behavioral Practice* 26 no. 1 (2019): 46–62.
Kalin, Ned H. "The Critical Relationship between Anxiety and Depression." *American Journal of Psychiatry* 177, no. 5 (2020): 365–367.
Kearney, Christopher A. "Forms and Functions of School Refusal Behavior in Youth: An Empirical Analysis of Absenteeism Severity." *Journal of Child Psychology & Psychiatry* 48, no. 1 (2007): 53–61.
Kearney, Christopher A., and Anne Marie Albano. "The Functional Profiles of School Refusal Behavior. Diagnostic Aspects." *Behavior Modification* 28, no. 1 (2004): 147–161.
Kearney, Christopher A., and Wendy K. Silverman. "A Preliminary Analysis of a Functional Model of Assessment and Treatment for School Refusal Behavior." *Behavior Modification* 14, no. 3 (1990): 340–366.
Keppens, Gil, and Bram Spruyt. "The Development of Persistent Truant Behaviour: An Exploratory Analysis of Adolescents' Perspectives." *Educational Research* 59, no. 3 (2017): 353–370.
Lingenfelter, Nannette, and Sheila Hartung. "School Refusal Behavior." *NASN School Nurse* 30, no. 5 (2015): 269–273.
Sobba, Kristen N. "Correlates and Buffers of School Avoidance: A Review of School Avoidance Literature and Applying Social Capital as a Potential Safeguard." *International Journal of Adolescence & Youth* 24, no. 3 (2018): 380–394.
U.S. Department of Education, Office for Civil Rights. "2015–16 Civil Rights Data Collection: A First Look." Report. 2018.
Wimmer, Mary. "School Refusal." *Principal Leadership* 8, no. 8 (2008): 10–14.
Yu, Rondy, Aaron Haddock, and Tyler Womack. "Integrating Supports for Students with Wraparound." *Contemporary School Psychology* 26 (2020): 155–163.

3 Solid Attachment to a School Community Boosts Academic Success

Brandon was a middle-school student in a small school district sandwiched between two larger school districts half an hour outside of a large urban area. His district had 3,000 students attending one of two elementary schools, one middle school, and one high school. Nearly all of the high school students graduated and went on to college and other postsecondary learning institutions. The average SAT score in the district was 1310 (out of a possible 1600 for math and English) and the average ACT score was 29 (out of a possible 36). Over 60% of the student population was White, and the remainder were Asian, Hispanic, African American, and multiracial. The majority of classrooms had a ratio of 11 students to 1 teacher. The school district exemplified a tight-knit community, with students progressing together through the grades, culminating with graduation in the twelfth grade. It was not uncommon for students to be in the same classes with their friends for the duration of their academic journey.

The tight-knit community also included students' families and school personnel, who maintained close relationships both in and outside of the school community. Parents coached the teacher's children in Little League games and community members bumped into one another at the local supermarket or other stores on Main Street. Like so many other families who lived in the district, Brandon's family were long-term residents of the community, and his mother, maternal grandparents, and maternal aunts had attended and graduated from the same school system. Brandon lived with his older sister, younger brother, and maternal grandparents in the same house his mother had grown up in. His two maternal aunts lived nearby, and they often got together for family events or family dinner.

Brandon and his family moved back to his mother's house after his parents divorced when he was 4 years old. The divorce was contentious, and ended with Brandon's mother gaining full legal custody of Brandon and his two siblings. His father, who was emotionally abusive, was provided with scheduled supervised visitations, as well as a restraining order. Brandon's

DOI: 10.4324/9781003731221-3

mother felt this was an anxious time for the family, and her family home offered them a safe place. But the feeling of safety was elusive, as Brandon's father moved nearby and insisted on maintaining contact, igniting feelings of anxiety for Brandon's mother. Her anxiety never abated, as she constantly feared that her ex-husband would insist on joint custody. These intensified feelings of anxiety caused Brandon's attachment to his mother to develop with extreme intensity.

After the family moved, Brandon began school as a kindergartner and did not have any academic or social concerns. He was a smart, quiet student and an active participant in every grade and classroom. He would engage with his teachers in a Socratic method, questioning thoughts and processes in his classes. He loved social studies and learning about ancient civilizations. He had typical, healthy relationships with both his peers and the greater school community until middle school, when problems began to emerge. Up to that time, Brandon had been able to control his feelings of anxiety throughout elementary school, but after having a fight with a friend, he began to lose control in middle school.

Brandon's social connections began to fray in the seventh grade when he made a hurtful comment about his friend's appearance and clothes, which resulted in hurt feelings and caused a rift in his social group of friends. Brandon was shut out of his peer group and had very limited opportunities to maintain his social connections within the middle school. He began to self-isolate, narrowing his interests to connections via video games, where he would remotely connect with other players. Brandon was also becoming emotionally inflexible and stubborn and reacting poorly to changes in routine. He would have frequent temper tantrums and refuse to wake up in the morning to attend school. He was having difficulty concentrating in class, not participating in classroom activities, and not handing in assignments. And, most importantly, he was starting to refuse to attend school.

Given all of these maladaptive behaviors, Brandon's mother sought assistance from the school psychologist and eighth-grade guidance counselor, who suggested that Brandon receive support in the classroom with a 504 plan to better address these concerns. Brandon's 504 plan included extended time to complete homework and assignments, preferential seating so he could sit wherever he wanted in the classroom, and teacher check-ins to ensure he understood the assignment and when it was due. However, this plan only addressed classroom concerns, not the maladaptive behaviors such as the avoidance and anxiety that prevented him from making and maintaining social connections, or attending school and completing assignments.

Things only got worse when Brandon was in the eighth grade as schools shut down in March 2020 due to COVID-19 mandates. He was having difficulty logging on and engaging with remote learning, often missing classes throughout the day. When school reopened in the fall of 2020 for in-person instruction, Brandon began ninth grade refusing to attend school, or would go to only a few classes for an hour or two. When he was in school, he was polite and participated in class, but would do the minimum amount of work, often spending his free time with a school social worker or the school psychologist. He felt disconnected, and moved his bedroom down to the basement where he could sleep when he wanted, altering his circadian rhythm.

Brandon's behavior continued throughout the fall, and by the winter of 2021, his mother became more concerned. He was not attending school, and it was clear that the 504 plan, which only provided for accommodations in a general education classroom, was not offering enough support to keep him in school. As a result, Brandon's mother requested that the school provide more assistance, and sought to change the 504 plan to an Individualized Educational Plan (IEP) that could offer both academic and emotional support via measurable goals. The committee on special education reconvened to determine Brandon's eligibility for an IEP instead of maintaining his 504 plan. The meeting was contentious because the school team did not want to acknowledge Brandon's emotional state, believing he was consciously avoiding school to get out of testing and other evaluative assessments. Despite the team's opinion, Brandon was deemed eligible for an IEP due to his anxiety and school avoidance. Additionally, he was provided with an out-of-district placement, as he refused to return to the high school.

On the surface, Brandon became a school-avoidant student due to a rupture with his social network. However, beneath the surface, his school-avoidant behavior was a manifestation of his intense attachment to his mother. He wanted to help his mother feel safe by sharing the burden of her stress, which was two-fold: first, living at home with her parents was difficult, as constant arguments created tension, and second, his mother lived in ongoing fear that Brandon's father might return and interfere with their family life. Brandon had a strong attachment to his mother, and knowing that she was stressed and worried made it impossible for him to leave her alone while he was at school. His commitment to ensuring his mother's emotional safety prevented him from feeling safe anywhere but at home. Attending school was not possible for him, so he believed he was making the only choice he could.

Brandon's story exemplifies how school avoidance can be understood within attachment theory. Attachment is a deep and enduring emotional bond that provides a feeling of security and comfort, allowing children to safely take risks while exploring the world beyond their caregivers. Brandon's type of attachment—an insecure and disorganized attachment—hindered his ability to form healthy relationships outside of the home. Nor was he able to modulate his feelings of anxiety and stress as his feelings mirrored those of his mother. Brandon felt that being home, where he could be with his mother, was his only option.

What Is Attachment Theory?

Attachment is a bond between a child and caregiver in which there is a sense of trust and predictability. As developed by John Bowlby, the fundamental component of attachment is the need to be close to a specific person or attachment figure whose proximity helps to calm feelings of insecurity or fear.[1] Attachment begins in infancy or early childhood when a child establishes a variety of strategies to maintain proximity to an attachment figure, using the attachment figure as a secure base from which to explore and return to for reassurances and comfort.[2] As the infant or young child begins to explore, the hope is that the curious exploration can be a positive, stress-free experience because the secure base can be trusted to reassure and protect. Thus, when a child feels secure in the availability of the attachment figure, the child develops social skills with an ever-widening world. This feeling of support becomes the foundation for future social interactions[3] and allows for a continual dyadic interaction in which the attachment regulates between the need to explore and the need for proximity.

One of the central components of attachment theory is the concept of attachment as a behavioral system in which the child learns that a variety of behaviors can provide and allow for proximity to the attachment figure. This behavioral system teaches young children to be flexible in their responses to environmental changes,[4] as the goal of maintaining proximity to the attachment figure never changes. The behavioral system is based on both the desire to explore as well as the fear of exploring. The exploration is not based upon whether or not the attachment figure is physically present, but rather, upon the young child feeling that the attachment figure is available if needed. Another component of the behavioral system is the role of emotion, as emotion influences the response, communication, and regulation of feelings of stress or anxiety by the attachment figure to the child. When attachment figures can modulate this emotional response, it enables young children to re-regulate their feelings of stress and anxiety.

Ultimately, this behavioral system is in constant motion as it seeks to maintain homeostasis between the child's need to explore as well as the need to remain close to the attachment figure. The goal is to reinforce the importance of regulating emotions, providing guidance, and fostering feelings of safety and security. The regulation of emotions is defined by four basic attachment styles: secure, anxious-avoidant, anxious-ambivalent, and disorganized. Although children may exhibit characteristics of two attachment styles, they usually prefer one that best reflects their relationship with the caregiver: for example, a child with a secure attachment instinctively knows that the attachment figure is physically and emotionally available. A secure child can signal attachment needs through various cues, allowing for exploration with the assurance of available protection when necessary.[5]

However, a child with an insecure attachment is unable to tolerate adverse conditions, as the attachment figure may be emotionally unavailable or provide intermittent responses. Children who experience this type of relationship will either blunt their emotions or intensify their needs using maladaptive behaviors.[6] These children maintain defensive strategies to protect themselves from intense emotional distress, resulting in a disorganized attachment with the attachment figure. Young children who experience insecure attachments are at a higher risk for internalizing and externalizing behaviors,[7] and since children with insecure and disorganized attachments tend to maintain rigid defensive thought patterns, their new experiences take longer to intermingle with past experiences, reinforcing feelings of the self as being unworthy or incompetent.[8]

The foundation of children's bond with their attachment figures revolves around a mental representation of themselves and the attachment figures, known as an internal working model.[9] An internal working model allows the child and the attachment figure to anticipate, interpret, and guide interactions. The internal working model is also dependent upon the strength of the attachment and its ability to continuously fulfill exploration and secure base functions.[10] An internal working model is a reflection of the self and others and is based on day-to-day interactions between young children and their attachment figures in which young children learn that their attachment figures are both dependable and consistent in meeting their needs.[11] This relationship is complementary and mutually affirming, as the attachment figure is loving and protective and the young child/self feels loved and secure.[12] As young children continue to grow, the relationships between them and their attachment figures evolve, allowing for reciprocal adjustments and revisions of the internal working model. Previous experiences intermingle with present realities, providing opportunities to reshape the sense of self and others and adjust the attachment accordingly. This constant revision helps the young child learn how to adapt and cope with stress, especially if the caregiver's response to the change is positive and supportive.[13]

Attachments are important throughout our lifespans, and evolve over time. For securely attached children and adolescents, attachment needs will diminish as the child matures and is able to self-regulate, activating the need for attachment only when necessary. Children with avoidant or disorganized attachments have a limited repertoire of strategies for self-regulation, and when their attachment needs are activated, instead of seeking the attachment figure, these children will resort to using defensive tactics such as dysregulation and dissociation so as to not feel at a loss.

These children and adolescents are not able to develop effective strategies to manage stress and anxiety, and do not feel able to depend on a social network or view others as dependable. Rather, these children and adolescents feel socially and emotionally isolated. As a result, they cannot cope with their stress, and become restless and easily frustrated.

The Ego as a Protective Emotional Barrier

To understand why an insecure attachment can be problematic, it is helpful to understand how an individual's ego influences and negotiates between the internal emotional needs of the individual and external stressors. Ego functions are how individuals adapt to the world and their environment[14] and are an essential part of an individual's personality. The ego is responsible for negotiating between the internal needs of the individual and the demands of the outside world. Ego development progresses sequentially, and is complete when an individual masters developmental tasks and effectively copes with internal needs and environmental stressors at each stage. Ego development is also influenced by hereditary factors, the quality of interpersonal relationships, environmental impacts, sociocultural values, and socioeconomic conditions.

The component parts of an ego are made up of a tripartite of the id, ego, and superego. The id propels instinctual drives for sex and aggression, although, since it is not always appropriate to act on these drives, the superego morally represses them. Since the id demands discharge of these sexual and aggressive drives, the ego negotiates or tempers the id and permits the discharge of these drives in a socially appropriate manner.[15] In other words, the ego acts as a go between, negotiating between the id and the superego and tempering the drives using ego defenses. The use of defenses modulates, controls, and protects individuals from feeling anxiety to enhance more effective coping capabilities. This then enables the individual to communicate thoughts and feelings clearly, logically, and in an organized fashion oriented toward a shared reality. Ultimately, the ego augments problem-solving skills toward mastery and self-actualization.

There are 12 ego functions: reality testing; judgment; sense of reality and of the self; regulation and control of drives, affects and impulses; object relations; thought processes; adaptive regression in the service of the ego; defensive functioning; stimulus barrier; autonomous functioning; mastery-competence; and synthetic-integrative functioning. These ego functions enable individuals to maintain homeostasis between internal needs and external or environmental stresses. There is always variability in ego functioning, with some aspects being more stable than others. Even if an individual exhibits overall ego strength, regression can occur in some functions, such as during illness or transitions. It is important to recognize that not all difficulties result from an impairment in ego functioning, although, at times, an emotional conflict between the id and the superego can arise, resulting in anxiety and leading to the activation of defenses.

When an individual feels emotional stress, the ego is protected by a series of defense mechanisms that protect against feelings of anxiety by keeping intolerable thoughts and emotions away from conscious awareness.[16] The use of a defense mechanism can restore emotional equilibrium without impairing a person's ability to test reality. However, for others, the fragility of the defense mechanism will cause an individual to feel overwhelmed and disorganized. In this instance, the defense mechanism is rigid and will activate immature defenses and thought processes and distort reality. Efforts to modify or resist defenses may intensify feelings of stress and anxiety, as these individuals feel uncertain about the change they are seeking. While it may seem that these individuals want to change, their maladaptive defenses also act as a buffer, protecting them from intense feelings.[17]

The use of defenses during times of emotional distress is unconscious and often employed without thought or choice. These defenses are rigid, and rooted in the past rather than focused on the present or future. They distort the current situation instead of stemming from its reality. Defenses rely on primary thinking, which is unconscious and keeps intolerable or unacceptable thoughts from surfacing, preventing organized resolution and hindering the individual's ability to move forward.

How Does Disorganized Attachment Affect School-Avoidant Students?

Attachment does not terminate at a certain age; it is an integral component of the developmental process. How attachment between the child and the attachment figure transitions throughout this process can dictate the success or failure of later attachments, especially during adolescence. During this developmental timeframe, the adolescent evolves from being a receiver of care to becoming a self-sufficient adult, profoundly changing the attachment relationship.[18] As adolescence begins, individuals experience a change in cognitive and emotional thinking, providing adolescents with an opportunity to redefine their sense of self and their relationships with their caregivers or other adults in their lives. Attachment figures become less prominent as the adolescents learn how to balance the need to explore outside the confines of the safety of their attachment figures while at the same time determining and developing their own autonomy.[19]

Adolescence is a time of balancing the adolescent's desire for less attachment with the attachment figure's wish to maintain established and habitual patterns of response. This balancing act can result in conflict as adolescents seek to explore outside the bounds of their attachment with the attachment figure. As adolescents gain more autonomy, they begin to reassess their relationships with their attachment figures, becoming less reliant on the attachment to maintain homeostasis. How the adolescent manages the tension—or the push and pull between the desire for autonomy and the need to remain connected to the attachment figure—is dependent on the type of attachment that defines the relationship.

Adolescents with secure attachments will handle the transition in a productive manner using problem-solving skills. In secure attachments, attachment figures are able to provide opportunities for adolescents to explore their autonomous selves. A secure attachment occurs when adolescents feel they are in control of their life decisions, while in an insecure attachment, adolescents have a complicated relationship with their attachment figures. When attachment needs are triggered, defensive tactics such as partitioning of feelings, controlling behaviors, and dysregulation are utilized to help calm the feelings of stress and anxiety.[20] However, once in a state of dysregulation, and with no attachment figure able to help with regulation, the adolescent's stress response system becomes more reactive and less able to cope with the stress. Thus, adolescents with insecure attachment handle conflict in a disorganized, disoriented manner that can result in metacognitive deficits.[21]

Although attachment theory is defined by the dyadic relationship between a young child and a caregiver, attachment theory can also apply to the relationship between children and a school environment that includes teachers, peers, and staff. If students have a secure base with their school environment, they can build a repertoire of patterned internal responses when feeling stressed to help them regulate their feelings to better tolerate social, academic, and performance challenges they face throughout the school day.[22] These students will be able to develop an internal working model that provides a solid framework for them to experience fewer behavior problems, have more secure social network systems, and fulfill higher academic achievements. However, students whose internal working models are based on insecure or disorganized-disoriented relationships with their school environment will experience increased behavioral problems, poor academic performance, and social isolation from peers, staff, and the school community. And, even students with secure attachment can experience similar problems if the school system maintains a disorganized-disoriented attachment style between members of the system. If the school system or school community does not act as a sanctuary and is inflexible in meeting a student's needs, that student may become disillusioned and disengaged.

School-avoidant students with insecure or disorganized-disoriented attachments to a school community will hide their emotions, fears, and anxieties to avoid interacting with their school environment. This type of attachment avoidance acts as protective buffering, an emotional barrier that is erected when hiding one's worry or anxiety from others.[23] Hiding their feelings of distress enables school-avoidant students to protect themselves against possible rebuff from others or from actively engaging with their school environment. In essence, attachment avoidance is the degree to which a student doubts or questions the responsiveness of the school community during their times of emotional crisis and need. As a result, school-avoidant students will utilize a variety of strategies to deactivate the attachment system[24] as a self-protective adjustment to their feelings of stress and anxiety, or their anticipation of feelings of stress and anxiety.

Students' relationship with teachers may be as important as their relationships with caregivers. A secure attachment between a student and a teacher will encourage and support the development of self-confidence, encourage resilience, and promote autonomy.[25] When students begin elementary school, they learn how to behave and what to expect in a relationship with their teachers because teachers provide a secure base from which students can explore and take risks. Students learn that the teacher, and thereby the school environment, is a solid anchor that will help them to regulate emotions, understand how to relate with peers, and learn to regulate their behaviors during times of stress. Even children who may have entered school with insecure attachments to their caregivers will be ready to learn and take risks when they have a secure attachment with a teacher at school,[26] while insecure attachments to a teacher can result in poor school performance and becoming socially distanced from peers.[27] How adolescents define their attachment relationships with the school community, teachers, and peers will determine how they cope with stress and anxiety. For instance, does the attachment enable the adolescent to modulate, control, and tolerate stress and anxiety without becoming overwhelmed, or does the adolescent resort to maladaptive coping responses when feeling overwhelmed, stressed, or anxious?[28] Developing a thoughtful approach to a newly defined attachment allows the adolescent to mature and form other secure, attached relationships with others.

When the ego functions of a school-avoidant student are weak, impaired, or too fragile to withstand intolerable feelings, the defense maintains a rigid set of thoughts that focus on the past rather than the future. A school-avoidant student's defense mechanism can distort reality, which allows room for only primary thought process rather than secondary thought process, and for repressing any unwanted thoughts or feelings out of conscious awareness. Thus, when a student has a disorganized attachment along with a weak ego, it can lead to issues maintaining coping and modulating reactions to stress and anxiety.

A solid attachment to a school environment provides a student with the knowledge that there are a few select individuals who can be considered safe havens.[29] Each of these select individuals will be ranked in order of importance of their ability to ensure proximity, support, and security. School-avoidant students do not have these select few individuals who can provide safety from the emotional turmoil they experience in the school building, so they disconnect from a stressful, anxiety-producing school environment. Although school avoidance is about anxiety, at its root, it is about how students are unable to regulate their attachment to a secure school base. If they lack the ability to maintain a stabilized relationship or develop a secure inner working model, they will be unable to overcome an attachment that is insecure and disorganized. The student will ultimately feel that there is no one who can provide a safety net for emotional distress. Their bedroom at home becomes a sanctuary—a protective barrier from feeling overwhelmed.

How Did Brandon Repair His Attachment to a School Community?

Brandon slowly began to repair his attachment to his new school community when his attachment to his mother changed. The purpose of the intense attachment between Brandon and his mother was based on the need to feel safe and secure against the threat of his father. If his father was nearby, Brandon felt responsible for ensuring that his mother and siblings were safe and secure. Thus, Brandon and his mother always made sure to stay near one another for their emotional safety. As Brandon moved into high school, the threat of his father began to dissipate, as there was no relationship between them. Once his father was removed from the family system, the anxiety and the stress began to significantly lessen. Brandon was able to modulate his emotional responses rationally, which enabled him to return to a feeling of safety to explore beyond the boundaries of the attachment. As the quality of Brandon's relationship with his mother improved, so too did their communication, which began to reflect sensitivity to the other's internal emotional states. There was no need for them to maintain the protective barrier, and school attendance became a possibility. Brandon was able to internalize his mother's emotional strength and resilience, allowing him to trust his own instincts and autonomous self. Gradually, he began to define himself outside of his attachment with his mother.

Initially, Brandon did not trust that the new school community could help him reconnect or rebuild his sense of attachment to school. For the first six weeks in his new school, Brandon purposely remained awake all night, falling asleep at six a.m. to avoid the bus. It took a team effort to convince him to leave the basement, a team that included the principal of his new school, the school therapeutic team made up of the school social worker and school psychologist, a teacher, and his mother. Ultimately,

Brandon was convinced to leave the basement because the team validated and acknowledged his feelings and let him know that he would feel connected and supported in his new school community.

By encouraging and inviting Brandon to become part of the team, he was able to become part of the solution. On the first day at his new school, Brandon was immediately placed in classes where he could learn and discuss with peers and teachers in the Socratic method. To meet the socioemotional goals of his IEP, Brandon was connected with the school social worker and school psychologist and began the intense process of exploring his fears using a cognitive behavior paradigm. As part of the school program, the school offered him an opportunity to learn a trade in addition to his academic classes. Since his mother's family was in the restaurant business, Brandon took this opportunity to learn culinary arts, as he hoped to one day become a chef at his own restaurant.

His reattachment to the new school community was solidified when he connected to a peer group that provided him with important sources of feedback about acceptable social behavior, social influence, and information about expected behaviors. He made friends and became part of a social group that socialized both within and outside of school. He became a student mentor and enjoyed helping peers when they did not understand a topic, and became a reliable member of the school cooking team, which won two national awards due to Brandon's organization and ability to run a kitchen. And he never missed a day of school, as he enjoyed the school community and felt safe learning.

Brandon's successful reattachment with the new school community was the result of a support system that included academic support, therapeutic support, and a stable and accepting peer group. Ultimately, he learned that he could have a variety of attachments, each one allowing him to expand his sense of self. His primary attachment would always be with his mother, but knowing that she was dependable and available created a space for him to trust that the world beyond his mother would also be supportive. While his fragile ego regained strength and meditated more effectively between his id and superego, he developed a set pattern of defensive responses that could calm him down, and more importantly, began to develop secondary thought patterns that enabled him to connect to actual realities.

Attachment is a bond that encapsulates a sense of trust and predictability. Its fundamental component is being close to a specific person or attachment figure whose proximity helps to calm feelings of insecurity or fears. For Brandon, being close to his mother was vitally important, helping him to maintain a sense of calm. A secure base allows individuals to feel secure to explore and be flexible knowing that the attachment provides a sense of well-being and calms fears, although if the secure base is stressed, that stress will ripple out to those who are emotionally dependent on it.

A solid attachment regulates emotions toward always feeling safe and secure. An insecure or disorganized attachment is the opposite, where the individual remains in a heightened state of fear, flee, or fight. An insecure or disorganized attachment causes an individual to maintain rigid thinking where stress and anxiety cannot be tolerated, leading to a blunting of emotions. These defensive strategies allow the individual to avoid feeling extreme distress or anxiety, and do not allow for the individual to develop or maintain strategies toward healthier mechanisms of self-regulation. Brandon's need to be close to his mother led to an insecure and disorganized attachment where he could not strategize how to feel safe, making his basement the safest space where he could allow himself to feel less anxious. His school avoidance was a result of an insecure attachment that affected all areas of his life. When he was able to resolve his attachment to his mother, he was able to develop self-confidence, be resilient, and promote autonomy, all of which were necessary for successful transition to adulthood.

Notes

1 John Bowlby, "Grief and Mourning in Infancy and Early Childhood," *Psychoanalytic Study of the Child* 15 (1969).
2 Karen Zilberstein, "The Use and Limitations of Attachment Theory in Child Psychotherapy," *Psychotherapy* 51, no. 1 (2014).
3 Monica L. Mandell, "Attachment Theory as a Lens for Examining the School Avoidant Student" (Dissertation, Yeshiva University, 2022), 42.
4 Bowlby, "Grief and Mourning"; Jude Cassidy, "The Nature of the Child's Ties," in *Handbook of Attachment: Theory, Research, and Clinical Applications* (2nd ed.), ed. Jude Cassidy and Phillip R. Shaver (New York: The Guilford Press, 2008).
5 Zilberstein, "Use and Limitations of Attachment Theory."
6 Zilberstein, "Use and Limitations of Attachment Theory."
7 Janice H. Kennedy, and Charles E. Kennedy, "Attachment Theory: Implications for School Psychology," *Psychology in Schools* 41, no. 2 (2004).
8 Inge Bretherton, "The Origins of Attachment Theory: John Bowlby and Mary Ainsworth," *Developmental Psychology* 28, no. 5 (1992).
9 Bowlby, "Grief and Mourning."
10 Bowlby, "Grief and Mourning"; Inge Bretherton and Kristine A. Munholland, "Internal Working Models in Attachment Relationships: Elaborating a Central Construct in Attachment Theory," in *Handbook of Attachment: Theory, Research, and Clinical Applications* (2nd ed.), ed. Jude Cassidy and Phillip R. Shaver (New York: The Guilford Press, 2008).
11 Kennedy and Kennedy, "Attachment Theory."
12 Bretherton and Munholland, "Internal Working Models."
13 Bretherton and Munholland, "Internal Working Models."
14 Eda Goldstein, *Ego Psychology and Social Work Practice* (New York: The Free Press, 1984).
15 Graham Danzer, "Integrating Ego Psychology and Strengths-Based Social Work," *Journal of Theory Construction & Testing* 16, no. 1 (2012).
16 Goldstein, *Ego Psychology*.

17 Goldstein, *Ego Psychology*.
18 Joseph P. Allen, "The Attachment System in Adolescence," in *Handbook of Attachment: Theory, Research, and Clinical Applications* (2nd ed.), ed. Jude Cassidy and Phillip R. Shaver (New York: The Guilford Press, 2008).
19 Allen, "The Attachment System in Adolescence."
20 Zilberstein, "Use and Limitations of Attachment Theory."
21 Karlen Lyons-Ruth and Deborah Jacobvitz, "Attachment Disorganization: Genetic Factors, Parenting Contexts, and Developmental Transformation from Infancy to Adulthood," in *Handbook of Attachment: Theory, Research, and Clinical Applications* (2nd ed.), ed. Jude Cassidy and Phillip R. Shaver (New York: The Guilford Press, 2008).
22 Kennedy and Kennedy, "Attachment Theory."
23 Heike A. Winterheld, "Hiding Feelings for Whose Sake? Attachment Avoidance, Relationship Connectedness, Protective Buffering Intentions," *Emotion* 17, no. 6 (2017).
24 Winterheld, "Hiding Feelings."
25 Bretherton and Munholland, "Internal Working Models"; Michelle Sumner Howard and Frederic J. Medway, "Adolescents' Attachment and Coping with Stress," *Psychology in the Schools* 41, no. 3 (2004); Kennedy and Kennedy, "Attachment Theory"; Robert F. Marcus and Joanne Sanders-Reio, "The Influence of Attachment on School Completion," *School Psychology Quarterly* 16, no. 4 (2001).
26 Marcus and Sanders-Reio, "The Influence of Attachment."
27 Allen, "The Attachment System in Adolescence"; Lyons-Ruth and Jacobvitz, "Attachment Disorganization"; Marcus and Sanders-Reio, "The Influence of Attachment."
28 Goldstein, *Ego Psychology*.
29 Lara K. Kammrath et al., "What Predicts Who We Approach for Social Support? Tests of the Attachment Figure and Strong Ties Hypotheses," *Journal of Personality and Social Psychology* 118, no. 3 (2020).

Reference List

Allen, Joseph P. "The Attachment System in Adolescence." In *Handbook of Attachment: Theory, Research, and Clinical Applications* (2nd ed.), edited by Jude Cassidy and Phillip R. Shaver, 419–435. New York: The Guilford Press, 2008.

Bowlby, John. "Grief and Mourning in Infancy and Early Childhood." *Psychoanalytic Study of the Child* 15 (1969): 9–52.

Bretherton, Inge. "The Origins of Attachment Theory: John Bowlby and Mary Ainsworth." *Developmental Psychology* 28, no. 5 (1992): 759–775.

Bretherton, Inge, and Kristine A. Munholland. "Internal Working Models in Attachment Relationships: Elaborating a Central Construct in Attachment Theory." In *Handbook of Attachment: Theory, Research, and Clinical Applications* (2nd ed.), edited by Jude Cassidy and Phillip R. Shaver, 102–127. New York: The Guilford Press, 2008.

Cassidy, Jude. "The Nature of the Child's Ties." In *Handbook of Attachment: Theory, Research, and Clinical Applications* (2nd ed.), edited by Jude Cassidy and Phillip R. Shaver, 3–22. New York: The Guilford Press, 2008.

Danzer, Graham. "Integrating Ego Psychology and Strengths-Based Social Work." *Journal of Theory Construction & Testing* 16, no. 1 (2012): 9–15.

Goldstein, Eda. *Ego Psychology and Social Work Practice*. New York: The Free Press, 1984.

Howard, Michelle Sumner, and Frederic J. Medway. "Adolescents' Attachment and Coping with Stress." *Psychology in the Schools* 41, no. 3 (2004): 391–402.

Kammrath, Lara K., Benjamin F. Armstrong, Sean P. Lane et al. "What Predicts Who We Approach for Social Support? Tests of the Attachment Figure and Strong Ties Hypotheses." *Journal of Personality and Social Psychology* 118, no. 3 (2020): 481–500.

Kennedy, Janice H., and Charles E. Kennedy. "Attachment Theory: Implications for School Psychology." *Psychology in Schools* 41, no. 2 (2004): 247–259.

Lyons-Ruth, Karlen, and Deborah Jacobvitz. "Attachment Disorganization: Genetic Factors, Parenting Contexts, and Developmental Transformation from Infancy to Adulthood." In *Handbook of Attachment: Theory, Research, and Clinical Applications* (2nd ed.), edited by Jude Cassidy and Phillip R. Shaver, 666–697. New York: The Guilford Press, 2008.

Mandell, Monica L. "Attachment Theory as a Lens for Examining the School Avoidant Student." Dissertation, Yeshiva University, 2022.

Marcus, Robert F., and Joanne Sanders-Reio. "The Influence of Attachment on School Completion." *School Psychology Quarterly* 16, no. 4 (2001): 427–444.

Winterheld, Heike A. "Hiding Feelings for Whose Sake? Attachment Avoidance, Relationship Connectedness, Protective Buffering Intentions." *Emotion* 17, no. 6 (2017): 965–980.

Zilberstein, Karen. "The Use and Limitations of Attachment Theory in Child Psychotherapy." *Psychotherapy* 51, no. 1 (2014): 93–103.

4 The Impact of COVID-19 on Students with Social Anxiety

In March 2020, all schools in the United States serving kindergarten to grade 12, as well as early childhood, day care centers, and colleges shut their doors to help mitigate the spread of COVID–19. These closures affected 21 million children in childcare, 57 million students in kindergarten to grade 12, and 20 million college students.[1] It was the first time students in the United States experienced a prolonged closure of school buildings, and it affected all members of the school community. Initially, school closures were thought to be a temporary solution to minimize the spread of COVID-19, but schools stayed shut for the remainder of the school year, an average of 85 school days. The enforced closures forced school systems to create new online learning environments, which led to unforeseen consequences.

Both the sudden nature and the prolonged length of school closures affected students' well-being and mental health, especially for students in middle and high school. It also affected their motivation and concentration, thereby reducing academic performances. More importantly, neither staff nor students were prepared for the new method of online learning. New online classrooms came with a steep learning curve, and success or failure was contingent upon a teacher's use of technology, the students' ability to easily access Wi-Fi, and parents' participation. Both staff and students had to adapt to this new virtual classroom, and students had to remain motivated to learn, especially when they were alone without the physical presence of peer support.

Clearly, social distancing, the suspension of both in- and out-of-school learning and activities, and changes in work and home environments profoundly affected students' feelings of well-being. The absence of peer socialization, limited access to school mental health counselors, and constrained opportunities for social learning undoubtedly stand out as critical factors that may have significantly contributed to a range of health and emotional well-being concerns. Over the past five years, research has consistently demonstrated that the COVID-19 pandemic significantly

DOI: 10.4324/9781003731221-4

disrupted students' academic progress and hindered the development of their socialization skills worldwide.[2] The result is that school closures have left an enduring, profound impact on all students, staff, and parents. One student's story, Sandra, mirrors that of countless students around the world whose mental health and academic development were directly impacted by COVID–19.

COVID-19 Impact on Schools and Students

Like all schools in the United States, Greenwood Bell Elementary—a small elementary school nestled among shady, majestic trees and historic homes—immediately shut down due to the COVID-19 pandemic. Greenwood Bell is located in a small town that can trace its origins back to an Indigenous population. It was founded as a town by the Dutch and played a significant role in the Revolutionary War. Homes date back to the 1800s, and its Main Street has been designated as a national historic district. It is considered a bedroom community, as it is half an hour away from a large urban city. People there live in an intermingling mix of modern and historic homes overlooking a mighty river.

The school district that serves the town prides itself on providing individual attention to students, fostering a community where both teachers and parents connect personally. It has 1,770 students spread between one elementary school that houses grades K-3, a second elementary school that houses grades 4-5, and one middle school and high school that are combined in the same building. Three-quarters of the student population is White, and the remainder are racially mixed. There is a ratio of 18 students to one teacher, and nearly the entire student population is proficient in both English and math. It is a high-achieving school district dedicated to preparing students for college and other postsecondary opportunities. Prior to the COVID-19 closure, students and staff were learning as a community and planning for the weeks ahead, eager for the arrival of spring. The community was looking forward to spring concerts, state assessments, learning about immigration, and an upcoming health fair. At the middle and high school, spring sports teams were announcing spring tryout dates, and fifth, eighth, and twelfth graders were starting to plan for their graduations. There was no hint of a pending problem, and the entire school community was buzzing along like an active beehive.

Then, with no warning and a sense of urgency, the school shut down in March 2020 with few details given. Parents and students were provided with little information and told that school closure would only last for a few weeks. In the blink of an eye, the community had to switch from in-person to online Zoom classrooms. School learning took place via a screen at home with limited opportunities for organic social interactions. As the three-week mark ended, it was clear that schools would not reopen until the fall of 2020. When school finally reopened after the summer break, students were given options to return or to maintain distance learning. Classes were half full as some parents worried about allowing their children to return to school, as they were concerned about possible exposure to COVID-19 despite mask and social distancing regulations.

For one 10-year-old named Sandra, the elimination of daily in-person school attendance due to the mandated school closures for COVID-19 scared her so much that she simply stopped participating in school-related learning activities. Prior to the school closures, Sandra was a fifth grader during the 2019–2020 school year who enjoyed going to school, where she felt safe to learn and interact with her friends. She was the first person to raise her hand in class, and was a voracious reader, an eager learner, and an active member of the school community. She participated fully in school activities and enjoyed all aspects of the school community. She had a comfortable home with two loving parents and one older brother. Her attachments were secure, both within her home and with external relationships, and she was able to adapt to stressors, knowing that she had a secure base.

However, Sandra had a difficult time adjusting to the new learning format when the school was forced to shut down all school functions. The swift change in daily routines with no apparent understandable reason set off a wave of panic for Sandra. From the start, Sandra did not like learning from home, as she felt isolated and did not like being on camera, which made her feel exposed. She preferred to be in a classroom, sitting next to her friends and actively listening and participating in a supportive learning environment. She had never experienced remote learning, and it felt uncomfortable for her. She refused to turn on the camera because she felt overwhelmed by all of the faces on the computer screen and began to participate with no camera, preferring just to listen. During the summer break, Sandra, like many other students nationwide, had some much-needed vacation time. In September, when school reopened, her parents were reluctant to send her or her older brother back to school, even with everyone wearing masks, as her older brother had an immuno-compromised disorder and they were concerned about transmission of COVID–19. Not returning to school perpetuated Sandra's fear of interacting with the school community. Although she continued as a virtual student, she never felt comfortable turning on her camera while her classmates were in the classroom, leaving her feeling more exposed than ever.

Sandra's parents' decision to have her remain at home instead of starting sixth grade in September 2020 with her peers had significant emotional consequences for her. Although Sandra had been learning online since March 2020, she continued to feel uncomfortable using Zoom as a learning platform when school resumed in September. And, her feeling of discomfort never abated. From the moment the school day began at 8:40 a.m., Sandra would spend her day crying, becoming agitated and unable to calm down. She began to pick at her skin and refused to turn on the camera during online class sessions, losing whole days of school and quickly falling behind in her schoolwork. She socially isolated herself because she felt she no longer shared any common activities with her peers, and her overwhelming worry led her to avoid contact with them. By October 2020, Sandra stopped attending school, both in person and virtually, as it triggered her feelings of anxiety and avoidance.

Sandra's refusal to attend either in-person or virtually led to the decision to place her in a small private school program near her home designed to help students with intense anxiety. However, this plan did not work, as Sandra had one-to-one teaching sessions that did not provide any opportunity to socialize with peers. As a result, she continued to feel isolated and alone, only feeling safe at home, where she was able to decide what to do, along with when and with whom she would do an activity. She spent much of her day with her dog and with her parents, who tried to provide her with activities that would be of interest to her. She continued to refuse to socialize with peers and became agoraphobic, which led her parents to initiate both individual and family therapy to address not only her social anxiety, but their frustration as well.

Sandra's parents knew she needed to be in a school environment. Because Sandra was no longer attending the small private school, the only option available was a referral to the special education committee, where she was evaluated and found eligible for special education services. She was classified as a student with an emotional disturbance and provided with an out-of-district placement, as her local school could not provide her with sufficient social-emotional support such as therapy and individualization to manage her social anxiety. The educational decision made by the committee for special education provided Sandra with an opportunity to be in a school setting that acknowledged her feelings of avoidance and anxiety. This setting offered the specialized attention she needed to thrive both academically and emotionally, as it would allow her to not feel exposed when she felt anxious. Moreover, the provision of specialized attention would envelope Sandra in a soft embrace that would make her feel safe and secure.

Defining Social Anxiety

Social anxiety, or social anxiety disorder as defined by the *DSM-5*,[3] is a persistent fear of one or more social or performance situations in which the individual is either exposed to unfamiliar people or could be judged, embarrassed, or humiliated by others. Exposure provokes anxiety, and the individual avoids the feared situations—or, at the very least, endures them with intense anxiety or distress. The avoidance, fear, or anxiety typically lasts for at least six months and significantly interferes with daily functioning and social interactions that are perceived as threatening. Interactions that can be considered stressful include family tension, being bullied, public embarrassment, or significant changes in daily routines, all of which may contribute to and/or increase the risk of developing social anxiety.

Social anxiety is the third most common psychiatric condition in the United States, with major depression and alcoholism being the other two most common psychiatric disorders.[4] Generally, social anxiety has an average age of onset at mid-adolescence but can emerge in childhood.[5] Social anxiety can be defined by three factors: the first is parental overprotection, where children learn to fear the world and believe they cannot manage or cope with threats without parental supervision or oversight. The second is genetic or environmental factors such as experiencing childhood illness or having a member of the family with a chronic condition. The third is that social anxiety tends to emerge during adolescence when there is an increase in autonomy and the peer group replaces parents as a source of identity and approval, with onset usually occurring around ages 11 or 12. Social anxiety can also be defined as direct conditioning, observational learning, and information transfer. Direct conditioning is a fear that can develop from exposure to a traumatic event; observational learning is observing someone else in a traumatic event; and information transfer is when information regarding social situations is either verbally or nonverbally transmitted. Social anxiety can also emanate from heritable genetic factors that can also play a role in the development of social anxiety.

Social anxiety can present as either a fear of one or two situations with multiple feared outcomes, or multiple feared situations with one feared outcome. Regardless of the pattern, adolescents with social anxiety often struggle to form and maintain friendships, leading them to have fewer friends overall. Moreover, adolescents with social anxiety fear a broad range of activities outside of the home, preferring instead the safety that their home provides. They may present with moments of crying or behavioral outbursts such as tantrums, and struggle to participate in classroom activities, ask for help, attend social events, or navigate a school day without feeling paralyzed or frozen in place. Overall, social anxiety reflects intense feelings of inhibition to interact in social or performative situations. It is often confused with shyness, with the assumption that the adolescent will outgrow the shyness around others.

Students who are socially anxious can feel lonely and have a poor sense of self or self-esteem. Low self-esteem is a significant contributing factor toward developing social anxiety. Self-esteem is defined as our ability to value ourselves, along with how we feel and behave about ourselves.

Healthy self-esteem enables an individual to be resilient during times of change or transition, whereas an impaired or low self-esteem impacts one's ability to manage stress, adversity, or difficult transitions. With feelings of low self-esteem, individuals become hypersensitive to criticism and trying new things because of potential failure. For an adolescent, self-esteem comes from validation of individual abilities and self-worth from peer interactions.[6] Adolescents with low self-esteem will have thoughts of feeling inadequate compared to their peers and will become either passive in social interactions or avoid them. These adolescents will withdraw and isolate themselves from peer groups, thereby hindering the development of age-appropriate social skills and reinforcing negative self-appraisals. Self-esteem may reflect gender differences, as boys reported lower social anxiety than girls. This could be because girls tend to experience higher vulnerability to social anxiety, which potentially stems from lower levels of self-worth and self-esteem compared to boys.[7]

Students who were socially anxious before COVID-19 had resources such as social skills groups and individual counseling, which helped them adjust to new school situations. However, when schools shut down and later reopened with social distancing rules, students who may have felt socially anxious prior to COVID-19 came back to a school community unable to manage the stress and transition to a new learning format, either via online learning or learning in the classroom six feet apart while wearing masks. Thus, their ability to remain connected to others was significantly compromised, as social interactions with peers were stilted. It became increasingly challenging to sustain and foster peer support networks and meaningful social bonds, potentially contributing to an apparent lack of support. Moreover, parents were afraid to send their child back to school, as they feared transmission of the virus to more vulnerable family members. Thus, as schools slowly reopened, those students who were fearful of the world outside of their home were overwhelmed with feelings of social anxiety and felt exposed and vulnerable when they left their homes. It was not possible to attend school either partially or in person, and feeling emotionally safe became paramount.

How Did COVID-19 Impact the School Community?

In 2021, a year after the mandated shutdown, the United States Surgeon General's office issued an advisory statement in their report titled Protecting Youth Mental Health. The advisory statement noted that the rates of anxiety, depression, and other mental health disorders nearly doubled during the COVID-19 pandemic. It called for a coordinated response to better address the relationship between education and mental health. Students who quarantined and were separated from their peer groups developed acute stress disorders, adjustment disorders, and even feelings of grief and loss.[8] Additional data from a survey of school district leaders throughout the United States corroborated the Protecting Youth Mental Health advisory statement, noting that students had fallen behind in their social-emotional development as a result of school closures.[9]

School districts throughout the United States, as well as internationally, were significantly impacted by school closures due to the COVID-19 shutdown. With limited access to a school environment and social interactions, students and the larger school community had to learn how to manage and navigate new challenges within a technological space. Although the school community tried to recreate an easily accessible learning environment online, it became clear that being physically present in school is vitally important to maintaining a sense of belonging to a community. Specifically, the school community allows students to feel accepted, connected, and valued.[10] Actively connected students participate in school-related clubs and sports and maintain social connections. COVID-19 mandates leading to school closures significantly compromised these social and academic activities, forcing school personnel and students to adjust both how instruction was provided and how they could maintain social connections as a school community. More importantly, school closures due to COVID-19 mandates illustrated that adequate peer interactions within a school community enable students to feel less traumatized by catastrophic events or events out of their control.

Children and adolescents throughout the United States shared similar experiences during school shutdowns.[11] The radical change in daily routines due to COVID-19, the strict social distancing measures, lengthy school closures, parental stress, and long stretches of social isolation resulted in significantly elevated stress levels. For children and adolescents, the availability of stable routines and access to social interactions and friendships is the foundation upon which healthy emotional and social attachments can flourish, fostering a sense of security and belonging that positively shapes their overall well-being. With forced isolation due to COVID-19 restrictions, maintaining stable routines and access to social interactions became either very limited or nonexistent.[12]

During the months of school closure, students experienced a constant sense of unpredictability because daily life activities were halted. As a result, there was a marked increase in feelings of loneliness, isolation, and social anxiety among students. And, even when schools reopened, these symptoms persisted, as the maintenance of strict guidelines toward social distancing and mask use remained for the entire 2020–2021 school year. Because COVID-19 lockdowns disrupted daily routines and social interactions and forced children and adolescents to be isolated from one another, studies have noted that children and adolescents are more likely to develop acute stress disorders, adjustment disorders, and feelings of loss and mourning.[13] In fact, adolescents were particularly sensitive to the changes brought on by COVID-19 and were more likely to feel symptoms of depression, anxiety, and post-traumatic stress, and to experience intrafamilial violence.[14] Adolescents experienced mental and physical health challenges, as well as difficulty sustaining social relationships.

The disruption in daily life activities due to the COVID-19 school closures had a profound impact on adolescents, affecting their social bonds with teachers and peers. Even if the actual support system remained intact through virtual means, some adolescents perceived this break as a lack of support, leading to feelings of loneliness. As a result, this perception could potentially lead to the adoption of maladaptive coping strategies to manage feelings of anxiety, thereby allowing the adolescent to avoid exposure to social situations.

Social-Emotional Learning to Help Mitigate COVID-19 Repercussions

What exactly helped to mitigate the effects of social isolation on children during the COVID-19 pandemic and school closures? While all students were participating in a school environment from home, some students with preexisting social anxiety experienced a reduction in symptoms due to the mandated school closures, as everyone had to maintain limited engagement with peers and school activities.[15] However, mandated school closures had profound effects on mental health for a significant number of students. In a national survey conducted in April of 2020, 36% of 13- to 19-year-olds expressed concerns about their mental health, with over 40% reporting difficulties concentrating, making decisions, and feeling happy.[16] For many students, social isolation and loneliness precipitated the development of social anxiety.

For important reasons, focus and attention has been primarily on academic loss during COVID-19 school closures, with academic loss defined as either delayed learning progress or a loss of already obtained knowledge.[17] And, despite additional remedial services, students were not able to easily reverse the learning deficits. While academic loss is difficult to recoup, it is clear that social-emotional losses during school closures are as significant as academic losses. Without the structure of daily school attendance and a lack of daily structured activities, students felt disconnected, which led to poor sleeping habits and lack of hygiene. This combined with declining academic performance and limited social-emotional connectedness led to an increase in social anxiety, feelings of loneliness, and social isolation.

Social-Emotional Learning in a School Community

Understanding that school closures due to COVID-19 mandates greatly impact a school community and all of its members, a focus on how to reengage the community is crucial for fostering a supportive and inclusive environment that addresses the social and emotional needs of students. Students with strong social-emotional skills have better academic performances, fewer behavior problems, and better social and familial relationships.[18] In contrast, students who lack social-emotional skills may develop disruptive behaviors that will impact collaboration with peers and thereby impact the school community. Thus, school communities are a natural setting to implement interventions to manage mental health needs related to social anxiety and social withdrawal because they are open environments that foster a sense of shared vision and mutual responsibility among and between students, teachers, staff, parents, and local organizations.

Prior to school closures due to COVID-19, a third of the US student population experienced some form of emotional or behavioral concerns.[19] A year after school closures, statistics from the Center for Disease Control's Healthy Youth Data Summary Trends revealed that in 2021, more than 42% of students nationwide reported feeling persistently sad or hopeless, with one third experiencing some form of poor mental health.[20] These data indicate a significant increase in students experiencing mental health issues since schools reopened post-COVID-19 closures. Given the data, learning and improving social and emotional skills can serve as the cornerstone of enhancing academic performance, improving self-esteem, and bettering social behaviors. Social and Emotional Learning develops and maintains positive self-image and increases students' sense of self by teaching them valuable skills and strategies to reduce intense feelings of anxiety by focusing on a sense of resiliency. The ultimate goal is to help students become capable of integrating into a school community, which can have a positive effect on students experiencing social anxiety and social withdrawal.[21]

Social and Emotional Learning has five competencies that are hierarchical, so that each stage has to develop to gain a higher level of functioning. First is self-regulation, which promotes critical thinking and mental flexibility, and leads toward the development of self-efficacy and executive functioning. These stages then lead to compassion, and to the final stage of understanding how to collaborate and work with others. Developing through the hierarchy of these competencies enables students to develop the necessary skills to manage emotions, set and achieve positive goals, show caring for others and their communities, maintain positive relationships, and make responsible decisions.

Social Anxiety + School Avoidance + Social-Emotional Learning

Social anxiety can cause students to avoid attending school because of intense feelings of emotional distress. It is an inappropriate reaction to a perceived danger or consequence of attending school.[22] There is no reason or cause that can explain why the student is avoiding the school community and jeopardizing both academic and social pursuits. Social anxiety in a school setting is reflective of feelings of inadequacies, as these students will perceive themselves as less than the others. To mitigate these feelings and strengthen resiliency, social, and emotional learning can help students lessen intense feelings of distress by incorporating self-awareness, self-management, social awareness, relationship skills, and responsible decision-making on both an intrapersonal and interpersonal level. It will provide an emotional toolkit for enabling the socially anxious student to reengage and not isolate from the school community.

Social-emotional learning involves and engages a school community that requires both the adults and the students to possess the competence and awareness to interact in a healthy and positive manner.[23] A classroom that is student-centered and incorporates self-reflection, cooperation, and meaningful discussion will promote academic achievement, as adolescents will feel valued and heard in the classroom. Adolescents who experience positive and supportive classrooms have lower levels of internalizing and externalizing symptoms. A school community that has high expectations and supports for academic rigor, caring relationships, and a commitment for safety among all community members will augment a sense of belonging, where students feel safe to learn.

Social-emotional learning in the classroom is guided by the Collaborative for Academic, Social, and Emotional Learning (CASEL), which provides specific guidance and curriculum for implementing and sustaining a supportive learning environment. CASEL's framework focuses on providing opportunities for students to learn and apply knowledge, skills, and attitudes to aid in the development of healthy identities, help them to manage emotions, achieve personal and school goals, develop empathy for themselves and others, establish and maintain mutually supportive relationships, and make caring decisions. CASEL utilizes four approaches that reflect the five competencies of self-awareness, self-management, social awareness, relationship skills, and responsible decision-making. The first approach is utilized in the classroom, where the goal is to develop positive relationships—both between the teacher and the students, and between students themselves—to promote inclusivity. Using age-appropriate topics and lesson plans within each age group (elementary, middle, and high school), students learn how to label feelings, cope with anxiety or stress, set, and achieve goals, develop empathy, resolve conflicts, and make responsible decisions. Lessons are provided using explicit instruction and opportunities for practice. The second approach is to create classroom and school-wide opportunities to support emotional connections and provide authentic feedback, while the third approach pertains to curriculum development and the fourth covers policies and organizational structures.[24]

Research has shown that providing social-emotional learning in a school community is beneficial for all students.[25] Specific implementation of CASEL uses five core competencies: the first is self-awareness, which is the ability to recognize one's emotions to accurately assess how they influence behavior. The second is self-management, which refers to regulating one's behavior with regard to managing stress, controlling impulses, and managing motivation. The third competency, social awareness, promotes empathy for others, and the fourth, relationship skills, builds toward creating and maintaining appropriate social relationships with others. Finally, the fifth competency, responsible decision-making, refers to making the right choice in any situation.

At the classroom level, a social-emotional learning framework uses teaching practices that are student-centered and promote the five competencies of self-reflection, cooperation, meaningful discussion, and promoting engagement in learning. Students are more likely to be motivated to learn if they feel seen, known, and valued.[26] This allows students to feel connected to all aspects of the classroom and lower levels of both internalizing and externalizing behaviors. However, despite its aspirations for connections, social-emotional learning does not always help all students, especially those with social anxiety. Students with social anxiety feel intense emotional distress and are not able to regulate their feelings of stress. For a student such as Sandra, the shift from in-person to online learning was emotionally overwhelming: she felt that all eyes were upon her and that there was no safe space within the Zoom classroom. Over time, she began to feel less valued, and wished only to disappear from view.

Sandra's Somewhat Successful Reintegration into a School Community

COVID-19 school closures changed the school community from one of togetherness to one of individuals whose only connection was via a screen at home while wearing pajamas. For Sandra, this created a significant rupture in her daily routines and led to feelings of isolation and loneliness. Sandra was not able to adjust to a new virtual and remote school environment, even if the school community remained the same during the mandated COVID-19 school shutdown. This new learning experience—one that she had never experienced—left her bereft of coping strategies, affecting her ability to be resilient in the face of change and transition. Her social anxiety was so overwhelming that she could not participate and refused to turn on the camera, even though her peers were also learning remotely. She became attached to her home, playing with her dog and refusing to engage in any activity where she did not feel comfortable.

After she was classified and referred to an out-of-district placement, Sandra lost her voice when speaking to strangers or people she did not know. She would whisper to her mother, who would speak on her behalf. The longer Sandra remained at home separated from the world outside, the quieter she became. Finding a school placement that could support her social-emotional needs took a long time, as Sandra would only whisper in her mother's ear to share whether or not she felt comfortable. Her mother would then relay the information, stating that Sandra wanted to be assured that her new classroom would only have a few students, that she did not have to raise her hand if she did not want to participate, and that she could signal the teacher if she felt overwhelmed and needed to leave. She chose a small school near her home with space to sit and relax, one that had a small farm with animals such as chinchillas and chickens that she could care for when she felt the need to leave the classroom.

The new school program incorporated a social-emotional learning environment that was supported by a therapeutic program. In this school, Sandra was provided with a community where she felt safe to learn academically, as well as learn how to manage and tolerate her feelings of social anxiety. Using a collaborative and cooperative learning environment, Sandra was able to relearn how to be a member of a classroom with peers and how to self-regulate her anxiety. She enhanced her critical thinking skills by using mindful practice about being in the present, and was in a classroom that did not force her to participate and where she could learn at her own pace. She was guided toward using her own strength to learn tolerance and regain a sense of resiliency.

Although Sandra's behavior may have been at the extreme end, for many students, social anxiety enveloped them in a state of fear. Avoiding the school community was the only coping method available that allowed some students to feel safe, especially when they felt that the world was turned upside down. However, Sandra, as well as many other students, learned to navigate their social anxieties, building resilience, and finding their place within the school community.

Notes

1 Julia M. Donohue and Elizabeth Miller, "COVID-19 and School Closures," *JAMA: Journal of the American Medical Association* 324, no. 9 (2020).
2 Samantha Bates and Danielle R. Harrell, "COVID-19 School Closures: Disruptions in School-Based Support Services and Socioemotional Loss among Middle

School Students," *Journal of School Health* 94, no. 3 (2024); Deni Mazrekaj and Kristof De Witte, "The Impact of School Closures on Learning and Mental Health of Children: Lessons from the COVID-19 Pandemic," *Perspectives on Psychological Science* 19, no. 4 (2023); Sarah S. Sobalvarro et al., "The Impact of COVID-19 on Emotional, Social, and Behavioral Health in Adolescents with Preexisting Mental Health Concerns: A Qualitative Study," *Clinical Practice in Pediatric Psychology* 11, no. 2 (2023).

3 American Psychiatric Association, *Diagnostic and Statistical Manual of Mental Disorders: DSM-5-TR* (5th ed., text revision) (Washington, DC: American Psychiatric Association Publishing, 2022).

4 Monika Yadav and Tahura Ahmad. "Social Anxiety Disorder: Fear of Being Judged," *Homoeopathic Heritage* 49, no. 4 (2022).

5 Deborah C. Beidel, "Social Anxiety Disorder: Etiology and Early Clinical Presentation," *Journal of Clinical Psychiatry* 59, no. 17 (1998).

6 Sara Cruz et al., "Trajectories of Social Withdrawal and Social Anxiety and Their Relationship with Self-Esteem before, during, and after the School Lockdowns," *Scientific Reports* 13, no. 1 (2023).

7 Cruz et al., "Trajectories of Social Withdrawal."

8 Office of the Surgeon General, "Protecting Youth Mental Health: The U.S. Surgeon General's Advisory," U.S. Department of Health and Human Services, 2021, https://www.hhs.gov/sites/default/files/surgeon-general-youth-mental-health-advisory.pdf.

9 Bates and Harrell, "COVID-19 School Closures."

10 Iniussah Mahama et al., "Attached or Not Attached: Does Different Learning Styles Exist among Students with or without Sense of Belonging Amidst COVID-19?" *Journal of Educational Technology and Online Learning* 4, no. 2 (2021).

11 Cruz et al., "Trajectories of Social Withdrawal"; Nazish Imran et al., "Psychological Burden of Quarantine in Children and Adolescents: A Rapid Systematic Review and Proposed Solutions," *Pakistan Journal of Medical Sciences* 36, no. 5 (2020).

12 Imran et al., "Psychological Burden."

13 Imran et al., "Psychological Burden."

14 Sobalvarro et al., "Impact of COVID–19."

15 V. Sousa et al., "Can an Universal School-Based Social Emotional Learning Program Reduce Adolescents' Social Withdrawal and Social Anxiety," *Journal of Youth and Adolescence:* 52, no. 11 (2023): 2404–2416.

16 Laura Hamilton and Betheny Gross, "How Has the Pandemic Affected Students' Social-Emotional Well-Being? A Review of the Evidence to Date," *Center on Reinventing Public Education* (2021). https://eric.ed.gov/?id=ED614131

17 Mazrekaj and De Witte, "Impact of School Closures."

18 Bates and Harrell, "COVID-19 School Closures."

19 Bates and Harrell, "COVID-19 School Closures."

20 Centers for Disease Control and Prevention, "2023 Youth Risk Behavior Survey Results," Youth Risk Behavior Surveillance System (YRBSS), 2023, https://www.cdc.gov/yrbs/results/2023-yrbs-results.html

21 Mickayla Dussault and Robert B. Thompson, "Fundamental Themes in Social–Emotional Learning: A Theoretical Framework for Inclusivity," *International Journal of Environmental Research and Public Health* 21, no. 4 (2024).

22 Larry D. Evans, "Functional School Refusal Subtypes: Anxiety, Avoidance, and Malingering," *Psychology in the Schools* 37, no. 2 (2000).

23 Celene E. Domitrovich et al., "Promoting Social and Emotional Learning in Middle School: Intervention Effects of Facing History and Ourselves," *Journal of Youth and Adolescence* 51, no. 7 (2022).

24 Linda Dusenbury et al., "What Does Evidence-Based Instruction in Social and Emotional Learning Actually Look Like in Practice? A Brief on Findings from CASEL's Program Reviews," *Collaborative for Academic, Social, and Emotional Learning* (2015). https://eric.ed.gov/?id=ED574862
25 Charley Todd et al., "Implementing SEL in the Classroom: A Practitioner Perspective," *Clearing House: A Journal of Educational Strategies, Issues and Ideas* 95, no. 1 (2022).
26 Domitrovich et al., "Promoting Social and Emotional Learning."

Reference List

American Psychiatric Association. *Diagnostic and Statistical Manual of Mental Disorders: DSM-5-TR* (5th ed., text revision). Washington, DC: American Psychiatric Association Publishing, 2022.

Bates, Samantha, and Danielle R. Harrell. "COVID-19 School Closures: Disruptions in School-Based Support Services and Socioemotional Loss among Middle School Students." *Journal of School Health* 94, no. 3 (2024): 209–218.

Beidel, Deborah C. "Social Anxiety Disorder: Etiology and Early Clinical Presentation." *Journal of Clinical Psychiatry* 59, no. 17 (1998): 27–32.

Centers for Disease Control and Prevention. "2023 Youth Risk Behavior Survey Results." Youth Risk Behavior Surveillance System (YRBSS), 2023. https://www.cdc.gov/yrbs/results/2023-yrbs-results.html

Cruz, Sara, Mariana Sousa, Marta Marchante, and Vítor Alexandre Coelho. "Trajectories of Social Withdrawal and Social Anxiety and Their Relationship with Self-Esteem before, during, and after the School Lockdowns." *Scientific Reports* 13, no. 1 (2023): 1–10.

Domitrovich, Celene E., Alexis R. Harris, Amy K. Syvertsen et al. "Promoting Social and Emotional Learning in Middle School: Intervention Effects of Facing History and Ourselves." *Journal of Youth and Adolescence* 51, no. 7 (2022): 1426–1441.

Donohue, Julia M., and Elizabeth Miller. "COVID-19 and School Closures." *JAMA: Journal of the American Medical Association* 324, no. 9 (2020): 845–847.

Dusenbury, Linda, Sophia Calin, Celene Domitrovich, and Roger P. Weissberg. "What Does Evidence-Based Instruction in Social and Emotional Learning Actually Look Like in Practice? A Brief on Findings from CASEL's Program Reviews." *Collaborative for Academic, Social, and Emotional Learning* (2015). https://eric.ed.gov/?id=ED574862

Dussault, Mickayla, and Robert B. Thompson. "Fundamental Themes in Social–Emotional Learning: A Theoretical Framework for Inclusivity." *International Journal of Environmental Research and Public Health* 21, no. 4 (2024): 506.

Evans, Larry D. "Functional School Refusal Subtypes: Anxiety, Avoidance, and Malingering." *Psychology in the Schools* 37, no. 2 (2000): 183–191.

Hamilton, Laura, and Betheny Gross. "How Has the Pandemic Affected Students' Social-Emotional Well-Being? A Review of the Evidence to Date." *Center on Reinventing Public Education* (2021). https://eric.ed.gov/?id=ED614131

Imran, Nazish, Irum Aamer, Muhammad Imran Sharif, Zubair Hassan Bodla, and Sadiq Naveed. "Psychological Burden of Quarantine in Children and Adolescents: A Rapid Systematic Review and Proposed Solutions." *Pakistan Journal of Medical Sciences* 36, no. 5 (2020): 1106–1116.

Mahama, Iniussah, Felix Larbe Asante, Jonathan Kwame Mensah et al. "Attached or Not Attached: Does Different Learning Styles Exist among Students with or without Sense of Belonging Amidst COVID-19?" *Journal of Educational Technology and Online Learning* 4, no. 2 (2021): 175–192.

Mazrekaj, Deni, and Kristof De Witte. "The Impact of School Closures on Learning and Mental Health of Children: Lessons from the COVID-19 Pandemic." *Perspectives on Psychological Science* 19, no. 4 (2023): 686–693.
Office of the Surgeon General. "Protecting Youth Mental Health: The U.S. Surgeon General's Advisory." U.S. Department of Health and Human Services, 2021. https://www.hhs.gov/sites/default/files/surgeon-general-youth-mental-health-advisory.pdf.
Sobalvarro, Sarah S., Javier A. Cepeda, Janelle T. Garcia et al. "The Impact of COVID-19 on Emotional, Social, and Behavioral Health in Adolescents with Preexisting Mental Health Concerns: A Qualitative Study." *Clinical Practice in Pediatric Psychology* 11, no. 2 (2023): 228–238.
Sousa, V., P. R. Silva, A. M. Romão et al. "Can an Universal School-Based Social Emotional Learning Program Reduce Adolescents' Social Withdrawal and Social Anxiety?" *Journal of Youth Adolescence* 52 (2023): 2404–2416. https://doi.org/10.1007/s10964-023-01840-4
Todd, Charley, Moriah Smothers, and Tori Colson. "Implementing SEL in the Classroom: A Practitioner Perspective." *Clearing House: A Journal of Educational Strategies, Issues and Ideas* 95, no. 1 (2022): 18–25.
Yadav, Monika, and Tahura Ahmad. "Social Anxiety Disorder: Fear of Being Judged." *Homoeopathic Heritage* 49, no. 4 (2022): 55–58.

5 Is Suspension Just Another Pathway to School Avoidance?

Data released in 2020–2021 by the Education Office of Civil Rights focusing on discipline showed that out of 49.4 million public school students nationwide, 786,000 students from kindergarten to twelfth grade received one or more in-school suspensions, 638,700 received one or more out-of-school suspensions, and 28,300 were expelled.[1] Suspension, also referred to as exclusionary discipline, involves removing a student from the classroom or school as a punishment for violating the school code of conduct. Every school district has a code of conduct that all students are expected to follow, as it defines acceptable forms of behaviors and interactions within the school community. Students who are suspended are more likely to suffer academically, miss educational opportunities, or repeat a grade and are less likely to graduate from high school, preferring instead to stop attending school.[2] Suspensions also disproportionately impact students of color and students with disabilities.

In one small school, situated in the northeastern United States, the national data comes into stark reality. The school district is located in a small city covering 4.4 square miles and is home to nearly 74,000 residents with a low to middle-class median income. Most families live in multifamily homes or public housing. Homes that are well-kept are located next to homes that are dilapidated, giving the neighborhood a lopsided appearance. There is a constant flow of people in and out, as many neighborhoods are not safe and there is a need to seek safer places to live. The city is situated in an inner-ring suburb within a wealthy county. Despite the affluence of its surroundings, the district is marred by violence and drug-related activities and characterized by poverty in terms of wealth, healthcare, and housing, and the lack of all three directly impacts educational opportunities for students. The school district serves 7,000 students situated in 12 elementary schools, three middle schools, and three high schools. The graduation rate is 74%, and many students do not pursue college or other postsecondary education options. Nearly three-quarters of the student population qualify for reduced or free breakfast and lunch programs. Less than half of the

DOI: 10.4324/9781003731221-5

students are proficient in reading, and only one-quarter are proficient in math. There are 12 students for every one teacher, and the student body is nearly three-quarters Black, a little less than one-quarter Hispanic, and the remainder are multiracial.

The school district is overwhelmed by problems and under significant financial stress. The teacher's union is demanding an increase in salary, and the city cannot support the school system, as it has been unable to collect enough property taxes. As a result, the district struggles to provide an adequate education to its students. Students who have difficulty understanding or completing tasks and require additional assistance will not receive appropriate support, as the special education department is overwhelmed and understaffed. As a result, many students slip through the cracks, go unidentified as needing extra support, and gradually disengage—finding the school hallways far more enticing than the classroom. Although roaming the hallways is a violation of the school's code of conduct—which states that all students shall be in class during class time—these students feel unsupported, as they have not been provided adequate academic or social-emotional support, and feel their needs have been ignored by school staff. In addition, their parents also have a difficult time contacting office staff for special education services, as no one answers the phone to provide answers.

For many of these students, the hallways become their classroom. However, since this behavior violates the code of conduct, they are unfairly suspended, resulting in even greater loss of learning opportunities. Among this population is one student who has never experienced academic support and has been suspended so many times that daily attendance became impossible.

Nathan's Suspension Begins in First Grade

Nathan was born in the school district and is the youngest of three siblings, with an older sister who is 22 years old and an older brother who is 25 years old. His parents, who were born in Columbia, have been living in the United States for nearly 25 years. The family visits Columbia frequently, and Nathan spends summers with his maternal and paternal family members. Both of his parents are high school educated and value education. They are hardworking, with Nathan's mother employed as a babysitter and Nathan's father self-employed as a painter. His older sister graduated from the local high school and is attending college, while his older brother also finished high school and decided not to attend college, preferring to work as a bartender.

The family resides in a modest home with three bedrooms on the first floor of a two-story house. There is a large cat that roams the house, and

Nathan shares a bedroom with his older brother while his sister and his parents each have their own room. There is a small backyard, and his father parks the truck that he uses for painting in the driveway. Across the street are apartments for families that are below the median income and require housing assistance, while up the block are private homes as well as homes for rent. It is also close to a local hospital, downtown main street, and public transportation. The family feels safe in their neighborhood and has friends who live nearby.

Nathan has enjoyed boxing since he was in the sixth grade, and helps out at a local gym when he has free time. He is bilingual, speaking English and Spanish with his friends and siblings and only Spanish with his parents. During times when he is suspended from school, Nathan will either remain at home watching videos, or his father will take him to work so as not to leave him alone all day long. Although Nathan does not have a large social network or support system, he maintains friendships with a small circle of friends he has known for many years.

Nathan's story begins at birth, when he had to remain in intensive care due to heart concerns that required surgery when he was three weeks old. The surgery was successful, and he was sent home. Although he was reported to have obtained developmental milestones within normal range, he was a colicky baby who was not easily soothed. By 17 months, Nathan's parents were concerned, and he was referred for evaluations due to his limited language skills in speaking and understanding both Spanish and English. The evaluator noted that Nathan had certain activities such as blocks and puzzles that he preferred, and would not sit for activities that he did not enjoy. He required constant redirection and refocusing on tasks, and could not verbally identify objects. As a result, he was referred for services to improve his speech and language abilities. These services continued through preschool and into elementary school, where he was identified as a student with a disability and provided with an Individualized Educational Plan (IEP) with a classification of Other Health Impairment. Nathan's IEP focused on continuing to develop speech and language skills, as well as having teachers monitor his attention when completing tasks in the classroom.

While in kindergarten, Nathan was a student who was not easily soothed, as he wanted to be home with his mother. In the classroom, Nathan had trouble understanding content and classroom direction, as his language deficits were significant. He would only participate in preferred activities such as recess or gym, and would not sit for activities that he did not enjoy such as writing or math. He also required constant redirection and refocusing on a task. Thus, he would easily become frustrated and throw tantrums, which included yelling, crying, and throwing objects. It would take a while for him to calm down and rejoin classroom activities. The school staff were at a loss as to how to best manage him in the classroom, and decided to develop an in-school behavior plan. The plan included understanding what was triggering Nathan's tantrums and how to assist him with emotional regulation. The plan moved forward with Nathan into the first grade, where his behaviors continued to escalate and his dysregulated behavior led to an in-school suspension. In-school suspension refers to being placed in a classroom with other students who have also been suspended and provided with work to complete. It is a more structured and supervised classroom with a teacher, and the student remains in the classroom for the duration of the school day.

Nathan's dysregulated behaviors never abated as he moved up through the grade levels, and school staff focused exclusively on his maladaptive behaviors rather than recognizing that they were a result of his significant speech and language delays and inability to maintain attention long enough to complete tasks. By third grade, Nathan had been referred for special education services, provided with an IEP, classified with emotional disturbance, was receiving mental health services via a local agency as well as at school, and had already been diagnosed with Disruptive Mood Dysregulation, Intermittent Explosive Disorder, and Attention Deficit Hyperactivity Disorder. Additionally, he was hospitalized for five days when he was 9 years old, during which time he was prescribed medications for his multiple diagnoses. Despite receiving therapeutic treatment both in and outside of school, Nathan was unable to internalize strategies to manage his feelings, leading him to act out when he felt angry or frustrated. He had difficulty with emotional regulation, staying focused, and processing language efficiently to acquire knowledge. Thus, his elementary school experience was unsuccessful due to a variety of factors that included his maladaptive behaviors—which led to both his in-school and out-of-school suspension at least once every six weeks—and his attendance at a school that was hyper-focused on these behaviors rather than the underlying academic needs that contributed to them. In fact, by the time Nathan reached middle school, he had already missed a full year of schooling due to the number of suspensions he had received from first to fifth grade.

What Is the Purpose of Suspending a Student?

The purpose of suspension is the removal of a disruptive student from a school community to maintain or improve the learning environment.[3] The removal is due to the student's failure to follow the code of conduct, which all students must follow and is printed and available online to the school community. While school districts in each state have different regulations regarding discipline, all students have the statutory right under federal education law known as the Individuals with Disabilities Education Act to be notified of the code of conduct, the right to a notice of any charges made against them, and the right to be heard under proper circumstances. In addition to following federal regulations, school districts also adhere to their state regulations concerning discipline for students who are insubordinate, disorderly, violent, disruptive, or whose conduct endangers the safety, morals, health, or welfare of others.

In general, discipline may begin with a conversation with the principal and can result in a few hours of detention or an in-school suspension as described in the previous section, where the student attends school but remains in a separate class that is structured and supervised by a teacher. For more serious violations of the code of conduct, the student may be suspended, meaning they are not allowed to attend classes or remain on school grounds for a specified period. If the violation is serious, two forms of suspension can result: the first is a short-term suspension that is referred to as a principal's suspension, and can last from one to five days. The second is referred to as a superintendent suspension, which can last from six days to more than a year. In either case, a parent or guardian has the right to meet with the school staff and discuss what happened and to present evidence in the student's defense to argue against the suspension. Students who are suspended are legally entitled to home instruction for several hours each day where they can continue with classroom expectations for the curriculum.

Specific to a student receiving special education, Federal Education Law 20 U.S.C. § 1415 (k) provides the legal definition for procedural safeguards that protect the rights of a student with a disability. Among the procedural safeguards are those that pertain to discipline, such as the requirements for due process hearings, as well as procedures that allow school personnel to place students with a disability in an alternative educational setting when they have violated a code of student conduct. Discipline procedures are also noted in Federal Education Law 20 U.S.C. § 300.530, which explain the rights of children with disabilities when being disciplined and the authority of school personnel when suspending, expelling, or temporarily placing a student in an interim educational setting for disciplinary purposes.

Suspending Students with Disabilities

Educational law states that students with disabilities can be disciplined in the same way as all students in the school community. However, when a student with a disability has violated the code of conduct and is suspended for ten days and/or there is a change in placement, the student with the disability has due process rights and protections. Due process refers to substantive procedural rights guaranteed by the Fifth Amendment of the U.S. Constitution, as well as the Fourteenth Amendment, which guarantees equal protection and due process. For students with disabilities, this means that when they are accused of either misconduct or violating the code of conduct, they have the legal right to defend themselves prior to being suspended.

If the student is suspended for a short period, that student's due process includes notification of the alleged misconduct and proposed punishment in a written statement, an explanation of the evidence, and the opportunity to challenge the allegations and present their side of the story. If the proposed penalty is longer than ten days, the district must hold a manifestation determination meeting to decide whether the behavior that caused the suspension was a manifestation of the student's disability or a weakness in the IEP.

A manifestation determination meeting is a review of relevant information, such as the educational file, the IEP, evaluations, teacher observations, and any diagnostic information that will answer whether the conduct in question was caused by the student's disability or the direct result of the school's failure to implement the IEP. The meeting includes the IEP team from the school, the parent/guardian, the student, and any other relevant individuals who can provide additional information. If either the student's disability or failure to implement the IEP as written is answered affirmatively, the behavior is found to be a manifestation of the student's disability. If the team determines that the student conduct is a manifestation of the disability, the IEP team must conduct a functional behavioral assessment, review and modify any existing behavioral intervention plan, and reinstate the student's current placement or consider an alternative, out-of-district placement.

If the team determines that the behavior was not a manifestation of the disability, then the student is entitled to the same disciplinary procedures as all other students and proceeds to the next step, which is a due process hearing. A due process hearing is a formal hearing with the superintendent of the school district to determine whether the student will be suspended and for how long. Prior to the due process hearing, the student is usually suspended for a short period (more than five days) and has the right to a prior written notice that indicates the time, date, and place of the hearing, as well as the rule that was violated, how it was violated, and an explanation of the student's legal rights. The school district must also explain that the student is entitled to legal counsel and provide names of low-cost or free legal counsel. The student and the student's family should also meet with the school principal, who can withdraw the suspension. The superintendent of the school district then appoints a hearing officer to officiate at the hearing. Testimony is provided under oath and both evidence and witnesses can be presented by either side. The hearing is closed to the public to protect the student's privacy.

If the hearing officer decides to suspend the student, alternatives to an educational setting are discussed, and the student is offered home instruction and will receive all of the services as stated in the IEP. A letter with the decision will then be sent to the family. These procedures are described in both federal and state laws requiring that all school districts throughout the United States follow the same procedures. Despite this legal framework, and although suspension rates vary from state to state, the reality is that racial disparities have persisted for years and students with disabilities are suspended at higher rates than students without disabilities, substantially impacting a student's risk of suspension.

Zero Tolerance for Misbehavior

Data from the Office of Civil Rights (OCR) states that in 2020–2021, there were 49.2 million K-12 students in the United States, of whom 2% had received in-school suspension and 1% had received out-of-school suspension. Black boys, White boys, and boys of mixed race were overrepresented in the suspension data, with Black boys nearly two times more likely than White boys to receive out of school suspension or expulsion. Students with disabilities represented 17% of total student enrollment, with 24% receiving in-school suspension and 29% receiving out-of-school suspension. Students with an IEP represented 14% of the total student enrollment, with 18% receiving in-school suspensions and 24% receiving out-of-school suspensions. Students with a 504 plan represented 3% of the total student enrollment, with 6% receiving in-school suspensions and 5% receiving out-of-school suspensions. In total, according to the data collected by OCR, public school students who received one or more out of school suspensions missed a total of 2 million school days.[4]

These data illustrate that certain groups of students, such as students of color and students with disabilities, are disproportionately suspended. As a result, these students miss significant portions of academic time compared to their peers and are not given opportunities to catch up. Students who are suspended are more likely to repeat a grade, less likely to graduate from high school and pursue further education, and more likely to be involved in the criminal justice system. Thus, while the objective of suspension is to maintain safety in a school environment by deterring future misbehavior, in reality, it often proves ineffective in preventing further violations of the code of conduct. Suspension fails to address the underlying reasons for the behavior, and does not provide students with alternative methods to modulate their behaviors or create opportunities to learn how to communicate and resolve conflicts more effectively.

Suspensions significantly contribute to unequal educational outcomes, as they reflect a zero-tolerance policy in which any misbehavior is criminalized rather than understood within a normative, age-appropriate developmental process.[5] Zero tolerance for misbehavior has its roots in the nineteenth century, when education focused not only on academics but also on training children how to behave and be good citizens. For nearly a century, school discipline was guided by the legal term *in loco parentis*, which translates to *in place of a parent*, providing teachers discretion in defining good versus bad behavior and disciplining with corporal punishment. This changed in the mid-twentieth century when school enrollment increased, shifting the responsibility for discipline from teachers to principals. Additionally, rules for discipline were standardized within individual school districts, and the legal framework of *in loco parentis* was eliminated.

The nature of school suspension changed in the 1980s and early 1990s, becoming more reflective of a new deterrence policy for drug violence used by the criminal justice system. Known as zero-tolerance policies, any major or minor violation for drug-related offenses resulted in a referral to the criminal justice system. These zero-tolerance policies for drugs were part of the Reagan-era War on Drugs and were institutionalized in Reagan's Drug-Free Schools Act of 1986. By 1994, due to rising concerns about gun and gang violence, the U.S. government passed the Federal Gun-Free Schools Act as part of the America's Schools Act of 1994. The America's Schools Act reauthorized the Elementary and Secondary Education Act of 1965 to provide compensatory education to disadvantaged students by targeting schools with high needs and focusing on emerging educational and social interests. Thus, as a result, any student found in possession of a firearm on school property would be expelled for one year and referred to local law enforcement.[6]

This law marked the first time the federal government tried to influence how schools suspended students and for what reasons. It also created the perception that school communities were unsafe and that students were violent offenders who needed to be controlled.[7] However, the federal government does not have the authority to decide disciplinary actions for local school districts. Instead, it influenced compliance via the America's Schools Act of 1994 by offering financial incentives for adhering to federal policies and imposing penalties for noncompliance to enhance school safety. Federal funds were allocated to increase school security measures, such as hiring police officers and school resource officers, installing metal detectors, and patrolling hallways.

In many instances, the roles of these officers were poorly defined, leading to an increase in the criminalization of school code of conduct violations.[8] This also resulted in the expansion of zero-tolerance policies where individual school districts determine their own rules for appropriate behavior, codes of conduct, and what constitutes a violation of either the rules for behavior or the code of conduct. This has led to an increase in the number of students subjected to punitive disciplinary actions. In essence, school discipline operates under the presumption of guilt rather than a presumption of innocence. The zero tolerance policy is more egregious in school districts with higher proportions of students of color and students with disabilities. These students are more likely to be disciplined and receive a harsher punishment than their peers, leading to negative perceptions that the school community is neither welcoming nor interested in assisting students in attaining their educational goals or a diploma.

Do Zero-Tolerance Policies Increase the Likelihood of School Avoidance?

The primary objective of school-based regulations regarding suspension has been the continued enforcement of zero-tolerance policies for any type of infraction. Infractions can range from minor violations of the code of conduct such as talking back to a teacher to aggressive behaviors that pose safety concerns for both the student and others. The general premise of zero-tolerance suspension policies is that students who receive the suspension will learn that there are consequences to their misbehavior and that the student will decrease the frequency of the behavior to avoid future suspensions. However, the result is usually not a decrease but rather repeated suspensions, as these policies presume that students will adhere to the code of conduct to avoid punitive consequences. However, for a zero-tolerance policy to be effective, all members of the school community must understand the code of conduct and the consequences of violating it. If not all members know or understand the code of conduct, it is difficult to ascertain the intent behind the behavior, especially if it is assumed that all misbehavior should be punished.

Zero-tolerance policies have proven to be ineffective in preventing misbehaviors and keeping a school community safe. Students who have experienced punitive zero-tolerance discipline are more likely to experience frequent suspensions that contribute to poor academic performance and grade retention as the student loses classroom learning opportunities and assignment completion. Students who have been suspended may be offered alternative educational settings, which are often academically less rigorous. Thus, students who have been suspended will have incomplete academic records and miss out on educational opportunities for continued growth, leading to long-lasting negative outcomes for success later in life.[9]

One unintended consequence of zero-tolerance suspension policies is that they fail to account for the developmental stages and unique challenges of adolescence. Adolescence is a time of great change, as it is the onset of puberty as well as a time when cognitive and social skills become more complex and sophisticated. It is the time when an adolescent begins to use reason and logic and acknowledge the perspective of others.[10] At the same time, the prefrontal cortex continues to mature, resulting in an adolescent having limited logic, judgment, reasoning, and decision-making. Emotionally, adolescents have a harder time managing and controlling their emotions, leading to impulsive and overactive behaviors that may cause the adolescent to misinterpret situations or the emotions of others.[11] Adolescence is a period when students are not able to plan or weigh the consequences of their actions, and will test boundaries and engage in risk-taking behaviors. This sense of newfound freedom goes against the rules and code of conduct of a school system.

One of the most important components of adolescence is establishing autonomy and gaining acceptance from peers while at the same time testing limits for school-specific boundaries. In fact, challenging authority is a sign that an adolescent is developing a healthy level of independence.[12] Punitive zero-tolerance policies that are defined within a criminal framework are in direct contrast to the developmental needs of adolescents. By merging the school community with law enforcement and positioning schools as enforcers of punishment, students may begin to associate educators with discipline rather than support, fostering defiance and ultimately leading to school disengagement.[13] School disciplinary responses that are punitive influence and inform whether the student perceives the school community as a supportive environment where there is equity in fostering academic engagement and promoting academic success.[14]

Does Zero-Tolerance Skew Discipline?

Thus, when the school community adheres to zero-tolerance policies in enforcing punishments, students view discipline as unfair or inconsistently applied. Often, their view is a result of not only the punitive nature of zero-tolerance policies but of the disproportionality of out-of-school suspensions by race, socioeconomic status, gender, and disability, all of which are well documented.[15] Such disparities send a powerful message to students that they are not valued or treated equitably, undermining their trust in educators and weakening their sense of belonging in the school environment.

Moreover, there is an intersectionality between race and special education classification of emotional disturbance, as these students receive out-of-school suspensions at a higher rate than students without disabilities. As per the 2020–2021 Civil Rights data collection on Student Discipline and School Climate in U.S. Public Schools, students with disabilities were overrepresented in discipline outcomes as they accounted for 17% of the total student population in the United States.[16] The data show that there is a higher proportion of racial minority students such as Nathan who are often disproportionately impacted and are more likely to be disciplined and severely punished compared to their White counterparts. Thus, schools do not make daily school attendance a priority for these students, as the school community defines them through a lens of maladaptive, dysregulated behaviors rather than as students who want to learn. As a result, due to their repeated suspensions, these students will not only have lower academic achievement in all content areas, but may be more likely to drop out.[17]

All students are expected to follow the school's code of conduct to maintain safety. Violations such as fighting, leaving school grounds, or talking back to staff typically result in in-school or out-of-school suspensions. While some students may receive only one or two suspensions during their school career, others experience repeated suspensions for the same behaviors over multiple years, which can impede the development of emotional regulation and anxiety management skills during the school day. Supporting these students is more effective when schools implement mediation and restorative practices—such as dialogue and community service—rather than relying solely on punitive measures. Prevention is further strengthened through positive behavioral interventions that engage the entire school community in defining expectations, addressing violations constructively, and supporting peers during moments of struggle.

Feeling connected to a school community allows for the creation and maintenance of social networks, an important component of an adolescent's normative developmental needs.[18] A social network can provide cohesion and a sense of trust that the student will be taken care of by the school community. If there is a paucity of connections, the student is less likely to engage, leading to loss of academic gains and social connections. More importantly, when school discipline is punitive and has a zero-sum gain, it significantly impacts how safe students feel to engage, interact, and trust that the school community will take care of their needs.

Was Suspension a Form of School Avoidance for Nathan?

By the time Nathan finished elementary school, he had been suspended so frequently that he had lost the equivalent of more than a full school year of classroom learning and social opportunities. By eleventh grade, his total number of days of suspension added up to nearly three years of lost instruction. The school district made no effort to understand the root causes of his behavior or to teach him strategies for emotional regulation. Instead, they showed zero tolerance for his struggles and little willingness to collaborate with him or his family.

Nathan's loss of classroom learning and social opportunities continued in the sixth grade when he was referred for special education services, given an IEP, and placed in an out-of-district school forty-five minutes from his home, which was done to provide therapeutic interventions that would teach him how to manage his emotions and build frustration tolerance. Nathan attended his new school faithfully, hopeful that the new placement would help him catch up academically. The school served students with learning disabilities, as well as those with significant mental health diagnoses, including mood dysregulation disorder, trauma-related disorders such as PTSD, anxiety, depression, and bipolar disorder. However, although the staff were well-intentioned, they were unable to provide assistance in helping Nathan build tolerance for frustration, nor were they able to catch him up academically. Nathan also struggled to develop and maintain peer relationships, as many students in the school were prone to explosive behavior and physical fighting rather than resolving conflicts verbally. This left him constantly on guard, uncertain of who was a friend and who might become an adversary.

Nathan remained at this school for three years, completing sixth, seventh, and eighth grades. Throughout this three-year period, he was given out-of-school suspensions multiple times, each of which was no longer than two or three days. During a meeting with Nathan, his parents, the out-of-district school, and Nathan's home school district, it was decided that this placement was no longer viable, and he was given another out-of-district placement for ninth grade. Again, this second out-of-district placement was unable to provide any assistance for Nathan in building tolerance for frustration, and he struggled with peer interactions at his new school. After a fight with a peer, a verbal altercation with a school principal, and leaving school grounds, Nathan's home school district terminated the placement and Nathan was suspended for nearly five months for fighting. While suspended, he received home instruction, which amounted to two hours each day at the public library and the expectation that he log on to Google Classroom even though he had spotty Wi-Fi in his neighborhood. Thus, Nathan continued to lose academic time and did not complete his ninth grade year in a school setting.

Despite prolonged absences and multiple suspensions from school, Nathan was promoted to the tenth grade. The district convened a meeting with Nathan, his mother, and representatives from both his home district and another out-of-district school to determine a more appropriate placement while continuing his IEP. A school closer to home was selected, and Nathan started there the following day. Almost immediately, he began clashing with staff, security guards, and peers, and within two weeks, he was suspended for punching a wall and leaving campus, followed by several additional suspensions lasting one to two days each.

It took nearly two months before Nathan began to settle in, developing enough trust in the school community to feel supported in his learning. However, his repeated history of suspensions had left him nearly two years behind academically, with reading skills still at an elementary level. After six months, he again became dysregulated, fighting with both a peer and the school principal. As a result, he was asked to leave the school and suspended for ten months.

Nathan's experience exemplifies how suspension and zero-tolerance policies subjected him to punitive disciplinary actions that never addressed the root cause of his dysregulation. For Nathan, it was the presumption of guilt that resulted in him never feeling welcome in a school community, nor was he encouraged to learn or take academic risks to increase his knowledge. His experience illustrates how punitive discipline not only isolates students but also deprives them of the opportunity to build trust, belonging, and the academic confidence needed to thrive. Over time, Nathan's repeated suspensions caused him to avoid school altogether, as it no longer felt like a safe or welcoming environment. More importantly, his story reflects the profound cost of being judged rather than understood, which left him without the sense of safety and belonging every student needs to learn and grow.

Notes

1 U.S. Department of Education, "2020–21 Civil Rights Data Collection: Student Discipline and School Climate in U.S. Public Schools," Office for Civil Rights, 2023, https://www.ed.gov/media/document/crdc-discipline-school-climate-report pdf–21409.pdf U.S. Department of Education.
2 Melanie Leung-Gagné et al., "Pushed Out: Trends and Disparities in Out-of-School Suspension," Learning Policy Institute, 2022, https://learningpolicyinstitute.org/media/3885/download?file=CRDC_School_Suspension_REPORT.pdf.
3 Ming-Te Wang et al., "Does Anyone Benefit from Exclusionary Discipline? An Exploration on the Direct and Vicarious Links between Suspensions for Minor Infraction and Adolescents' Academic Achievement," *American Psychologist* 78, no. 1 (2023).
4 U.S. Dept. of Ed., "2020–21 Civil Rights Data Collection."
5 Talley Bettens, "The Risks and Consequences of Innocence in School Discipline: Implications for Policy and Research," *Psychology, Public Policy, and Law* 30, no. 3 (2024).
6 Kelly Welch and Allison Ann Payne, "Zero Tolerance School Policies," in *The Palgrave International Handbook of School Discipline, Surveillance, and Social Control*, ed. Jo Deakin, Emmeline Taylor, and Aaron Kupchik (New York: Palgrave Macmillan, 215–234).
7 Bettens, "Risks and Consequences."
8 Bettens, "Risks and Consequences"; Welch and Payne, "Zero Tolerance."
9 Welch and Payne, "Zero Tolerance."
10 Anissa Rogers, *Human Behavior in the Social Environment: Perspectives on Development and the Life Course* (New York: Routledge, 2016).

11 Rogers, *Human Behavior*.
12 Wang et al., "Does Anyone Benefit?"
13 Juan Del Toro et al., "The Spillover Effects of Classmates' Police Intrusion on Adolescents' School-Based Defiant Behaviors: The Mediating Role of Institutional Trust," *American Psychologist* 78, no. 8 (2023).
14 Wang et al., "Does Anyone Benefit?"
15 Bettens, "Risks and Consequences"; Leung-Gagné et al., "Pushed Out"; Wang et al., "Does Anyone Benefit?"
16 U.S. Dept. of Ed., "2020–21 Civil Rights Data Collection."
17 Bettens, "Risks and Consequences."
18 Kristen N. Sobba, "Correlates and Buffers of School Avoidance: A Review of School Avoidance Literature and Applying Social Capital as a Potential Safeguard," *International Journal of Adolescence & Youth* 24, no. 3 (2018).

Reference List

Bettens, Talley. "The Risks and Consequences of Innocence in School Discipline: Implications for Policy and Research." *Psychology, Public Policy, and Law* 30, no. 3 (2024): 260–272.

Del Toro, Juan, Dylan B. Jackson, Alexander Testa, and Ming-Te Wang. "The Spillover Effects of Classmates' Police Intrusion on Adolescents' School-Based Defiant Behaviors: The Mediating Role of Institutional Trust." *American Psychologist* 78, no. 8 (2023): 941–954.

Leung-Gagné, Melanie, Jennifer McCombs, Caitlin Scott, and Daniel J. Losen. "Pushed Out: Trends and Disparities in Out-of-School Suspension." Learning Policy Institute, 2022. https://learningpolicyinstitute.org/media/3885/download?file=CRDC_School_Suspension_REPORT.pdf.

Rogers, Anissa. *Human Behavior in the Social Environment: Perspectives on Development and the Life Course*. New York: Routledge, 2016.

Sobba, Kristen N. "Correlates and Buffers of School Avoidance: A Review of School Avoidance Literature and Applying Social Capital as a Potential Safeguard." *International Journal of Adolescence & Youth* 24, no. 3 (2018): 380–394.

U.S. Department of Education. "2020–21 Civil Rights Data Collection: Student Discipline and School Climate in U.S. Public Schools." Office for Civil Rights, 2023. https://www.ed.gov/media/document/crdc-discipline-school-climate-report pdf–21409.pdf U.S. Department of Education

Wang, Ming-Te, Christina L. Scanlon, and Juan Del Toro. "Does Anyone Benefit from Exclusionary Discipline? An Exploration on the Direct and Vicarious Links between Suspensions for Minor Infraction and Adolescents' Academic Achievement." *American Psychologist* 78, no. 1 (2023): 20–35.

Welch, Kelly, and Allison Ann Payne. "Zero Tolerance School Policies." In *The Palgrave International Handbook of School Discipline, Surveillance, and Social Control*, edited by Jo Deakin, Emmeline Taylor, and Aaron Kupchik, 215–234. New York: Palgrave Macmillan.

6 Creating Space to Reclaim Student Voices

The common thread linking Alejandro, Brandon, Sandra, and Nathan was their fragile emotional attachment to their individual school communities, which, in turn, significantly impacted their academic and social growth. For each of these students, the ultimate goal shared by the school community and their parents was their reintegration back into the school community. However, for all of them, the return to school required that each was able to reach deep within themselves to draw on their own autonomy and decide how to best repair their attachment to their school community. Reintegration occurred only when they perceived themselves as ready, thereby requiring both the school community and their parents to recognize and accommodate their individual timelines. Although all four can be considered success stories, as they were able to reintegrate and reconnect with their school communities, this outcome was facilitated by a coordinated team that included home school staff, out-of-district school personnel, outside therapists, and parents. However, the process of aiding these four school-avoidant students' return was slow, as not every team member agreed with one another and, more often than not, the school-avoidant student was reluctant to engage in the process.

Successful reintegration back into a school community requires allowing school-avoidant students to be part of the process by listening to their specific needs. Most importantly, it also requires that the school-avoidant students be allowed to find their voices and autonomy toward helping to restore their fragile attachment to the school community. And, while these four students were successful in this, other students may struggle to find their voices or sense of autonomy—an essential component of feeling like a partner in the decision-making process about returning to school. This raises an important question: how can we, as a team of parents, peers, school social workers, school psychologists, outside therapists, nurses, and administrators support school-avoidant students in regaining their voices and autonomy? What values interplay and shape this critical process?

DOI: 10.4324/9781003731221-6

Providing an opportunity for school-avoidant students to use their voices begins with understanding their underlying values, priorities, and perspectives. Once these are identified and honored, appropriate resources and interventions can be integrated to support reintegration into the school community.

Was Ivan's Voice Ignored Despite His Insistence on Returning to His High School?

Ivan lives in a small community in a highly rated public school system where there are four thousand students in kindergarten through twelfth grade. The district has a student-teacher ratio of eleven to one and a little more than half of the students are proficient in math, while just under half are proficient in reading. The male to female ratio is 50%, with White students making up nearly 40% of the student population, Hispanic students nearly 38%, and Black students nearly 10%, with the rest being multiracial. It is a school district where nearly the entire high school senior population seeks and pursues secondary education.

Ivan's family moved to the United States from Ukraine prior to his birth. He lives with his mother, father, and older sister in a small, comfortable home. The family has a small network of family who reside nearby, as the extended family remained in the Ukraine. Both of his parents are employed, and Ivan and his family are close with their neighbors. They primarily speak Ukrainian at home, and Ivan easily moves between languages and culture. He has been attending school in his district since kindergarten, where he has been able to develop and maintain a small group of friends with whom he continues to socialize, often going to the local gym and playing video games with them. He seemingly progressed through each grade without too many academic difficulties, although trouble began for Ivan when schools shut down due to COVID-19 restrictions while he was in the seventh grade.

Like all of his peers, Ivan remained at home during the pandemic, learning through a computer. For him, this method was neither comfortable nor conducive to effective learning, as it became easy for him to disengage by turning off his camera, rather than remaining in view of his teachers and peers. Thus, although he may have logged on, it was difficult for his teachers to determine how much he either participated or paid attention during class instruction. When school reopened, Ivan was in the seventh grade, and the transition back to school proved to be difficult for him due to the continued distancing and mask regulations that remained in effect for most of the school year. As a result, his attachment to the school community began to quickly slip away, reaching a crisis point where he either refused to attend school or was unwilling to enter the school building even when his mother drove him to school. If he could be convinced to remain at school (sometimes by his teachers, but mostly by his mother), he would neither attend classes nor respond to teacher directives when in the classroom. Instead, he could most often be found in the school psychologist's office, where he could be alone.

By the end of seventh grade, Ivan had accumulated 73 unexcused absences, leading to concerns from his teachers, the school psychologist, and the school social worker regarding his intermittent and inconsistent daily attendance. These concerns led to his being referred to an intensive, supportive therapeutic program in another school where he could receive both academic and therapeutic interventions. Additionally, he was referred to a local hospital for a psychiatric risk assessment, as well as to the school district psychiatrist, who diagnosed him with Adjustment Disorder with Disturbance of Conduct. One of his teachers, along with his mother, also conducted a behavior assessment, and Ivan was found to have clinically significant areas of concern in withdrawal, adaptability, social skills, attention, and learning difficulties.

The following year, in eighth grade, Ivan attended only three classes from the first day of September to winter break in December, and did not participate in any school activities or learning opportunities. His teachers, the school psychologist, and the school social worker were all concerned about his withdrawal, limited adaptability, poor social skills, and problems with attention, and at their urging, Ivan's mother wrote a letter requesting that the Committee on Special Education meet to determine his initial eligibility for special education. The committee met in February of Ivan's eighth grade year, and those in attendance included the school district psychologist (who served as chair), two teachers, a second school psychologist, the school counselor, and Ivan's parents, along with an interpreter who spoke Ukrainian. In the meeting, it was noted that Ivan had already accumulated 54 absences and 39 days of tardy arrival and was significantly behind in his academic work. As a result, he was found eligible for special education and classified with emotional disturbance. Here, it should be noted that the Committee on Special Education concluded that Ivan's cognitive and academic skills were intact, and that his classification of emotional disturbance was because of his diagnosis of adjustment disorder with disturbance of conduct.

While the school team agreed with the decision, Ivan did not, although his mother convinced him that it was in his best interest to ensure that he would continue with his education. Ivan received special education services that included a class co-taught by two teachers and counseling with either a school psychologist or school social worker for the remainder of his eighth-grade year. The school team hoped that by placing Ivan in a classroom with two teachers, he would receive differentiated instructional support targeting his attendance. However, despite their best intentions, Ivan continued to refuse to be an active or engaged learner, and his absences slowly began to accumulate.

Ivan continued to accumulate more absences and refused to attend school through the fall of his freshman year of high school. And, he continued to indicate his disagreement with the school team's decision to his mother, resulting in conflict between the two of them. Ivan's mother felt torn—on the one hand, she understood the importance of both the IEP and daily school attendance, yet on the other, she wanted to honor Ivan's sense of choice and self-determination. In an effort to resolve their conflict, Ivan struck a deal with her: he would return to school if she withdrew her consent for special education services. Trusting his word, she agreed, and Ivan was declassified as a student with a disability and placed back into a general education classroom in the fall of his freshman year, leaving him without the special education support he had previously received. As the school year progressed, his situation worsened, so by the end of ninth grade, he had not attended any school counseling sessions, refused to participate in class, and had accumulated 88 absences and 51 days of tardy arrival. In response, the Committee on Special Education reconvened to reassess his needs.

Recognizing the severity of Ivan's school avoidance, the committee reinstated his special education services for the second time and referred him to his first out-of-district placement near his home, which offered an intensive therapeutic program. However, Ivan once again refused to attend the out-of-district placement, and the program staff grew increasingly concerned about his lack of communication and attendance. As a result, the committee met yet again to explore alternative placements and identified another out-of-district high school that could better address his withdrawal, limited adaptability, poor social skills, and attention difficulties.

At this meeting, it was clear that both Ivan and his mother were feeling frustrated as Ivan continued to insist that he wanted to return to his local high school. His continued insistence affected his mother, who increasingly felt at a loss and unsupported by either the home school team or the out-of-school placement team. She could not convince Ivan to attend the out-of-district placement even after having gone to visit the school and meet the team. In fact, during the interview with the out-of-district school, Ivan refused to acknowledge the team and would not engage in any reciprocal conversation. Once again, Ivan's mother pressed him to attend the out-of-district placement and, reluctant but wanting to ease his mother's distress, Ivan agreed, although his consent came with hesitation and uncertainty.

Once Ivan and his mother agreed to the placement, they requested a follow-up meeting in six weeks to determine whether it was a good fit. During the six weeks, Ivan's mother would drop him off at school, as Ivan refused to ride the school bus. Upon arrival, Ivan told his mother that he would only remain at school for an hour, and that she should wait for him in the car outside of the school building. When the hour had passed, Ivan would leave the school building and go home with his mother. He would not attend any classes, meet any students, or talk with the school team—he would only look at his phone, always refusing to engage in reciprocal contact. When the team reconvened six weeks later, the meeting was held virtually, and although Ivan did not turn on his camera, he voiced his refusal to attend the program and repeatedly expressed his desire to return to his local community high school. He was not upset or tearful, but forceful in his request to return. He provided no explanation for his school avoidance, indicating only that he felt ready to return.

Despite Ivan's request, both his home district and the team at the out-of-district school denied the return, stating that Ivan was not ready to return to his previous high school, as he had not proven that he could maintain daily attendance given that he had not attended a full day of school and that he showed a two-year history of school avoidance. Instead, both teams suggested a possible return in September the following year after he had successfully maintained daily school attendance. Although the reasons stated by both school teams may have been legitimate, the decision directly placed the blame on Ivan's behavior rather than acknowledging or validating his feelings or needs. This resulted in both Ivan and his mother becoming upset, as they felt that they were not being respected and had become alienated from the process.

Ivan's mother decided to end the meeting by revoking consent for the IEP and the out-of-district placement, and requested a mediation to be held between Ivan's family and the school district. Because mediation is a structured process of resolving conflicts using a neutral third-party mediator to promote communication, understanding, and cooperation, it promotes constructive dialogue and prevents escalation by empowering participants to have some control over the outcome, which in turn can foster autonomy and self-determination. The mediation between Ivan's family and his home school district resulted in Ivan returning to school in the ninth grade without any special education services.

Ivan's story illustrates the consequences of failing to create a supportive environment for reclaiming autonomy and voice. Despite his pleas and insistence to return to his local high school, he was marginalized in the process by both school teams—and, at times, by his mother—leaving him feeling even more disconnected. This raises important questions: Who was right in this situation? Was Ivan marginalized in the decision-making process? Was his voice overshadowed by the professionals in the meeting? What about his mother, who felt unsupported by the team and felt conflicted about what was best for Ivan? Whose values should take precedence—the professionals prioritizing academic readiness, or Ivan asserting his own agency? And ultimately, did any of the team members have the right to override Ivan's wishes, even if their reasoning was different from Ivan's or his mother's?

Autonomy, Self-Determination, and Values: Why They Are Essential

In following Ivan's story, it becomes clear that autonomy, self-determination, and values form the foundation upon which solutions, validation, and collaboration can emerge. His story illustrates the ethical conflict between obligations of duty and principles of self-determination and autonomy. The ethical conflict focuses on a student's decision to not attend school, thereby becoming school-avoidant. The harm in this decision is a loss of school community, loss of academic gain and knowledge, loss of partnerships, and an increase in conflict with peers and family systems. The decision made by the school-avoidant student affects many others, including parents, peers, school social workers, school psychologists, outside therapists, nurses, and administrators. Since the conflict manifests differently for each of these stakeholders, the shared ethical obligation to protect the school-avoidant student from harm creates a central dilemma that simultaneously challenges how much autonomy to grant the school-avoidant student. This tension shapes the relationships among the school-avoidant student and all of the stakeholders. Such conflicts emerge when stakeholder values collide, requiring that one value override another. Beyond the shared goal of educating the student, consensus often falters. However, when one key member of the team—the school-avoidant student—does not share the value of education, this raises the question of whether either the student's family, or the educational system, can truly honor the school-avoidant student's agency while still fulfilling its duty of care.

Supporting a school-avoidant student's autonomy begins with defining personal autonomy, the capacity to act freely with a self-chosen plan.[1] It is the liberty from controlling influences and agency for pursuing intentional self-action. Intentional self-actions require a plan for the execution of those actions (even if the plan is not successfully executed), as well as presupposing an understanding of the action. If the individual does not fully understand why they are pursuing intentional self-actions, they may become irrational and limit the decision-making process. For an action to qualify as autonomous, it must be free from both external and internal constraints, and involve the freedom to make a meaningful choice grounded in understanding.

However, individuals with limited autonomy, such as school-avoidant students, cannot act entirely independently, as they must comply with adult directives. Within this framework, the conflict of autonomy for school-avoidant students becomes evident in that conceptually, they should be able to decide according to their own reasoning, rather than submit to external parental or school authority. In practice, however, their decision to avoid school cannot be fully sustained as autonomous, because they are below the legal age of majority and therefore legally cannot act on their own. This dynamic creates an inherent inconsistency between the school-avoidant student's autonomy and the expectations of the family and educational systems, highlighting an ethical paradox: efforts to protect the school-avoidant student from harm may simultaneously undermine the very autonomy that ethical principles aim to respect.

For success to occur, there should be understanding and trust that every stakeholder—the school-avoidant student, parents, peers, school social workers, school psychologists, outside therapists, nurses, and administrators—has the right to hold a view, make choices, and act according to their values and beliefs.[2] Such acknowledgment fosters trust among members of the team, creating space for autonomous choice while easing fears of losing control of individual autonomy or intentional self-action.

Autonomy can be understood as both a negative and a positive obligation. On the one hand, the autonomous decision-making of a school-avoidant student may be constrained by the involvement of multiple stakeholders. Such constraints can include limitations on privacy, confidentiality, or informed consent. On the other hand, the capacity to act freely and autonomously requires that all stakeholders be treated with respect. Meaningful autonomous action often depends on cooperation among stakeholders, particularly when discussing options and sharing information in ways that are clear and easily understood. This ensures that both the school-avoidant student and parents and guardians can make decisions that reflect their values and beliefs. For this reason, the obligation to disclose information transparently from all of the stakeholders to ensure comprehension is essential to supporting adequate decision-making—and ultimately, meaningful self-determination.

Values

In considering how a school-avoidant student makes decisions about whether to attend school, it is important to examine the values that shape and guide those choices. Values allow us to mediate between ourselves and the environments in which we live and interact, influencing individual decision-making and ultimately impacting the capacity to act freely. Values reflect a preference for certain means, ends, and conditions, and can be asserted without proof, as they are subjective and feeling-based.[3] They differ from knowledge, as knowledge is based on fact, is objective, and can be tested for validity. A value follows a pattern, known as a value pattern,[4] which is defined as a direction of choice and commitment to action. Values are also action-oriented, enabling individuals to negotiate their environments toward building self-esteem and autonomy. The commitment to a set of values or a value pattern is important for all members involved in a situation where values play an important role. Values provide an opportunity to be respectful, maintain privacy, be empathic, act without judgment, maintain confidentiality, and most importantly, be supportive.

Overall, values represent neither a random set of norms nor a societal preference. Instead, they represent a standardized collective responsibility toward one another in society. A value is important in that it not only prescribes what a person ought to do but also provides a standard for evaluating behavior. In other words, if you value a certain outcome and are determined to pursue a course of action to obtain the outcome you value, then you have to be able to provide a reason for those actions. A conflict arises when the value that is being pursued toward autonomy and self-determination collides with the values of other stakeholders, each of whom have their own values for a specific outcome. Thus, value preferences continuously influence the process.[5]

Value preferences can be difficult to pursue when there is more than one value being pursued or activated. If the value preference is for self-determination and autonomy by the school-avoidant student, it competes against the value preferences of the other stakeholders (e.g., parents, peers, school social workers, school psychologists, outside therapists, nurses, administrators). Thus, when there are competing values at play, such as in the case of a school-avoidant student, the school-avoidant student's value preference of not attending school is not in the student's best interest, thus obligating the other stakeholders to select a course of action that the school-avoidant student disagrees with.

Ultimately, values can be viewed in two different ways. On the one hand, a decision regarding a value preference that results in an agreed-upon outcome will benefit everyone and can be regarded as serving the greater good. Actions based on this value prefer that the means justify the ends. On the other hand, value preferences that have a fixed moral set of rules will dictate and define whether or not the action is wrong or right regardless of the consequence, as adherence to the rules is very important in these systems. Value preferences that adhere to rules should never be disregarded, as the end is ultimately shaped by the rules.

Self-Determination Theory

Autonomy and self-determination can also be viewed within a theory of motivation known as self-determination theory. Within this theory, individuals are proactive regarding their own growth, mastering challenges and integrating new experiences.[6] To accomplish these goals requires support from the environment in which the individual resides. If the environment is not supportive, it will lead to lack of compliance, oppositional behaviors, and disengagement from the environment. When applying self-determination theory to school-avoidant students, the school environment plays a direct role in their ability to master challenges and integrate new experiences.

Self-determination theory provides a clear lens regarding autonomy within a school system. Students may be motivated to learn through external regulation—for example, seeking the pleasure and satisfaction of acquiring new knowledge, aligning schoolwork with personal interests that lead to positive outcomes, or working toward rewards such as a driver's license or participation in valued activities such as sports, theater, or the school newspaper. Others may be motivated by an integrated sense of self, in which they define and identify themselves as learners. For either external regulation or integrated sense of self, it is the student's autonomous motivation that fosters positive consequences and experiences. For school-avoidant students, however, anxiety, insecure attachment, or trauma-related stressors often interfere with their capacity to access either form of motivation. This leads to difficulty recognizing the value of growth, tolerating challenges, and integrating new experiences, reinforcing cycles of avoidance and disengagement from school.

Self-determination theory also emphasizes that all students have three core psychological needs—competence, relatedness, and autonomy—which are essential for motivation and well-being within the school environment. Competence is the desire to interact effectively with the environment; it motivates students to seek challenges because they perceive themselves to be competent and derive satisfaction from the challenge. Relatedness is the necessity for close and secure emotional bonds with others and feeling that they are part of a community, a collective whole. The third need, autonomy, refers to experiencing a choice: a willingness to behave within the confines of the environment. When students feel supported to make autonomous decisions, they are better able to internalize their school experience in a positive and supportive manner. School-avoidant students do not feel competent and are often scared to take on academic challenges, especially when they have missed many school days. Nor do school-avoidant students feel related and secure in their bonds with the school community, which leads to not feeling that they can make independent, autonomous choices.

Thus, encouraging a school-avoidant student back into the school environment requires all stakeholders to recognize the student as an autonomous decision maker and to remain mindful of the underlying value patterns that foster validation. A school-avoidant student holds a commitment to personal choices and values that may conflict with those of parents or professionals, often resulting in strong resistance to returning. While the school team has duties and obligations to ensure attendance, these responsibilities should not override the student's right to self-determination and autonomy.

How Can We Support Autonomy, Self-Determination, and Adherence to One's Values?

Ethical decision-making with regard to supporting autonomy, self-determination, and adherence to one's values is not a scientific endeavor. Rather, it is a day-to-day, situation-to-situation process of decision-making that involves analysis by all stakeholders involved. It is more often based on intuition rather than a set of prescribed actions or theories. However, despite the opaque nature of the process, where emotions often take precedence, information can be gathered in a holistic manner that is sensitive to the process and helps us to understand the situation.

A holistic approach—one that considers autonomy, self-determination, and individual value preferences—can serve as one more valuable tool for supporting school-avoidant students. Although the cases of Ivan, Alejandro, Brandon, Sandra, and Nathan are unique to the students themselves, each of them was determined to pursue autonomous decision-making that supported their self-determination and value preferences. In fact, these five students illustrate the importance of providing autonomy-supportive interventions that foster engagement, motivation, and a sense of belonging. Autonomy-supportive interventions also help to validate the school-avoidant student's experiences and help to reduce the persistent resistance to a return to school.

The implementation of autonomy-supportive interventions should involve both parents and teachers. Parents in particular are often the most significant influence on a student's development of autonomous motivation and self-determination. If a student has been able to benefit from autonomy support from home, they are more likely to be resilient and have a high success rate when facing challenges at school. However, school-avoidant students who have not been able to benefit from autonomy support at home will more likely face environmental, academic, or social difficulties that they are not able to tolerate.

Teachers also play a significant role, as they can have a profound influence on a student's autonomous motivation. A teacher who is flexible and can provide a consistent autonomy-supportive teaching style encourages students to focus on their abilities toward success. Examples that might be useful in a classroom are providing meaningful rationales for tasks, acknowledging student perspectives and feelings, and offering choices.[7]

Another method to help a school-avoidant student ensure autonomous decision-making is to uncover background information from all of the stakeholders involved to determine what each person views as an appropriate outcome. Questions for the school-avoidant student might include, but are not limited to:

- How do you define the purpose of the avoidance?
- What does school mean to you?
- Is there anything you find fun about school? Is there anything you find scary about school?
- What kind of interactions do you have with the other students?
- Is it easier to connect with a virtual community than with a real classroom?
- How much sleep are you getting each day? When do you sleep?
- Are you maintaining healthy habits?
- Can you describe any patterns or triggers that make school attendance harder?
- What do you need from the team?
- What does success look like for you?

Questions for parents and guardians might include, but are not limited to:

- What are school mornings like?
- How has your child's school avoidance affected your family life?
- What feelings come up for you when your child resists going to school?
- How do siblings or other family members respond to your child not going to school?
- What strategies have you tried at home to help? How have they worked?
- How would you describe your child's relationship with teachers or peers?
- Has your child shared any concerns about friendships, bullying, or social interactions?
- How supported do you feel by the school in addressing your child's school avoidance?
- Have you noticed patterns or triggers that make school attendance harder for your child?
- How does your child manage stress, anxiety, or feeling overwhelmed?
- What helps your child feel safe in stressful moments?
- What do you need from the team?
- What does success look like for you?

Question for the team might include, but are not limited to:

- What have you observed about the student's engagement when they are present at school?

- Are there particular classes, times of day, or environments that seem more difficult for the student?
- How does the student interact with peers and teachers while in school?
- What strengths, interests, or talents has the student demonstrated in the classroom or extracurricular activities?
- Have you noticed any consistent patterns around attendance (e.g., specific days, transitions, academic demands)?
- What situations seem to increase the student's stress or avoidance behaviors?
- What strategies have you attempted to ease transitions into the school day? How effective have they been?
- What supports are currently in place for this student (e.g., academic, social-emotional, behavioral)?
- How has the student responded to these supports?
- Are there flexible approaches (e.g., modified schedules, safe spaces, mentoring) that could be explored with the student?
- How does the school team coordinate with outside providers (e.g., therapists, doctors, community support)?
- How would you describe the student's connection to the school community?
- Does the student have a trusted adult in the building they can turn to?
- How does the team currently communicate with the student and family about absences and reengagement?
- What goals do you see as most realistic and meaningful for the student?
- How can the school partner with the family to build consistency and trust?
- What resources or professional development would help the team better support this student, as well as other students with school avoidance?

Ultimately, the ability to support autonomous decision-making and self-determination allows all of the stakeholders to identify the value preferences in a meaningful way. Once the value preferences have been identified, a common ground has been established, and decisions can be made regarding which priority or obligation justifies a course of action over other courses of action. All stakeholders should be able to explain and justify their decision and at all times ensure that the school-avoidant student—as well as their parents or guardians—are included, so that the decision-making process is made universally, rather than selectively.

Ivan Self-Advocates and Returns to His Local High School Community

Ivan's story began with his questioning whether or not any team member had the right to override his wishes, even if their reasons were different from his or his mother's. Was Ivan, as well as his mother, marginalized throughout the process?

The answer is complicated, as both the school team and Ivan were pursuing the same goal, but within different frameworks and values. This resulted in a process of returning Ivan to school that was tumultuous and lacked a sense of purpose and support because he felt that his voice was overshadowed by the voices of the team. As a result, he refused to speak to any member of the school team, either at his home school or at his two out-of-district placements. He refused to talk to any of his school therapists and would remain out of the picture during Zoom meetings. He would only speak with his mother, who was also growing frustrated and concerned about Ivan missing large amounts of school. In short, both Ivan and his mother felt marginalized in the decision-making process, with Ivan feeling that he was not allowed—and was in fact prohibited—from making autonomous decisions that would support his self-determination or value preferences.

Ivan stated his desire to return to his original high school, and the Committee on Special Education from both his home school and his out-of-district placement rejected his request. This decision devastated as well as infuriated Ivan because he did not feel that the committee supported him in returning to his home school. In fact, he specifically noted that the team was talking at him and not with or to him, and that his needs were not being met because he felt that no one was listening.

Thus, because Ivan was unable to reclaim his autonomy and self-determination, his values were suppressed, as the team viewed non-attendance as more harmful than recognizing his underlying need for autonomy, secure attachment, and emotional safety. At the same time, his mother also felt unsupported and conflicted in how to best help resolve her son's issue—she knew that school attendance was important, but she could not convince him to attend. And, she felt that she was not being heard, or that her feelings were not being validated by a committee that insisted on sending Ivan to another school rather than helping to return him to his own high school, where he felt connected.

In the end, Ivan had to fight for his autonomy, his values, and his self-determination. For him, the process—albeit arduous and often emotionally painful—provided an opportunity to find his voice and use it masterfully, allowing him to gain autonomous decision-making and strengthen his capacity for self-regulation and secure relational attachment, both with his mother and his school community. Because Ivan remained steadfast in his decision to return to his original school, the school team was compelled to acknowledge his request.

Perhaps a better way of helping school-avoidant students like Ivan is to create space for their voices rather than overriding their values. To support this process, a social contract with clear ground rules—ones that are agreed upon by all stakeholders—can help foster mutual respect. Questions such as those listed earlier in this chapter can also serve as a starting point for dialogue, helping school-avoidant students feel respected and validated while promoting autonomy and self-determination. Ultimately, Ivan's story illustrates that honoring student voice and autonomy is essential for reengaging school-avoidant students in ways that foster trust, validation, and growth.

Notes

1 Tom Beauchamp and James Childress, "Principles of Biomedical Ethics: Marking Its Fortieth Anniversary," *The American Journal of Bioethics* 19, no. 11 (2019).
2 Beauchamp and Childress, "Principles of Biomedical Ethics."
3 Charles S. Levy, "The Value Base of Social Work," *Journal of Education for Social Work* 9, no. 1 (1973); Norman Linzer, *Resolving Ethical Dilemmas in Social Work Practice* (Boston: Allyn and Bacon, 1999).
4 Levy, "Value Base of Social Work."
5 Marian Mattison, "Ethical Decision Making: The Person in the Process," *Social Work* 45, no. 3 (2000).
6 Frédéric Guay, "Applying Self-Determination Theory to Education: Regulations Types, Psychological Needs, and Autonomy Supporting Behaviors," *Canadian Journal of School Psychology* 37, no. 1 (2022).
7 Guay, "Applying Self-Determination Theory."

Reference List

Beauchamp, Tom, and James Childress. "Principles of Biomedical Ethics: Marking Its Fortieth Anniversary." *The American Journal of Bioethics* 19, no. 11 (2019): 9–12.

Guay, Frédéric. "Applying Self-Determination Theory to Education: Regulations Types, Psychological Needs, and Autonomy Supporting Behaviors." *Canadian Journal of School Psychology* 37, no. 1 (2022): 75–92.

Levy, Charles S. "The Value Base of Social Work." *Journal of Education for Social Work* 9, no. 1 (1973): 34–42.

Linzer, Norman. *Resolving Ethical Dilemmas in Social Work Practice*. Boston: Allyn and Bacon, 1999.

Mattison, Marian. "Ethical Decision Making: The Person in the Process." *Social Work* 45, no. 3 (2000): 201–212.

7 Providing a Helping Hand

For each of the students in this book, the critical component of encouraging and supporting their reengagement was the explicit affirmation that their presence was valued and that they held a meaningful place in their school community. Although each of their journeys differed, feeling safe and secure in the school environment was paramount. When these feelings were not maintained or the students felt that their feelings were not valued, it led to disengagement, disillusionment, and a diminished capacity to participate in the school community. Helping school-avoidant students reengage requires strategies that can provide students like Alejandro, Brandon, Sandra, Nathan, and Ivan with the tools necessary to help them feel that their school community values their presence.

The tools discussed in this chapter are not new, as they are widely available and easily accessible. However, they are perhaps the most important part of helping school-avoidant students reengage with either their local school communities or an out-of-district school placement. And, although these tools are widely known and in use, reviewing them will provide parents, peers, school social workers, school psychologists, outside therapists, school nurses, and administrators with guidance to effectively support a school-avoidant student.

The First Tool in the Toolbox: Wraparound Service Provision

It is clear that helping school-avoidant students return to the school community can be challenging, both for the school-avoidant student, and for all of the stakeholders: parents, peers, school social workers, school psychologists, outside therapists, nurses, and administrators. All of the stakeholders act within their own choices and value preferences, and unified consent can be hard to obtain. Thus, these differences often lead to fragmented and disconnected expectations for the student.[1] Merging the efforts of the school community, mental health professionals, and the family system provides a unified approach that considers the emotional needs of the

DOI: 10.4324/9781003731221-7

school-avoidant student. This multisystem approach is known as *wraparound service provision*.

Wraparound service provision entails a comprehensive approach that addresses an individual's needs across multiple interconnected domains of functioning. The philosophy is to provide services in a caring and supportive environment based on the needs of the student, focusing on the student's strength as well as highlighting and enumerating all of the connections the student maintains. There is also a commitment to students and their families of services being provided. Wraparound service provisions are effective when working with students with complex, multiple needs. Using a team-based approach that focuses on the specific needs of the student allows services to be flexible, comprehensive, and team-based, ensuring that the student remains involved.[2]

The framework for wraparound services is supported by the ecological systems theory as espoused by Uri Bronfenbrenner.[3] According to Bronfenbrenner, individuals, families, and communities work together within different systems that are more about the parts rather than the whole. It is a series of systems that are in constant flux, evolving and changing as members of the system interact within and without the systems. Specifically, for students, the ecological systems theory focuses on good communication between teachers and parents so that teachers can understand what is occurring within the family and stressors the students may be facing. Accordingly, if the teacher and the parents (or parent) maintain open and effective communication and collaborate with one another, this will benefit the student, since the student will know that they are supported, understood, and that their learning and well-being are a shared priority.

The idea for wraparound service began in the 1980s in North Carolina as part of the development of comprehensive community-based services to families in lieu of institutionalizing children who were in the foster care system. They were the outcome of *Willie M. v. Hunt*, a 1979 class-action lawsuit and settlement that was filed against the state of North Carolina on behalf of all institutionalized children who were assaultive, violent, or emotionally or behaviorally disturbed. The lawsuit stated that North Carolina had failed to provide adequate community-based treatment facilities, as these children were warehoused in either mental health institutions or juvenile training schools and denied meaningful treatment. Willie M. was one of the four plaintiffs, and as a result of the litigation, North Carolina recognized the right of these children to receive appropriate treatment in the least restrictive classroom setting. The least restrictive classroom setting refers to educating a child with disabilities in the general education environment to the greatest extent appropriate, providing opportunities for interaction and learning alongside typically developing peers. Additionally, the state was required to develop community-based facilities offering a continuum of social and mental health services. As a result, wraparound service provision became the preferred method for helping families with children who are emotionally or behaviorally dysregulated.

Wraparound is not a single service or a set of services. Rather, it is a consensus-building process that brings together a team of professionals, the family, the student, school providers, and other natural support systems to develop a plan of support.[4] Wraparound has three core features: it is a team-based approach, it fosters collaboration among all partners, and it is culturally responsive to the unique needs of each individual family. The primary goal of wraparound service is to literally wrap the student in care using supports, services, and interventions to ensure success at home, in school, and in the community.[5] Wraparound specifically promotes strong partnerships, shares accountability for mutually agreed upon results, sets high expectations for all members of the team, builds on the student's strengths, and embraces diversity.

Wraparound services consider students within their environment, recognizing and validating the student's complex emotional and behavioral needs.[6] It is a system of care where the intent is to improve outcomes by providing a guided service plan that develops tailored and targeted supports and interventions that are practical, realistic, and, most importantly, reflect the needs of the student. There are nine elements that are essential to the process: (1) it is community-based; (2) it is individualized and strength-based; (3) it is culturally competent; (4) it actively involves families as necessary and other active partners such as family; (5) it is a team that includes the family, child, natural supports, agencies, and community supports; (6) it promotes balancing of both informal and formal supports; (7) it offers unconditional commitment to the process; (8) members help to develop an individualized plan that best meets the needs of the students; and (9) it measures outcomes quantitatively.[7] A successful wraparound plan encourages the student's team to creatively come up with options and services that truly reflect the student and the student's family.

The wraparound process focuses on the design, implementation, and coordination of support networks between the school-avoidant student, the student's family, the school community, and mental health professionals.[8] Using wraparound services helps to create an atmosphere of collegiality and shared responsibility to target the specific area of need or stress for the school-avoidant student. The integration of different systems emphasizes a strength-based set of interventions that are committed to blending all perspectives to achieve consensus on desired outcomes.[9] The wraparound team seeks to think outside of the box to address the unique needs for each individual student.

Wraparound service provision can be considered one of the most effective options for supporting school-avoidant students in their reintegration back into a school community, as it maximizes the use of available resources. Although school-avoidant students represent only a small fraction of the school population, they often require intensive time and support to address their complex needs, and wraparound services provide a structured way to coordinate these resources. To illustrate the effectiveness of this approach, the cases of Alejandro and Brandon serve as strong examples of how wraparound service provision can foster successful outcomes. The process was set in motion when Alejandro and Brandon first met with their respective school communities toward the goal for collaboration.

The importance of wraparound service provision for Alejandro and Brandon became evident only after they had each experienced significant loss of instructional time and been school-avoidant for over one full school year. Both students expressed anger and frustration, feeling as though their voices had been disregarded. While they wanted to return to a school setting, they sought acknowledgment of their desire not to return to their home school, instead requesting a fresh start in an out-of-district placement. The wraparound service meetings provided the first context in which Alejandro and Brandon were able to articulate their needs directly to their school teams and begin the process of developing a plan that would bring multiple stakeholders together.

The Second Tool in the Toolbox: Wraparound Service Provision Using School Collaboration

The process of supporting Alejandro and Brandon could not proceed without collaboration from the school community, as designated members were responsible for making and implementing key decisions. A school community, in collaboration with parents and outside mental health providers, can effectively facilitate the wraparound process. Schools provide structure and daily routines, offer a wide range of student support services, implement special education services through Individualized Educational Plans (IEPs), integrate various learning models or environments, and foster positive school interactions.[10] The wraparound process encourages collaboration among all participants, focusing on positive, strengths-based interventions tailored to the needs of school-avoidant students, their families, and the school community. This approach is centered on creating academic and social supports that allow students to feel safe in school, enabling them to learn and succeed with the necessary support from both their families and communities.

The wraparound process initially assisted students with chronic and intensive emotional and behavioral needs[11] and has since evolved to assist students who have been identified as being at risk for chronic social-emotional problems. Effective implementation in a school setting begins with an interagency team that consists of a school-based planning team, outside agencies, and family who can identify and support the student in multiple ways. School settings are uniquely positioned to facilitate a wraparound, integrated, and interdisciplinary team (e.g., therapists, psychologists, psychiatrists) that incorporates both internal and external support. Within this framework, responsibilities can be clearly assigned, specifying who will provide support, what will be provided, and when it will occur.

Specifically, a wraparound team consists of the student, the student's family, teachers, relevant community providers, and private citizens such as extended family, neighbors, clergy, friends, or anyone who has a positive relationship with the student. The meeting occurs in the school building or remotely via Zoom or Teams. The focus is for all individuals to identify the strengths of the student and family across all systems and interactions within the community. Needs are prioritized to allow the student to stabilize behaviors and function with peers and adults. Based on the identified strengths, a set of flexible interventions and supports are developed to address the individual needs of the student, fostering engagement and success within both academic and social environments. It is important for goals and interventions to reflect the family system's values, traditions, and beliefs. Once the team is established, responsibilities and accountability measures are decided, along with check-ins that could be weekly, every other week, or monthly to adjust goals and interventions if needed. Once the goals have been met, a transition plan is developed to slowly fade out services, with a final meeting to celebrate all of the goals that were accomplished.

Alejandro and Brandon benefited from the initiation of a wraparound team that sought to work collaboratively to address their school-avoidant behaviors. Assembling this team at school took time, as neither student initially trusted the school community to support him in rebuilding connections and fostering attachment to their educational environment. Initially, the teams only included the student, his mother, the chairperson for the committee on special education, a general education classroom teacher, a special education classroom teacher, and a school psychologist.

Both Alejandro and Brandon met with their respective school teams several times. At the first meeting a wide range of support was offered using a positive, strength-based set of interventions. These interventions included a later start time, daily check-ins with the school psychologist, use of the school psychologist and school social worker's offices during lunch and free periods, an alternate gym class, time to catch up on missed classwork, and check-ins twice a month with their mothers. At the second and third meeting, outside members such as the therapist and an educational advocate were also invited to provide support outside of school.

Thus, from the first to the third meeting, the wraparound team sought to help Alejandro and Brandon with support and services toward reducing risk factors while incorporating effective clinical, medical, behavioral, and instructional strategies via daily contact with the student, family, school, and outside providers. These interactions are important in helping all of the team members focus on their specific set of responsibilities and also for checking in to change or enhance any intervention that may need tweaking. Additionally, because the focus is on the student, the wraparound school-based team can monitor and provide integrated opportunities for learning and developing positive relationships with staff and peers.

The Third Tool in the Toolbox: Wraparound Service Provision with Parent Involvement and Collaboration

A school-avoidant student's refusal to attend school—which is often driven by heightened emotional distress associated with disorganized attachment—will persist despite parental efforts to enforce daily attendance. This persistent avoidance is further complicated by the relational dynamics within the home, as families of school-avoidant students may experience complicated and dysfunctional patterns that are frequently shaped by poorly defined roles and enmeshed relationships.[12] Furthermore, parental psychopathology, such as depression, anxiety, and stress may exacerbate the challenges of managing a school-avoidant student's attendance, as the parent's psychopathology will impede the parent's ability to adequately support the child's emotional needs. Parental efficacy, or the level of knowledge and confidence parents have in their ability to parent effectively, is perhaps the most important cornerstone in supporting a school-avoidant student. Parents with high efficacy are more likely to provide a stable support system, while those with low efficacy may give up prematurely.

As part of the initial phase of the wraparound process, school officials should contact family members to discuss how best to assist the school-avoidant student. Engaging the family allows the team to explore their frustrations, the dynamics of family relationships, and their values and thoughts on reengaging the student with the school community. It empowers both the family and the student to be the drivers of the team process by making their personal set of experiences equally as important as those of the professionals and school personnel. Conversations with the family and student are crucial for identifying key information—such as strengths, weaknesses, and behavioral data—to design targeted interventions that address the student's specific needs. Involving family input early ensures that their voices are heard and incorporated into a solution-focused intervention.

Parent collaboration for Alejandro and Brandon was vital because if the mothers chose not to participate in the wraparound process, neither would their children. Both Alejandro and Brandon had complicated—and often dysfunctional—relationships with their mothers. Alejandro's mother had suddenly become a single parent and the sole breadwinner in the family, and was herself bereft when Alejandro's father left but had neither the time nor the energy to process her feelings of loss. Brandon's mother lived in a constant state of fear and anxiety that her ex-husband would take Brandon and his siblings away and sought the shelter of her childhood home, which reflected unresolved familial conflict between her and her father. Finally, neither mother had an opportunity to process how she felt about her child's decision to not attend school. They were both angry, and found themselves yelling and cajoling their sons to attend school, resulting in their feeling stymied and helpless.

When the wraparound team finally met, both mothers expressed feeling frustrated and emotionally exhausted. Each of them cried during the meeting as they stated how much they feared that too much time had passed and that each of their sons had sustained too much academic loss. They also both expressed how angry they were because they believed that school officials were blaming them for poor parenting despite their best efforts to get their sons into the school building. Both Alejandro and Brandon's mothers not only wanted a chance to express themselves, but, more importantly, wanted help in returning her son to school.

Each of the wraparound teams quickly embraced them and immediately set to work, creating interventions that would encourage Alejandro and Brandon back into the school building. The section that follows covers the interventions that they proposed.

The Fourth Tool in the Toolbox: Interventions

Interventions are another crucial tool for reintegrating a school-avoidant student with a disorganized attachment to the school community. The goal of an intervention is to acknowledge the multiple factors contributing to the student's refusal to attend school while working toward increasing the student's coping skills and improving daily attendance. By addressing the student's concerns related to school avoidance, interventions use preventive measures to alleviate the effects of these challenges. As school-avoidant behaviors start to significantly impact daily attendance and academic achievement, school personnel will begin the process of identifying the behavior or behaviors to assess how best to reintegrate the student back into the school community. Although this can be a long process, it is a necessary first step.

Identifying what interventions would be most helpful begins with assessment methods that can include structured diagnostic interviews, questionnaires, behavioral observations, behavior rating scales, functional behavior assessments, and a review of any school-related attendance data. Overall, the assessments will examine the function of the school-avoidant behavior as to whether it seeks to avoid, escape, gain attention, or pursue a desired activity outside of school.[13] Identifying the function of the behavior will also help the student to address feelings of disorganized and insecure attachment to the school community.

Intervention: Cognitive Behavioral Therapy

One intervention that is often effective with school-avoidant students and can be provided both in and out of school is cognitive-behavioral therapy (CBT). CBT is a useful tool that offers behavioral approaches to address the anxiety and depression that school-avoidant students may experience by teaching coping skills that can improve daily attendance. CBT guides the school-avoidant student in developing coping strategies such as relaxation techniques, cognitive restructuring to modify irrational thoughts, and replacing negative self-talk with positive and healthy self-talk, as well as exposure-based techniques and problem-solving. Medication may also be prescribed as part of the CBT process to help reduce intense feelings of anxiety or depression. CBT also includes a family component in which daily routines are strengthened to improve communication and create incentives toward daily school attendance. As part of the wraparound service provision framework, the goal of CBT is to support school personnel, outside service providers, and the family system in helping school-avoidant students recognize signs of stress and anxiety, and to implement healthier cognitive patterns and coping strategies that increase their tolerance for these emotions.

Intervention: Gradual Reentry

Given that forcing a school-avoidant student back into a school community can be very stressful, a gradual reentry is often recommended. Gradual reentry is a process that slowly decreases feelings of anxiety and depression while at the same time increasing tolerance for these feelings. The process begins by helping students identify which part of their morning routine is most stressful: Is it getting up in the morning, getting ready for school, eating or not eating breakfast, or getting on the school bus? Would it be more helpful and less anxiety provoking if the school-avoidant student arrived earlier or later than the other students? Would it be more helpful to leave class earlier or later to avoid crowds in the hallway? How about sitting in the corner, middle, or front of the classroom, or eating lunch in the library? These are only a few examples that can ensure that school-avoidant students play an active role in determining best practices for their support. Keeping the needs of school-avoidant students at the center of the discussion not only validates their perspective but also strengthens their motivation by giving them voice and autonomy within the process.

Another part of gradual reentry is identifying which classroom feels the safest and which staff members (e.g., the school nurse, school social workers, school psychologists, teachers, or administrators) or friends can provide a safe harbor to help the student to decompress, allowing the wave of anxiety or depression to abate and return to homeostasis. The intention of providing a safe harbor with staff members is important because it creates and envelopes the school-avoidant student in safety, both emotionally and physically. The feeling of safety can lead to feeling connected to a school community, which, in turn, enables school-avoidant students to begin to engage as learners and view themselves as valued members of the school community.

Intervention: Response to Intervention

Another effective intervention is the use of Response to Intervention (RTI), a model used in all school districts to address academic and other related school-based problems. It is a systematic, hierarchical decision-making process that uses evidenced-based strategies and regular progress monitoring. Although RTI varies from district to district, there are key principles that schools should practice with fealty, including a systems-level approach, proactive and preventive programming, alignment with student needs, data-driven decision-making and problem solving, and the implementation of school-wide practices that have demonstrated effectiveness.[14]

RTIs are used with students with academic needs such as learning difficulties in reading, writing, or math, or with students who have disruptive behaviors, emotional disturbances, or problematic social behaviors. It is a three-tiered program with universal and targeted interventions. Tier 1 is for all students, and uses a set of strategies and regular screenings to determine who may benefit from more intervention. Tier 2 is targeted intervention toward at-risk students who require additional support via small group instruction, and uses more frequent progress monitoring. Tier 3 is intensive interventions for students with severe or complex needs who require a more individualized set of services.

RTI can be helpful for a school-avoidant student, as it emphasizes early identification and treatment. If a school-based team can identify a student who has been chronically absent, there is a continuum of positive behavior interventions that can be implemented. These interventions can include conducting a formal functional behavioral assessment or implementing behavior intervention programs. A program may focus on the development of anger management skills or peer mediation. Examples of assessments include the Behavior Assessment System for Children (BASC), the Student Risk Screening Scale, and the School-avoidant Scale. These programs, interventions, and assessments allow the school community and family to begin to address the school-avoidant behavior by implementing structures that provide behavior modifications, aligning interventions with a student's needs.[15]

An RTI model, with its three tiers, is well-suited for addressing the needs of a school-avoidant student. It includes a functional behavior assessment to analyze the behavior by answering key questions about the nature of the problem, its function, and the best intervention.[16] RTI uses a purpose-driven, problem-solving approach to specifically identify either internalizing or externalizing behaviors that interfere with daily attendance, and is also compatible with other interventions a school may use such as social-emotional learning programs or positive behavior intervention programs.

Finally, RTI is a team approach that suits any wraparound service framework for a school-avoidant student. It requires a team to identify the stressor or the student's concerns, implement interventions, and monitor the interventions.

Intervention: Special Education

As mentioned earlier, one intervention that is the most commonly used—and may even be considered the most important component of wraparound services—is integrating the wraparound process with the provision of special education services. Through a team approach, support and services can be combined to reduce risk factors while incorporating effective clinical, medical, behavioral, and instructional strategies. When support and services are provided within the school setting, the school team—including nurses, psychologists, social workers, teachers, and administrators—can maintain consistent daily contact with school-avoidant students and their families. By centering the school-avoidant student, the wraparound team is able to monitor progress, provide integrated learning opportunities, and foster positive relationships with both staff and peers. Furthermore, if a school-avoidant student has fallen behind academically or continues to experience social-emotional dysregulation, the team can initiate a referral for special education service.

Specifically, when the school-based team provides and maintains wraparound services, they have firsthand knowledge of the student's strengths and weaknesses and can guide the development of an effective Individualized Education Plan (IEP) that reflects the student's academic and emotional needs. An IEP is the provision of special instruction taught by a specialized instructor for a student who has been classified with a disability (e.g., a learning disability, anxiety, depression, ADHD, speech and language disabilities, cognitive impairment) that adversely affects the student's ability to easily access or gain a meaningful education without assistance from a special education teacher or related service provider, such as a speech and language therapist, an occupational or physical therapist, or a counselor. The IEP is a legally binding document that binds the school district to provide a series of specific services to the student to ensure Free and Appropriate Public Education (FAPE) and access to the curriculum. It provides the what, who, where and how: who will provide the education, where the services will be provided, what services will be provided, and how the goals for each of the services will be provided. An IEP is specific to a student's academic or social-emotional needs and will ensure there are goals and specific timeframes to accomplish those goals.

A school-avoidant student who is found to be eligible for an IEP with an emotional disturbance classification would benefit from modifications and accommodations, as they can provide a meaningful set of interventions that will enable the student to be successful in a school-based setting. The many types of accommodations and modifications available are too numerous to list here, although here are a few that are useful for school-avoidant students: a quiet area in which to complete work; preferential seating, early dismissal from class, permission to leave class when needed, small group instruction, advanced notice of transitions, copies of class notes, extended time for tests, quiet locations for testing, graphic organizers, and fidget tools.

The purpose of the IEP is to provide specialized instruction from a specialized instructor to help gain access to the curriculum. The IEP provides additional tools that the wraparound team feels is needed as part of an overall intervention plan for the school-avoidant student.

How Did These Interventions Help Alejandro and Brandon Return to School?

Once the wraparound service provision team unified as a cohesive unit, both Alejandro and Brandon finally had opportunities to voice their concerns and fears of returning to their home school. The first step was to refer both students to the committee on special education to review any diagnostic information and school-related attendance data to aid in deciding the provisions of an IEP with a classification of emotional disturbance. Both students attended their initial meetings for eligibility, and both requested and were granted out-of-district placements where they could close their chapter at one school community and open a new chapter in another.

In both of their IEPs, Alejandro and Brandon were provided a specialized classroom with fifteen students, goals encompassing academic as well as social-emotional development, counseling with a school psychologist or school social worker, and modifications and accommodations such as a quiet area to complete work, permission to leave class when needed, advanced notice of transitions, extended time for tests, a quiet location for testing, and fidget tools. Once Alejandro and Brandon were accepted at their new schools, CBT became the preferred behavioral paradigm to help address the intense feelings of anxiety and depression both of them experienced. Their CBT goals included relaxation techniques, cognitive reframing, and replacing negative self-talk with positive and healthy self-talk. They were also offered a gradual reentry and given the opportunity to define their school day; each of them felt that early morning was difficult, so they were offered late starts for the first three weeks of school and then began attending full days after that. They were also allowed to leave earlier from a class if needed, and were asked by the team if there was a space in the building that they would prefer to go to when they needed to. Alejandro indicated that he wanted permission to visit the school nurse to talk about medical-related topics, while Brandon indicated that he preferred to go to the music room and talk with the music teacher because he wanted to learn to play the drums. At both of their schools, they were offered RTI to track their daily attendance as well as begin to help them understand the function of their avoidance and reduce the stressors around school.

Both Alejandro and Brandon thrived at their new schools and graduated with all of their peers. They were provided a safe haven where they could reengage with a school community and find joy in learning and interacting with peers and teachers.

Wraparound Services Effectively Address Complex Student Needs

School-avoidant students have a complex relationship with a school community: on the one hand, school represents a shared space where all students strive toward future goals, while on the other hand, a school community can also feel like a prison where the academic and social rules of engagement are rigid. If the school community feels unwelcoming, then daily attendance becomes an impossibility.

Creating a strong and healthy bond with a school community is a team effort between the school-avoidant student, stakeholders from the school, the student's home, and other individuals who know the student. It is a multitiered, multipronged approach that addresses the needs of the school-avoidant student in a caring and supportive manner. There is a commitment to helping the school-avoidant student, focusing on that student's strength. This team-based approach allows for flexibility and ensures that the school-avoidant student remains involved, promoting the development of self-confidence and autonomy. Ultimately, through this approach, school-avoidant students such as Alejandro and Brandon will learn that when using wraparound service provision, they are supported, understood, and their presence at school is valued.

Notes

1 Lucille Eber and C. Michael Nelson, "School-based Wraparound Planning: Integrating Services for Students with Emotional and Behavioral Needs," *American Journal of Orthopsychiatry* 67, no. 3 (1997); Lucille Eber et al., "Wraparound and Positive Behavioral Interventions and Supports in the Schools," *Journal of Emotional and Behavioral Disorders* 10, no. 3 (2002); Rondy Yu et al., "Integrating Supports for Students with Wraparound," *Contemporary School Psychology* 26 (2022).
2 Yu et al., "Integrating Supports."
3 Uri Bronfenbrenner, *The Ecology of Human Development: Experiments by Nature and Design* (Cambridge, MA: Harvard University Press, 1979).
4 Eber et al., "Wraparound and Positive Behavioral Interventions."
5 Ruth Alisha Hill, "Wraparound: A Key Component of School-Wide Culture Competence to Support Academics and Socio-Emotional Well-Being," *Peabody Journal of Education* 95, no. 1 (2020).
6 Eber and Nelson, "School-Based Wraparound Planning."
7 Eber et al., "Wraparound and Positive Behavioral Interventions."
8 Eber et al., "Wraparound and Positive Behavioral Interventions"; Yu et al., "Integrating Supports."
9 Eber et al., "Wraparound and Positive Behavioral Interventions."
10 Yu et al., "Integrating Supports."
11 Eber et al., "Wraparound and Positive Behavioral Interventions."
12 Belinda Carless et al., "The Role of Parental Self-Efficacy in Adolescent School-Refusal," *Journal of Family Psychology* 29, no. 2 (2015).
13 Christopher A. Kearney and Michelle Bates, "Addressing School Refusal Behavior: Suggestions for Frontline Professionals," *Children & Schools* 27, no. 4 (2005); Mary Wimmer, "School Refusal," *Principal Leadership* 8, no. 8 (2008).
14 Christopher A. Kearney and Patricia Graczyk, "A Response to Intervention Model to Promote School Attendance and Decrease School Absenteeism," *Child & Youth Care Forum* 43, no. 1 (2014).
15 Kearney and Graczyk, "Response to Intervention Model."
16 Kearney and Bates, "Addressing School Refusal Behavior."

Reference List

Bronfenbrenner, Urie. *The Ecology of Human Development: Experiments by Nature and Design*. Cambridge, MA: Harvard University Press, 1979.
Carless, Belinda, Glenn A. Melvin, Bruce J. Tonge, and Louise K. Newman. "The Role of Parental Self-Efficacy in Adolescent School-Refusal." *Journal of Family Psychology* 29, no. 2 (2015): 162–170.
Eber, Lucille, and C. Michael Nelson. "School-based Wraparound Planning: Integrating Services for Students with Emotional and Behavioral Needs." *American Journal of Orthopsychiatry* 67, no. 3 (1997): 385–395.
Eber, Lucille, George Sugai, Carl R. Smith, and Terrance M. Scott. "Wraparound and Positive Behavioral Interventions and Supports in the Schools." *Journal of Emotional and Behavioral Disorders* 10, no. 3 (2002): 171–180.
Graczyk, Patricia A., and Christopher A. Kearney. "Roadmap for Implementing a Multi-Tiered System of Supports Framework to Improve School Attendance." *Current Psychology* 43, no. 17 (2024): 15286–15307.

Hill, Ruth Alisha. "Wraparound: A Key Component of School-Wide Culture Competence to Support Academics and Socio-Emotional Well-Being." *Peabody Journal of Education* 95, no. 1 (2020): 66–72.

Kearney, Christopher A., and Michelle Bates. "Addressing School Refusal Behavior: Suggestions for Frontline Professionals." *Children & Schools* 27, no. 4 (2005): 207–216.

Kearney, Christopher A., and Patricia Graczyk. "A Response to Intervention Model to Promote School Attendance and Decrease School Absenteeism." *Child & Youth Care Forum* 43, no. 1 (2014): 1–25.

Wimmer, Mary. "School Refusal." *Principal Leadership* 8, no. 8 (2008): 10–14.

Yu, Rondy, Aaron Haddock, and Tyler Womack. "Integrating Supports for Students with Wraparound." *Contemporary School Psychology* 26 (2022).

8 Successful Outcomes on Their Own Terms

Alejandro, Brandon, Sandra, Nathan, and Ivan each felt isolated, disconnected, and unattached from their school communities, leading to a frayed relationship where they no longer felt safe to take social or academic risks. These five students' inability to regulate their feelings prevented them from maintaining stable relationships, and their intense feelings of anxiety led to insecure and disorganized attachments. Disengagement became a form of emotional survival, not an act of defiance. Convincing these five students that going back to school was in their best interest was both challenging and demanding, as each of them not only had to face their anxieties but also had to acknowledge that they missed being in school, missed the social interactions, and missed the academic pursuits. Most importantly, they missed the attachment they had with the community because remaining at home, isolated from the school community, was neither fun nor productive. Reintegration into school occurred only when each of them demonstrated readiness, with their voices validated and their roles recognized as integral members of the team rather than peripheral participants.

The process of returning these five students to school was challenging, as each remained steadfast in their refusal to attend. Often, for every step forward, there were three steps back. Their return to the school community was bumpy, as none of the students could find a clear path back. They felt the bridge had been broken, with lost connections deepening their sense of withdrawal from the school community. However, despite the slow progression, once they began to perceive school as a safe place, their attachments gradually shifted from insecure to secure. Each student's journey back to the school community was different, reflecting the unique nature of their attachment.

Alejandro

Alejandro was approved for a school program outside of his local school district. However, convincing him to attend school on a daily basis required

DOI: 10.4324/9781003731221-8

the efforts of staff from his home school district, staff from his new school, his mother, and an outside therapist. Moreover, Alejandro was starting in the new therapeutic school as a tenth grader at the same time that schools were beginning to reopen after the mandated school closures due to the COVID-19 pandemic, and daily in-person attendance was not required. Alejandro would often refuse to come in person and would have to be picked up at home by a school official, who would often wait for nearly an hour for Alejandro to come to the car. Or, his mother, upon her return from work early in the morning, would take Alejandro to school, and he would arrive well after the school day started. This remained his daily routine for nearly an entire school year. Throughout that school year, school staff encouraged Alejandro to attend school every day, even if he attended remotely. With the support and encouragement of a team that included his home district, his new school, his mother, and an outside therapist, Alejandro began to trust that the school community was in fact able to provide an environment where he could take academic and social risks, allowing his attachment to grow stronger and more stable.

Moreover, Alejandro began to make connections with peers, finding common interest in the medical field. He had expressed an interest in pursuing a career as a nurse, and would visit the school nurse or talk with other students who were thinking about careers that encompassed care for others. The school staff never penalized Alejandro for nonattendance, and instead, would talk with him and encourage attendance, even if it was only for half a day. By the end of his high school career, Alejandro had won an award for the most persistent and dedicated student in his grade. He was also granted a scholarship for books at the community college he planned to attend in the fall after graduation. Although Alejandro's journey back to school was slow, the school team made great efforts to encourage him and respected his pace of return.

Brandon

Brandon was also approved for an out-of-district school placement after a committee on special education meeting where he refused to return to the local high school. And, because Brandon spoke on his own behalf, he self-advocated, and the district approved his placement into a therapeutic school setting, also as a tenth grader. Although Brandon requested the school transfer, he still refused to wake up in the morning, switching his sleep time from evening to early morning. Waking him up was nearly impossible, and when he did wake up, he was grumpy, cantankerous, and argumentative with his family. The school bus would arrive every day only to have his mother send it away, and, each time it came, his mother would let Brandon know it had arrived despite his refusal to attend school. After several weeks of this, the principal of Brandon's new school drove to his home and spoke to Brandon about the need for daily attendance and the structure that school provided to students. He described to Brandon the activities and classes that he could attend, hoping it would spark a new interest in learning.

Brandon finally did begin to return to school, and for the first few weeks, he would reluctantly attend, arriving an hour after the school day had started, driven by his mother. This went on until Brandon met a few other students, who quickly embraced him and included him into their friendship circle, as they had mutual interests in music and social media as well as a shared sense of humor about why they were attending a therapeutic school. His teachers praised him and encouraged him to participate and learn new things in the culinary department that were of interest to him such as knife skills, along with topics such as the Civil War. And, similar to Alejandro, when Brandon felt supported, he was able to reorganize his attachment from one that was insecure to one that was secure.

Sandra

Sandra's journey back to school, meanwhile, has been slow and arduous. Her disengagement was a result of school closures due to the COVID-19 pandemic that led to intense feelings of social anxiety. Sandra, like the other students, was also provided with an out-of-district placement; however, unlike Alejandro and Brandon, Sandra immediately felt supported and validated at her new placement and was excited to start. She attended school on a daily basis, and although she initially did not feel comfortable at her new school, she soon realized that she was safe and could leave the classroom when feeling anxious and would visit the animals at the farm. The farm animals were an integral component of the therapeutic process at the school, as caring for them allowed students to nurture another living being, helping them to shift their focus away from their own anxieties toward empathy and responsibility. Sandra loved petting the chinchillas and stroking their soft fur, as well as feeding the chickens who roamed outside of the barn.

Sandra remained at this program for nearly a full school year. However, despite her secure attachment to the school community and the farm animals that she cared for, her feelings of social anxiety became so overwhelming that they became physical symptoms and required her to be hospitalized. Her anxiety had become so intense that it affected the neural transmitters in her brain that focused on ambulation and she became unable to walk independently, necessitating that she use a wheelchair. She also became unable to get up without assistance, and had to wait until her parents were able to lift her out of bed. Her feelings of social anxiety had resulted in a physical disability, and as a result, she was unable to return to the school or the farm and remained at home for nearly six months, where she received in-person home instruction.

After she recuperated, Sandra returned to a new school placement as she aged out of her previous one, and she began ninth grade in an emotionally supportive out-of-district high school placement that focuses on mental health, where she remains today.

Nathan

Nathan has little reason to feel any secure attachment to his school community, given the numerous times he has been suspended since kindergarten. Over the past ten years, he has been psychiatrically hospitalized for maladaptive behaviors, diagnosed with multiple psychiatric conditions, placed in several out-of-district programs where he was suspended from each, and has had to fight his way back into the school community. His experience and repeated suspensions resulted in him never feeling welcome, encouraged, or validated to learn, and he was defined as an uncooperative and angry student who refused to adhere to the code of conduct. Because Nathan was suspended so many times, he never remained in one out-of-district school placement long enough to make connections with staff or peers; in fact, his attachment to the school community began to waver starting in kindergarten. Thus, his early experiences taught him that school was a place of punishment rather than support, leaving him feeling unwelcome from the very start.

However, despite these challenges, Nathan remained determined to learn and graduate. Even though he had experienced a long history of school officials defining him within a negative and punitive lens, his determination to graduate grew stronger each year. After his final suspension, which lasted ten months, he asked to return to his local community high school, but the principal denied his request. Forced to pivot, he decided that his best course of action was to pursue a GED as an alternative to a high school diploma. He understood that his future success began with a diploma, and when he could not obtain one within his local school community, he sought an alternative path.

Ultimately, Nathan was denied the chance to experience a supportive education, leaving him alone to navigate his future without the guidance and belonging every student deserves. Thus, instead of fostering growth, the school environment reinforced disconnection, shaping a trajectory of struggle that might have been avoided with early intervention and understanding.

Ivan

Finally, Ivan's experience is the story of the dogged pursuit for self-determination and autonomy that can lead to a successful reintegration back into a school community. His return to his home school was not an easy journey, and highlighted the importance of recognizing and acknowledging a school-avoidant student's desire for autonomy and self-determination. Ivan never shared why he chose to not attend school, and his decision to not share resulted in a loss of academic skills, a loss of partnerships and peer groups, and a strained relationship with his mother. More importantly, his insistence on self-determination created an ethical dilemma, as educators were challenged to respect his autonomy while still fulfilling their responsibility to ensure his presence in school.

After a contentious meeting that included the district school team, the district attorney, Ivan, his mother, and the family's attorney, Ivan was allowed to return to school with the caveat that he begin in the ninth grade. He accepted, and returned to school the next day.

Ivan held strong to his desire that he wanted to return to his local high school community. And, he compelled all of the stakeholders involved to acknowledge his autonomy and commitment to his personal choices. His case illustrates how the recognition of student autonomy can serve as a critical factor in reengagement, highlighting the necessity for schools to balance institutional obligations with the developmental need for self-determination.

Conclusion: School Avoidance Is Not an Act of Defiance

A school-avoidant student is not a defiant student. There is no secondary emotional gain in remaining at home, isolated and disconnected from the school community. There is also no single profile of a school-avoidant student; each arrives at the decision to avoid school based on their own emotional experiences and capacity to regulate stress and anxiety. Some may have learning disabilities that were not identified or addressed early enough, while others struggle with social interactions and feel overwhelmed by the demands of peer engagement. Regardless of the underlying cause, a school-avoidant student seeks to be heard, validated, and welcomed back into the school community on their own terms.

Helping school-avoidant students return to a school community requires that we view them not in a deficit model, but rather in a supportive and empathic manner. It requires recognizing that their attachment to a school community can be complicated by family stress, trauma history, learning disabilities, mental health concerns, lack of connections, and feeling emotionally and physically unsafe. For school-avoidant students, it may be easier to hide under the covers rather than attend school and maintain their focus and attention.

Most school-avoidant students want to return to school, but often find the road back filled with potholes. School teams, parents, therapists, and others should be encouraged to provide the school-avoidant student a voice and listen to what they need and want from a school experience. A school-avoidant student seeks attachments, and the more positive the attachment, the more likely they are to return to school, ready to learn and tackle new challenges.

School-avoidant students must be cared for and nurtured to allow them to develop a sense of trust that their emotional needs will be cared for by the school team. Building healthy attachment to the school community can ease feelings of insecurity or fear, fostering greater flexibility in thoughts and actions toward others. In contrast, an insecure or disorganized attachment amplifies feelings of fear and the fight-or-flight response, dulling emotions and hindering stable relationships within the school community. It also inhibits school-avoidant students' ability to self-regulate and gradually increase their tolerance for anxiety. Ultimately, fostering secure attachment within the school community is not simply an act of support, but a foundational step toward enabling school-avoidant students to regulate their emotions, build resilience, engage meaningfully in relationships, and achieve academic success.

Robbery and Redemption: Cancer as Identity Theft

Craig Fiedler, PhD, JD
Edited and with an Epilogue by
Kent L. Koppelman

Death, Value, and Meaning Series
Series Editor: Dale A. Lund

Routledge
Taylor & Francis Group
LONDON AND NEW YORK

First published 2012 by Baywood Publishing Company, Inc.

2 Park Square, Milton Park, Abingdon, Oxfordshire OX14 4RN
605 Third Avenue, New York, NY 10017

Routledge is an imprint of the Taylor & Francis Group, an informa business

First issued in hardback 2020

Library of Congress Catalog Number: 2011024622

ISBN 13: 978-0-89503-470-0 (hbk)
ISBN 13: 978-0-89503-473-1 (pbk)

Library of Congress Cataloging-in-Publication Data

Fiedler, Craig
Robbery and redemption : cancer as identity theft / Craig Fiedler ; edited and with an epilogue by Kent L. Koppelman.
p. cm. -- (Death, value, and meaning series)
Includes bibliographical references and index.
ISBN 978-0-89503-470-0 (cloth : alk. paper) -- ISBN 978-0-89503-473-1 (pbk. : alk. paper) 1. Cancer--Psychological aspects. I. Koppelman, Kent L., 1948- II. Title.
RC261.F43 2011
616.99'42400922--dc23

2011024622

Table of Contents

Foreword

The student became the teacher, and the reversal is remarkable. While grateful for Craig Fiedler's life lessons, we are deeply sorrowful that cancer instigated so many of them. We sorely miss Craig. We are comforted by the fact that his legacy embodied in this book will continue his incredible positive contributions to this world.

We have had the pleasure of knowing Craig both BC and AD—Before Cancer and After Diagnosis. BC, we were his faculty mentors while he earned his PhD in the Department of Special Education at the University of Kansas. We were immediately impressed by his intellect, strong commitment to social justice, and work ethic. Like us, he had a child with a significant disability; naturally, he and we shared from the outset the heart-to-heart connection that families of children with disabilities feel with each other. Beyond that powerful bond, we also shared a commitment to research and its use to improve the lives of people with disabilities and their families. That commitment took two paths: Craig had received his law degree and so had one of us; and Craig was studying in special education, and both of us were in that field.

Craig flourished in every dimension of his professional life: from graduate student to assistant professor and then to full professor and dean; from author of a family-focused dissertation to an author of one of the important books about families and policy; from the author of articles in journals to the role of editor in chief of the leading journal on disability policy. In his professional role, Craig consistently adhered to the values he proclaimed even as a student: to use research for the purposes of making significant and sustainable changes in policy and practice for people and families affected by disability.

Now for AD. We were shocked when we received an e-mail from Craig stating that he had lung cancer. We asked the obvious: How could this possibly have happened? He is a nonsmoker, at the top of his game, and has important work yet to do. The existential question arose for him and for us: Why does suffering exist for good people? Why do "bad" things happen?

Theologians offer answers. But so does Craig Fiedler. To understand why we rank him with the theologians, we must explain our response to reading his book.

Reading it—reading about Craig—was both a sobering and enlightening experience. It was sobering because Craig is so totally candid about the facts and feelings surrounding the diagnosis of and battle against cancer—a battle he waged with every ounce of his being. It was enlightening because Craig shares how he transformed his previous *knowledge* of family dynamics, coping strategies, and empowerment into *wisdom*. He shares his journey of taking the knowledge from the BC phase of his life, "testing it by fire" and, like an alchemist, converting one raw material—his life and his diagnosis and battle—into an element quite unlike the original. What once was iron is now gold; where knowledge once resided, wisdom now lives.

Robbery and Redemption: Cancer as Identity Theft is chock-full of wisdom that has been learned the old fashioned, visceral way—from lived experience and keen reflection. This personal, upfront, "rubber-hit-the-road" treatise is a gift from Craig to each reader. It is his wise interpretation of his own experiences of integrating values, problem solving, and coping strategies.

We are aware that, like Craig and our own family members, any day might be the day that we, too, move from BC to AD. So as we read about Craig, we made mental notes of how we could fortify ourselves now for a life-changing diagnosis.

But even if we do not experience cancer, we are certain that we will experience untoward challenges in our and our children's and grandchildren's lives. So we subscribe to Craig's lesson: "there's no time like the present" to live each day to the fullest. Even as others have been Craig's students, so we, too, now prosper from his teaching.

Years ago, when the threat of nuclear holocaust hung heavy over the world, the southern novelist William Faulkner accepted the Nobel Prize in Literature with words so deeply appropriate to Craig and his teachings:

> I believe that man will not merely endure. He will prevail. He is immortal, not because he alone among creatures has an inexhaustible voice, but because he has a soul, a spirit capable of compassion and sacrifice and endurance.

Craig did not merely endure his cancer, his stolen identity, he prevailed, turning that loss into a redemption, offering a voice that consists of not only strategies but, more existentially, of spirit—a spirit in which compassion, sacrifice, and endurance combine. In the end, Craig's spirit is his great legacy; this book memorializes it. For that reason alone, it is a book with a universal lesson: Regardless of your stage of life—BC, AD, or otherwise challenged—you too must not only endure but prevail.

Rud and Ann Turnbull, Distinguished Professors
The Department of Special Education and
Institute for Life Span Studies
University of Kansas, Lawrence

Acknowledgments

I shared drafts of this book with many family members, colleagues, and friends. I am particularly indebted to the following individuals who read earlier versions of my manuscript and offered useful feedback: Lynn Boreson, Jack Bortz, Candy Crandall, Sharon Fiedler, Susan Finkel, Mike Ford, Lou George, Bruce Javenkoski, John Kerrigan, Kent and Jan Koppelman, Michelina Manzi, Rick Prahler, Stu Robertshaw, Steve Rose, Michael Runner, Dan and Billie Jo Rylance, John Shaw, Rich Simpson, Wayne Swanger, Becky Thorson-Randall, Rud and Ann Turnbull, Teri Wegner, Lenore Wineberg, and Lisa Young. I am thankful to Steve Busalacchi for his assistance in the publication of this book. My wife and daughter, Lindsay, provided constant encouragement, support, and feedback in writing this book. My wife has been a wonderful partner and caregiver during this devastating illness. She has made this difficult journey tolerable. I owe a special thanks to Kent Koppelman for his extensive editorial suggestions. Finally, I am grateful for the competent and caring medical professionals who have waged this cancer battle with me.

Introduction

Your life can change in an instant. I learned that lesson on January 28, 2008, when I was diagnosed with terminal lung cancer. After spending 2 months in despair, depression, and self-pity, I decided to challenge myself. I needed a project to energize me and to focus on a goal. That project became this book. I wanted to leave a summary of my thoughts, feelings, and experiences as I struggled with my terminal illness. This was one gift I could give to my family and friends. Writing this book turned out to be very therapeutic for me. As a college professor, the writing process was always a refuge to gather my thoughts and reflect upon issues I cared about. This book became my refuge from the day-to-day struggles with cancer.

In the first chapter, I begin with a short summary of my life until my diagnosis with terminal lung cancer at age 55. The title of the chapter and the book ensues from a dream I had shortly after my diagnosis. That dream was about an individual who had his personal and professional lives subsumed and stolen by another person. I realized that this dream was a metaphor for the identity theft committed by my cancer.

The subsequent chapter takes the reader on my journey and life-shattering diagnosis of terminal lung cancer—all in the space of 2 weeks. I discuss the emotional toll on me and my family. The chapter concludes with my unsuccessful surgery to remove the golf ball-sized tumor from my right lung.

I also discuss my treatment regimen. After the unsuccessful surgery, I was devastated but had to pick myself up to begin radiation and chemotherapy. This was my entrance exam into "cancer world." It is a different universe that I describe in this chapter. The roller coaster ride that is radiation and chemotherapy is graphically depicted as the side effects of my treatments at times seemed worse than my cancer symptoms.

To supplement standard treatments, I needed to develop specific coping strategies. I chronicle the intellectual, physical, emotional, and spiritual resources I relied upon in my cancer battle, including the use of humor as my primary coping mechanism. I also address spirituality and how meditation became a major tool in fighting my cancer.

Chapter 5 addresses the lessons I learned as others interacted with me in my new circumstances. Cancer or any serious illness labels you, and many people view you differently as you struggle to regain your former life. I offer practical ideas on supporting and communicating with an individual stricken with a serious or terminal illness.

My goal during treatment was to become a proactive partner with my medical team. I offer a glimpse as to how I attempted to forge such partnerships. I discuss factors involved in forming effective patient-physician partnerships, communication issues, stressors, and characteristics of "exceptional patients."

The last chapter seeks to strike a positive tone by discussing the lessons cancer has taught me. Primarily, these lessons flow from an enhanced personal insight and appreciation for life. I identify more than 20 specific "lessons in redemption" that were most meaningful for me and were instrumental in maintaining a positive perspective.

Although a highly personal story and an autobiography of sorts, my experiences can inform and enlighten individuals with serious or terminal conditions as well as their loved ones and friends. I use a number of personal anecdotes and stories in illustrating issues and themes surrounding terminal illnesses. This has been an unexpected journey, and I do not know how long it will last. I am trying to make the most of every day of this journey.

Editor's Note

Craig Fiedler died at his "retirement home" south of Tucson, Arizona, on January 4, 2009. He originally self-published his book because he was afraid that he would not live long enough to see it in print. He was right. The book came out 5 days after he died. Having published in the field of death, dying, and bereavement, I asked Craig's wife to let me submit his manuscript to publishers in this field, and I was pleased when Baywood Publishing Company chose to publish Craig's book. I offered to take on the functions of the author from making the final revisions to providing marketing information. The revisions that have been made are minimal; the only major addition is the Epilogue. Those who reviewed the book were clearly impressed with the writing and did not suggest many changes to improve the book. I feel confident that Craig would approve of this final version, and I was glad to do it. Craig was my best friend, and I still haven't absorbed his loss. Working on this book brought back memories of his passion, his humor, and his love of life. My work on this book was not a labor of love; it was a gift of love. The labor left for me is to become reconciled to his death. There is much work for me to do before I will be done with that task.

Kent Koppelman
August 22, 2010

CHAPTER 1
The Dream

I like to dream. For me, dreaming has always been like going to the movies, only there were no admission fees or exorbitant prices for popcorn and soda. I was never especially analytical about any deep psychological meanings to my dreams; I simply enjoyed them, most of them anyway.

I had not been enjoying any nighttime dreams for several months, at least none that could be remembered the next morning. I could not understand why. Perhaps it was a result of stress, exhaustion, lack of ability to shut my brain off from day-to-day issues, or perhaps I was just no longer meant to be a dreamer.

It was mid-March of 2008 when my wife, Sheri, and I decided to stay at our cabin in northern Wisconsin for a weekend when I finally broke through my "dream barrier." That did not surprise me; it was normal for me to sleep better at the cabin. It is very dark because there are no streetlights, and very little noise because only a few houses are close to ours. We arrived on Friday, and on Saturday night I was lying in bed reading before going to sleep as is my normal routine. After turning off the light around 11:00 p.m., sleep came quickly and the dream came to me in a misty shroud. I was able to remember the outline of the dream because I woke up right after having it. A glance at the clock told me that it was 4:00 a.m. Unable to get back to sleep for the rest of the night, I sat in bed and mulled over the events in the dream, trying to make sense of it. At first, it didn't seem as if the dream really applied to me. Later, the dream would seem to be a harbinger of the changes I was soon to experience as a result of my lung cancer diagnosis less than 2 months earlier.

The essence of the dream involved a man, but it clearly was not me, in fact, it was nobody whom I could readily identify. For purposes of storytelling, let's call this man Michael. Michael was living a comfortable and successful life. He had a loving wife, three children, and a successful and satisfying career. He was not prepared for the way his life was about to change dramatically. Michael lost his identity, both personal and professional. Another person subsumed his life and identity, and it was as if Michael never existed. Michael's experience was similar to that of the Jimmy Stewart character, George Bailey, in the

Frank Capra movie, *It's a Wonderful Life*. In that classic film, a distraught and suicidal George Bailey is saved by his guardian angel, Clarence. Clarence shows George what life in his hometown of Bedford Falls would be like if George had never been born. George wanders around in a stupor and can barely recognize his hometown. Nobody, not his wife, mother, or friends, are able to identify him because he was never born. This experience demonstrates the impact George had on so many people. He understands that he is not a failure and has gained a new appreciation for his life when Clarence returns him to it. Unlike reality, Hollywood films can have a happy ending.

Unfortunately for Michael, there was no happy ending in my dream. Like George Bailey, he wandered unrecognized in a world as if he had never existed. Michael was devastated and lost. How does one restore a lost identity? Restore one's life? In my dream, there was no resolution for Michael. The dream simply ended with his life and identity shattered, lost to him forever.

By the time I got up the next morning, it had become apparent that the dream had, indeed, been about me, symbolizing my struggle with the recent diagnosis of lung cancer. It was as if the person I had been prior to January of 2008, no longer existed. In a matter of 2 weeks, as the requisite tests were conducted that led to the terminal lung cancer diagnosis, my life was forever and unalterably changed:

I took a medical leave of absence from my teaching position at the university.
—I was no longer a professor.

My plans for writing a new book on special education during my sabbatical the following year, were now completely up in the air.
—I was no longer an author.

I had to step down from my position as department chair.
—I was no longer an administrator.

I had always been healthy, never missing a class due to an illness.
—I was now sick; a "patient" who was being examined, poked, and prodded by lots of medical personnel.

My wife and I had been planning on retiring in the next few years and looking forward to splitting our time between our cabin in northern Wisconsin and a recently purchased new home just south of Tucson, Arizona.
—My retirement and how long I might live to enjoy it were now in serious jeopardy.

It had always been important to me to take care of myself and fulfill my responsibilities as a faculty member, husband, and father, but after starting chemotherapy and radiation, I lacked the energy to do simple household chores.
—I was no longer an independent person but had to rely on my wife as my caregiver.

In addition to nocturnal dreams, we all dream about our future. Most people have typical childhood dreams, and later adult ones where you fantasize about all of the great possibilities for your future and all that you hope to accomplish as you grow older. And I had lots of those fantasy dreams. As a child growing up in La Crosse, Wisconsin, my first dream was to become a star athlete. The 1950s and '60s were a good time to grow up. In my neighborhood, we always had plenty of kids to organize our own baseball, basketball, or football games. The only way our games ended was when we heard our mothers' voices calling their children home for dinner. First one, then another, and eventually we would lose so many players that the game would end. As I drive through neighborhoods now, the front lawns and playgrounds are "ghost towns" of missing children. Except they are not missing. Everyone knows where they are. Instead of kids playing games they have organized on their own, children today participate in adult-organized activities or in isolated or parallel-play computer games. Perhaps they're having as much fun as I did, but I still feel grateful for growing up in the 1950s and '60s.

I was competent in some sports such as baseball, basketball, and football, but I had the misfortune of attending a large high school where there were many athletes better than I was who got the letter jackets and garnered all of the female adulation. As a consequence, not only did my true athletic prowess go unrecognized, my dating life suffered. As an adolescent, I had romantic fantasies about finding that one special woman, and we would live a fairy tale existence of eternal bliss. Instead, from junior high, high school, college, law school and my early career as a lawyer, I experienced one romantic disappointment after another. I became a serial relationship casualty. My romantic luck finally changed just before turning 29 when I met Sharon (Sheri to her close friends), who would become my wife. She would undoubtedly snicker at my reference to being an "adolescent romantic" because over the years she has regularly accused me of not being romantic enough. Like a lot of other men, I have not been attentive enough to small things like bringing her flowers unexpectedly or giving her a big hug and kiss for no particular reason. So, my plea is guilty as charged, and it is just one more accumulating piece of evidence of how much most of us take for granted in our lives—our health, our loved ones, our career, our longevity.

When pursuing a bachelor's degree in economics in college, I dreamed of becoming a lawyer. The romantic in me envisioned myself as the champion of the disenfranchised, the poor and downtrodden, fighting for social justice. After college, I actually pursued this dream by attending law school, graduating from the University of Wisconsin in 1977, and I tried to become a champion of the poor and disenfranchised. My first job out of law school was as a legal services attorney in the heart of Appalachia. For 2 years I worked in the legal services office in southeastern Kentucky, representing low-income individuals in a number of civil legal matters—domestic relations, consumer claims, social security disability, black lung benefits, environmental litigation against strip mine coal companies, and other assorted legal issues. My legal services experience provided me with quite an education. Growing up in Wisconsin, my notion of poverty was based on people who lived on the north side of La Crosse, where some houses needed painting and the yards looked untidy at times. After moving to Appalachia and meeting some of my low-income clients, I discovered what an insulated and naïve existence I had lived. Some lived in tar paper shacks that technically qualified as residences but offered very little protection against the elements. Hopefully my legal expertise and skills helped some people there, but my only certain conclusion is that I was the main beneficiary of that 2-year experience. It shaped much of my thinking and my perspective on social and political issues. In the years since then, my activities have been focused on remaining true to the values that were inculcated in me as a result of that experience.

In the summer of 1979, I moved back to my hometown. A legal services program was being established in La Crosse and they hired me as a staff attorney. After about 5 months in that position, I realized that being a lawyer for the next 40 years was not appealing to me. Thus began a period of self-examination, some would call it a career crisis, and for several months I searched for another career that fit my skills and my temperament. In the spring of 1980, I was fortunate to find a position coordinating a volunteer program for individuals with disabilities. At La Crosse Citizen Advocacy, my primary task was to recruit local volunteers, match them with children and adults with disabilities, and train them to be advocates for their partners. The program also provided support to those in matched relationships. This turned out to be a good job for me. I was able to use some of my legal skills and hold true to many of the values formed during my days in Appalachia—community development, individual empowerment, social justice, inclusion, acceptance and celebration of human differences. As if this wasn't enough, my good luck even extended to my social life because I met Sheri, who served as one of the parents on the program's advisory committee. Sheri was recently divorced and the single parent of a 2-year-old daughter, Jennifer, who was born with severe and multiple disabilities. I fell in love with both of them at about the same time.

As serendipity works, when I began as coordinator for the Citizen Advocacy Program, another individual on the advisory committee was Stu Robertshaw. Stu was a professor of special education at the University of Wisconsin-La Crosse (UWL), and a few years earlier he had taken a sabbatical to earn a law degree from the University of Wisconsin-Madison. With his professional background, he was a major asset to the committee, but I especially appreciated him because he had tons of energy and an infectious laugh. As my friendship with Stu developed, he encouraged me to think about following his example by getting an advanced degree in special education to combine with my law background. With his assistance, I completed a teaching credential in secondary social studies and then enrolled in the master's program in special education at UWL. Although continuing in my full-time position as advocacy program coordinator, for 2 years I was also a part-time student until I completed my master's degree. It was now the summer of 1982, and being back in college had reminded me how enjoyable the life of a student could be and how well I performed in that role. After graduating with the master's degree, the question was whether to seek a special education teaching job in the public schools first or proceed right to a doctoral program in special education.

By this time, I had decided that my long-term goal was to teach at a university, so with Stu's encouragement, I applied to the doctoral program at Kansas University (KU). This program is perennially rated as the best graduate program in special education, and deservedly so. My application stated my intention of combining my legal background with an emphasis on family and policy studies and emotional/behavioral disorders. Not only did Kansas accept me, they gave me a research assistantship working on a grant project to foster the inclusion of students with disabilities into general education settings.

One of the best things about being at KU was the opportunity to work under the most able guidance of nationally recognized faculty such as Drs. Rich Simpson, Richard Whelan, Ann Turnbull, and Rud Turnbull. I relished my 3-year doctoral education at Kansas, but as it was coming to an end, reality intruded with my discovery that there was no pension program for full-time students. At the tender age of 33 years old, it would be necessary for me to venture back into the job market and face the inevitable stress of finding someone to employ me. That "someone" turned out to be the University of New Hampshire at Durham.

It was the summer of 1985, and by now Sheri and I were married. With my recently bestowed PhD in hand, we carted our few belongings in a U-Haul from Kansas City to New Hampshire with 8-year-old Jennifer. We moved into a rental duplex in Dover, about 10 miles from Durham, and before long, Sheri and I were celebrating the birth of our second daughter, Lindsay. Although we enjoyed New England, especially living only 10 miles from the ocean, we quickly discovered that we could not afford to raise a family on my university salary given the high cost of living in the area. After 2 years of teaching a number of special education courses at the University of New Hampshire, I was offered an opportunity to move back to Wisconsin. I accepted a faculty position in special education at the University of Wisconsin-Oshkosh (UWO), where I have been a professor (with a couple of interim administrative assignments) for 21 years. My career dream had been realized. I enjoyed teaching, research, and writing, and my efforts were acknowledged with several university awards over the years.

Since Sheri and I tend to be workaholics, we decided to purchase a little "get away" place in northern Wisconsin so we could relax a bit on weekends. We discovered that we could not afford lake frontage property, but that was not important since we were looking for a retreat that offered privacy and seclusion. In the summer of 1993, we bought a cabin and two acres of a wooded lot, and for the next 3 years we purchased adjoining parcels of land on both sides of our

Craig and Sheri get married (with daughter Jennifer).

cabin until we owned about seven acres around the cabin. My father-in-law stayed at our cabin for the first three summers, then he purchased a five-acre parcel of land right behind us and bought an old trailer that he lived in during the summer. The rest of the year he lived in a condominium in Phoenix, Arizona. At first, he did not have electricity in the trailer because he refused to pay the electric company to run a line to his property. I am not implying that my father-in-law was a little frugal with money, but as an example of his pecuniary ways, he ran an extension cord over 200 yards from an outside electrical outlet on our cabin to his trailer.

In 1997, my father-in-law was diagnosed with stage IV lung cancer. He had been a smoker but quit a number of years ago. By late December, only 2 months after being told of his cancer, he was dead at the age of 66. Sheri was just getting to know her father once again after several years of estrangement, so this was an especially devastating loss for her. Sheri and her brother inherited their father's five acres, and having this land seemed to give her a continuing connection to her father and to provide her with a measure of comfort.

In 2001, Sheri and I decided to add a bilevel addition to the original 600 square foot cabin. This addition almost tripled the size of our little "get away" place and made our Northwood's retreat even more comfortable. Almost every weekend from Memorial Day to Labor Day we made the 3-hour drive to our cabin. It has been a wise investment because it has helped to counter our workaholic tendencies as we had hoped. We loved being able to sit on our second floor deck and not see another house. We loved watching our English Springer Spaniel

Spencer—Craig's first and favorite English Springer Spaniel.

run in the woods. At least we did until Spencer tried to befriend a porcupine and came yelping back to the cabin with about 100 quills stuck in his head, including several in his mouth. The veterinarian had to give him a general anesthetic to extract all of the porcupine quills. Months later we were still discovering a few hidden quills. Unlike poor Spencer, my life seemed charmed for the first 55 years, and I felt blessed by all that had been given to me.

Achieving so many of my childhood, adolescent, and adult dreams served as a prelude for understanding my life to date. But in addition to dreams for the future, there are also simply the dreams that come during sleep, and about 7 years ago it occurred to me that I had not had such dreams in a long time, and I missed them. This was one of the few areas of my life that did not seem right. Since sleep researchers have determined that most dreams occur during rapid eye movement (REM) sleep stages, it concerned me that I perhaps was not experiencing REM sleep. Being very restless at night, my sleep tends to come in short spurts throughout the night. According to my wife, my snoring is quite loud, but fortunately she is virtually deaf in one ear so she can bury her good ear into the pillow to effectively block the sounds of the locomotive sleeping next to her. Several years ago, Sheri noticed that I would regularly stop breathing while sleeping, and then after a few seconds wake up gasping for air. With her encouragement, I went to a sleep disorders clinic and was diagnosed as having sleep apnea. During my "diagnostic sleepover," I stopped breathing over 100 times.

The standard treatment for sleep apnea is a bedside contraption called a continuous positive airway pressure (CPAP) machine. Continuous positive airway pressure therapy uses a machine to help a person with obstructive sleep apnea breathe more easily during sleep. A CPAP machine increases air pressure in your throat so that your airway does not collapse when you breathe in. It probably also prevents impending divorces from sleep-deprived partners. The machine sits on a nightstand next to the bed, and a long hose protrudes from it with a mask on the end that fits over the restless sleeper's nose and mouth, or just nose. In my case, I opted for the mask that only covered my nose. The CPAP machine makes a constant sound somewhat like a ventilator while it is running, but that was the least of the issues in trying to get acclimated to it. For example, I tend to be just a little claustrophobic—maybe more than a little. I rarely ride elevators and have told my wife not to bury me in a coffin, preferring the nonclaustrophobic method of cremation. The claustrophobia is a result of a second-grade prank when I climbed into a school locker and my friend Lou George accidentally slammed the locker door shut after another student bumped into him. Of course, the locker door got stuck and I spent about 10 minutes crammed into that locker, fearing I would forever have to look at the world through tiny slits in the door. A janitor finally extricated me from the locker but the psychological damage had been done. So, wearing the CPAP mask over my nose brought immediate panic feelings that were not conducive to falling asleep.

Another hurdle in using the CPAP machine was my habit of sleeping on my stomach. This was a challenge with a hose attached to my nose; in fact, it was impossible to find a comfortable position on my stomach while tethered to the machine. My natural restlessness at night quickly became a man-versus-machine struggle for supremacy. Since the man was the one floundering on the end of the hose, the machine prevailed. The final indignity of using the CPAP machine was that it made my voice sound like the robotic tones of Darth Vader from *Star Wars*. I could do a perfect rendition of Vader's heartfelt, "Luke, I am your father." This effect was a consequence of me breathing more through my mouth than nose while sleeping, so a wind tunnel effect was created every time my mouth would open. This accounted for my Darth Vader impersonation and a most peculiar whistling noise that was worse than the ventilator sounds of the CPAP machine. After struggling for several weeks with the CPAP, my conclusion was that I would sleep better without the machine despite constantly gasping for air. An alternative for dealing with sleep apnea was to lose weight and that seemed like a better option. My sleep apnea dilemma was one of the few significant problems in my version of *It's a Wonderful Life.* Little did I know that in the winter of 2008, the charm would end abruptly, and the life I had known would come crashing down around me.

Odd that my hope was simply to get a better night's sleep and perhaps to dream, and then when I did have a dream, it was the dream about Michael—the stranger who was me. When my dreams continued, the new dreams would reinforce the realities of my actual life. These dreams were not a refuge as they had been in the past, but a painful reminder of how fragile life is and how it can change so dramatically and quickly. As for my new reality, it was like suddenly stepping off a cliff and falling fast, not knowing where I might land. And after landing, where would I go from there?

CHAPTER 2

Through the Looking Glass

It started with a persistent dry cough in the fall of 2007. It was not debilitating, and I did not miss any time from work. It was more of a constant nuisance, and there seemed no need to worry, at worst it might be a touch of pneumonia. After fall semester was over, Sheri and I left in mid-December for a 3-week vacation at our home near Tucson, Arizona. The warmer weather was restorative as we read, lounged by a swimming pool, hiked in the mountains, and dined at fine restaurants. Lindsay and Colin, our daughter and her boyfriend, drove from Wisconsin to join us and enjoy a week of warm weather. All in all, it was a relaxing vacation and my continuing cough did not concern me.

To celebrate the new year, Sheri and I went to a jazz concert and gourmet dinner at one of the upscale hotels in Tucson. We ushered in the new year in grand style, even dancing together at midnight—a real concession for me. We both thought that life could not be any better. At the stroke of midnight, to celebrate the arrival of 2008, balloons were let loose from the ceiling. It seemed odd that most of the balloons were black, but perhaps the intent was to signify "out with the old, in with the new." In a few weeks, the memory of the black balloons seemed almost like an omen that what may happen to you in a "new" year may not necessarily signal better things to come.

Our 3-week vacation came to an end on January 9, but upon returning to Wisconsin, the stack of accumulated mail contained some good professional news. Three manuscripts that I had submitted to professional journals in the fall had all been accepted for publication with only minor revisions required. I began working on revisions for all three and began preparing for the start of the new semester on February 4.

I have had annual physical exams every year for the past 20 years; this year my exam was scheduled for January 11. Dr. Mark Heifner had been my primary-care physician for only 2 years, but we both seemed comfortable with our doctor-patient relationship. He always took the time to talk with me and was very thorough in asking health-related questions. After going through the routine physical check-up, I told Dr. Heifner about the cough that had persisted for several weeks. He asked if there was a lot of phlegm with the cough, but I said no, the cough was dry. He didn't think it sounded like pneumonia, but he wanted to take a chest X-ray to rule out other possibilities. He set up a chest X-ray for later that day and we met afterwards to discuss the X-ray film. Dr. Heifner pointed out a mass that showed up in the lower lobe of my right lung. In response to my question about what this mass was, he acknowledged that it might be a tumor, but he felt that further testing was necessary to be sure. He scheduled a computed tomography (CT) scan for me the following Friday, January 18.

Although it was a whole week before the CT scan, I was not particularly troubled. Surely the mass would turn out to be either benign or not a tumor at all. There appeared no reason for me to worry since I had never smoked in my entire life and there was no familial history of cancer. There was much to do at work, and I was confident that the explanation for what had appeared on the chest X-ray would allow my life to return to normal again. Some antibiotics to treat the cough, and my lung would be as good as new. The human capacity to deny that anything catastrophic could happen to you is unlimited. It is a useful coping mechanism when you hear so frequently about traumas and tragedies that happen to the other guy, you know, the one you do not know. But reality is much different. Reality improvises without a script, at times defies logic, and bad things happen to people all the time, often for no apparent reason.

That Friday was a typical winter day in Wisconsin as I drove to St. Elizabeth's Hospital in Appleton for my CT scan. Having a CT scan was a new experience. In 1997, my doctor ordered a magnetic resonance imaging scan (MRI) that found a herniated disk in my lower back. For someone with claustrophobia, the MRI scan can provoke emotions ranging from anxiety to panic. Arriving at the hospital, I was relieved to discover that the CT scanner was a much more open machine than the narrow MRI tube. While stretched out on my back, an IV was put into my arm to inject a dye into my body to enhance the images on the CT scan. The technician mentioned that the IV dye would cause a metallic taste in my mouth and create the sensation of needing to urinate. She was right on both counts. Fortunately, the CT scan only took a few minutes, and every couple of minutes a mechanical-sounding voice would say, "Take a deep breathe and hold it. Okay, you can breathe now." The process was a bit mysterious, making me wonder what this machine was doing and if it might possibly be causing any further damage to my body.

After the CT scan, I drove home and gathered some materials before setting off on a 3-hour drive to meet with a group of parents who had children with disabilities. For the past 8 years, I have been involved with Parents in Partnership. This program has special education professors meeting with families that include children with a variety of disabilities for 5 weekends during a school year. The program is designed to enhance the knowledge, confidence, and skills of parents so that they can serve as effective advocates for their children with disabilities. Facilitating these parent groups has been a source of great pride, but I also immensely enjoy working with these parents. This weekend was the second of our five meetings, and it served as a good diversion because it did not allow me to dwell on my CT scan and the possible results.

On the following Monday, Sheri and I met with a pulmonologist, Dr. Bryan Avery, to review the results of the CT scan. He entered the examination room with an animated and positive demeanor. I liked him immediately. He was easy to talk to, had a good sense of humor, and was very thorough in his questions about my symptoms and health history. After displaying the CT scan image on the computer monitor, Dr. Avery pointed to a white spot in the lower lobe of my right lung and explained that with CT scans you want to see all black because that meant no abnormalities. He said that the white spot was a golf ball-sized tumor. Well, now he had my attention—a tumor! It was as if a jolt of electricity shot through my body. For the first time, I began to be concerned and scared.

Dr. Avery indicated that the tumor could be the result of one of three different causes. It could be some kind of inflammation in my lung, but he did not think that was very likely. Another possibility was that it was the result of a fungal infection. He asked a number of questions about how much time I spent outdoors—digging in the dirt or working in the garden—and he also asked about any recent trips we had taken. I said that Sheri and I liked to walk in the woods together when we went up to our cabin in northern Wisconsin. We also told him about our recently purchased home in Arizona. He said that both areas could have had some fungal bacteria that might have caused my tumor, and if that was the cause, medication for a few months was the treatment that should resolve the problem. I asked if I could choose this cause right now and be done with it. He laughed, but then he went on to talk about the third and more ominous possible cause of the tumor—cancer. Further testing would be necessary before it was possible to determine the cause of the tumor.

On January 23, I had already been scheduled a gastroscopy to determine the cause of the chronic indigestion that had been bothering me over the past couple of months. Sheri has had acid reflux disease for several years so she knew all about this procedure. A gastroscopy is a diagnostic test that involves inserting a long, thin, flexible fiber optic tube that enables a gastroenterologist to look inside your stomach and digestive tract. The procedure is painless thanks to the intravenous injection of a painkiller, typically Demerol and Versed, a mild tranquilizer. Although the patient is not given a general anesthetic, the information the hospital provided indicated that during the gastroscopy procedure, the patient would experience a "pleasant twilight sleep." For me, the experience was more like a deep sleep, and afterward I remembered nothing about the procedure. What I remember was that when the procedure was over it took an hour or two to gather my senses and my throat felt sore. After being informed that it would take several days before we would get the results, Sheri drove us home to begin the waiting game that would become a familiar refrain over the coming months.

Sheri drove me back to the hospital again on the following day for another procedure, this time to determine the cause of my lung tumor. Dr. Avery performed a bronchoscopy, a diagnostic examination of the major air passages of the lungs. Once again, a thin, flexible tube called a bronchoscope was to be inserted through my nose or mouth and into my trachea and bronchial tubes. A small tube through the bronchoscope allows small specimens to be obtained from the lung that are used for a biopsy. Similar to the gastroscopy, an IV injection of a painkiller and a tranquilizer facilitated my entrance into a comfortable twilight sleep zone. By now, it was becoming clear that my life and health had suddenly been turned over to a variety of medical specialists. I would have preferred that all my health issues could have been addressed by my primary-care physician, but the more serious your health issues, the more medical specialists must be involved in your care and treatments. If your health issues can be treated by your primary-care physician, you are fortunate.

On the following Monday, Sheri and I met with Dr. Avery to go over the results of the bronchoscopy. There are certain dates that you will always remember—December 7, 1941, November 22, 1963, and September 11, 2001. To my personal list of unforgettable dates, I have added January 28, 2008. The one common

Dr. Avery, the pulmonologist who responded sympathetically to Craig's desire for a collaborative relationship with his physicians.

theme in all of these dates is that they involved disasters and death. Dr. Avery began by stating, "We have a lot to talk about." From the look on his face, this opening comment was not a good sign for the upcoming conversation, and my fear was confirmed when he said that the tumor in the lower lobe of my right lung was malignant. I had cancer! Although anyone would try to mentally prepare yourself for the worst-case scenario, it is not possible to be calm and unmoved when you hear the word "cancer" and your name in the same sentence. The effect was as if someone had punched me in the stomach. It was hard to breathe. I could not look at Sheri for fear that I would completely come unglued.

Dr. Avery gave us a moment to collect some semblance of composure before he continued. Specifically, I had non-small cell lung cancer, Aden carcinoma. Non-small cell lung cancer is more common than small cell lung cancer, and it generally grows and spreads more slowly. Was this supposed to be my single source of "good news"? As most people know, cancer is rated by stages: I, II, IIIA, IIIB, and IV, and the higher the stage, the more bleak the prognosis. Stage IV is when the original source of cancer has started to spread to other organs and locations in your body. Dr. Avery indicated I was probably at stage IIIA where surgery is still a viable option. The full extent of my cancer could not be determined until a surgeon went into my right lung, and he recommended that this lung surgery be scheduled as soon as possible.

By now, Sheri and I had recovered from the shock and we asked Dr. Avery for an explanation of my cancer diagnosis. Since I had never been a smoker, what could have caused my lung cancer? He shook his head, saying we would probably never have an answer to that question because several factors alone or in combination could be the cause. Possibilities included exposure to secondhand tobacco smoke, radon, asbestos, and environmental pollutants. My parents had been smokers for many years, but my father quit when I was young. My mother continued to be a heavy smoker, consuming a couple of packs of Kent cigarettes per day throughout my entire childhood. Eventually my mother suffered from emphysema, and for the last 4 years of her life she had to be on oxygen 24 hours a day. I was able to see her just before she died.

Sheri and I were spending a Christmas holiday with our good friends Kent and Jan Koppelman, sharing a condo right on the ocean in San Diego. The day after we arrived, my father called to say that mom had been admitted to the hospital. She had awakened that morning completely disoriented and incoherent. In response to my proposal to fly back to La Crosse, he said not yet, that he would call me every day with medical updates. Over the next 3 days it became clear that my mother's condition was progressively deteriorating. My sister and brother-in-law from Minneapolis had driven down to La Crosse, and the doctors indicated that our mother was likely not going to return home. On New Year's Eve, Sheri and I finally decided that it was critical for me to get on a plane to La Crosse. We hurriedly made arrangements for a flight that left San Diego early on the morning of January 1, 2000. This was the year of the Y2K scare with its exaggerated fears that computers would shut down as we entered the new millennium. So, in addition to worrying about my mother's health, there was this additional concern about taking a cross-country airplane flight on that particular New Year's Day.

To my great relief, the plane landed in La Crosse without incident. My brother-in-law picked me up at the airport and drove me to the hospital. It was 3:00 in the afternoon and my mother was basically in a coma. I held her hand and periodically told her that I loved her. Although she never regained consciousness to acknowledge my presence, I believe that she heard me talking and knew I was at her bedside. Friends and other family members came and went during the afternoon and early evening hours, but by 9:00 p.m. it was just my father and my sister with me in the hospital room. My mother had been receiving oxygen all of this time and her breathing was labored. My sister climbed into the hospital bed to lie next to her. She told my mother that the family would be all right, that we loved her, and that it was okay for her to leave us. Within a matter of minutes, my mother's rhythmic breathing ceased. A nurse was called and confirmed that my mother had passed away.

Being present for a baby's birth or a loved one's death are the two most emotionally charged experiences you can have as a human being. Watching my mother take her last breath, my feelings of loss and sadness were mixed with a sense of relief that her suffering was finally over. Everyone in the family knew that smoking contributed to my mother's death and that the damage to her lungs caused by emphysema meant that it was a terrible way to die. Grappling with my own diagnosis, memories of my mother's death returned. It seemed ironic that even though I had never acquired her smoking addiction, my lungs were now similarly damaged lungs and it was likely that I would have to face a similar outcome.

Radon was another possible cause of lung cancer. Radon is an invisible, odorless, and tasteless radioactive gas that occurs naturally in soil and rocks. My community happens to be an area where the potential for radon gas is high. People can purchase a kit at any hardware store to measure the radon levels in your home. About 15 years ago, Sheri had done that, and the radon test revealed a slightly elevated level of radon but still in the safe zone. After my cancer diagnosis, Sheri decided to check the basement of our home for radon again since she has her real estate appraisal office in our basement. The radon levels this time were even lower than before, so we felt some relief that Sheri's health was not placed in jeopardy by working in our basement office all of these years.

The doctor has also mentioned asbestos as another cause of cancer. Asbestos fibers tend to break into particles that can float in the air. When the particles are inhaled, they can lodge in the lungs, damaging cells and increasing the risk for lung cancer. Asbestos exposure is high in such jobs as shipbuilding, insulation work, and brake repair. It didn't seem likely that asbestos exposure would be a problem at my job, or so I thought. My work life has been spent in office buildings, and for the past 21 years my office and my classrooms have been in the Nursing

Education Building at my university. Recently the faculty and staff in that building had become increasingly concerned about air quality. There was visible mold in many of the ceiling and floor tiles, causing both faculty and staff to lobby the administration to conduct a comprehensive environmental assessment of the building. My colleague Dr. Billie Jo Rylance was spearheading this faculty/staff initiative, and she got the university administration to schedule an open public forum as the first step in a review process. This forum offered individuals an opportunity to express their concerns about the air quality in the building. Billie asked me to speak, but the forum was scheduled for the same day that Sheri and I were leaving for a 1-week vacation to New York and Pennsylvania. Instead of speaking, I submitted the following comments that were read at the end of the public forum by Becky Thorson-Randall, a good friend and colleague in the Special Education Department:

> An Institution of Higher Education should stand for basic principles such as the pursuit of truth and the promotion of the general welfare. This faculty/staff petition drive requesting a comprehensive audit of the environmental safety of the Nursing Education Building merely asks the administration to fulfill these basic principles of a university. The greatest asset of the university is the faculty and staff. At the very least, faculty and staff should have an expectation of safety in their work environment. Unfortunately, faculty and staff working in the Nursing Education Building no longer have confidence that their health and safety are being safeguarded.
>
> These concerns will continue to be a morale issue for faculty and staff. The administration must take decisive and swift action to investigate the concerns raised in the petition. Although I will never know the ultimate cause of my lung cancer, I know it was not behavioral. I have never smoked. Well, I did (unlike Bill Clinton) inhale some of those "funny cigarettes" during my undergraduate days! So, my cancer cause must be environmental. I spent 21 years in the Nursing Education Building. My career and life have been shortened by this dreadful cancer. No other university employee should have to experience this nightmare. I urge the administration to take seriously the faculty and staff concerns and to restore trust and confidence by conducting a comprehensive assessment of the Nursing Education Building and taking any necessary corrective actions.

Over the past several years, a number of individuals who worked in the Nursing Education Building had experienced severe illnesses, and now my cancer was added to the list. In terms of air pollutants, no one will probably ever know what I may have been exposed to or if it was anything that could have caused or contributed to my lung cancer. Certainly, with the incidence of cancer on the rise in the United States, everyone must be concerned about potential environmental causes. Although there is no way to know for certain, I will always wonder whether my work environment contributed to my cancer.

In response to my conclusion, Dr. Avery reinforced it by saying we would probably never know what caused my lung cancer. The best answer he could offer was, "It's just bad luck." Not much consolation there. I asked Dr. Avery if he could give me an idea of the survivability percentages with my type of cancer, but he was reluctant to quote such statistics. He noted that reliance on group survival statistics can be misleading because individuals with a wide variety of health histories and conditions are all a part of a larger group on which the survival rates are calculated. There were some factors working in my favor such as being a nonsmoker, being relatively young, and being in pretty good health. He suggested that the best way to look at my survival chances was to think in terms of 100% or 0%, meaning that I would either beat the odds and outlive the predicted survival time for most people with lung cancer, or I would not. This seemed a reasonable way to cognitively cope with such a devastating diagnosis, especially after searching the Internet for lung cancer Web sites and being distraught over the bleak survival statistics that were plastered all over these sites. It is not helpful to seek out such information; instead, I prefer to wake up each morning thinking that I will be the exception and beat the odds. That kind of thinking provides some peace of mind.

After Sheri and I ran out of questions, Dr. Avery left the examination room, telling us to take as much time as we needed before leaving. Sheri and I fell into each other's arms and wept together. Our bodies felt numb. Neither of us could believe what we had just heard; it was as if we were dreaming all of this. After several minutes, we left the examination room and the hospital. Neither of us spoke on the ride home. At this point, the thought of talking and using the word cancer was beyond my ability. When we got home, we cried some more and then started making plans.

We immediately initiated the process for scheduling my lung surgery. The first step was to meet with Dr. Avery's respiratory therapist, who conducted pulmonary function tests to measure how well my lungs were working. Included in these tests was a spirometry, which measures how much air the lungs can hold. In addition, a lung volume test was conducted to determine how much air was left in my lungs after exhaling, and finally, a lung diffusion test and pulse oximetry were administered to measure how much oxygen was being passed from the lungs to the blood vessels.

On January 29, Sheri and I met with the surgical team to discuss the procedure. Our first meeting was with the thoracic surgeon's physician assistant, who described the two incisions that would be made during my surgery. First, a mediastinoscopy would be performed, requiring an incision at the base of my neck to examine the mediastinum for additional tumors or cancerous lymph nodes. The mediastinum is the middle section of the chest cavity, the area that separates the two lungs. The second procedure is called a thoracotomy, where a larger incision would be made on the right side of my back below the arm to allow the surgeon to directly view the lungs and the area around them. The right lung has three lobes, the left lung has two lobes. The goal was to remove the golf ball-sized cancerous tumor in the lower lobe of my right lung. Removal of part or all of a lung is called a lung resection. It is possible to lead a fairly normal life with only one lung, and the optimistic hope was that I would only lose the lower lobe of my right lung. The physician's assistant was thorough in his description of the surgical procedure and answered all of our questions. I appreciated his positive and encouraging attitude and his assurance that the surgical team would take good care of me. After that, we met with the thoracic surgeon, who had been educated in Egypt, had a good reputation, and was highly recommended by Dr. Avery. He basically repeated the information already provided by the physician's assistant, but his manner was rather abrupt, unfortunately a perception that is not unusual for many surgeons. From reading and now from my experience, it is difficult to avoid the conclusion that teaching future physicians how to have a positive "bedside manner" and effective interpersonal communication with patients remains an often neglected aspect of medical school education.

It was late in the afternoon on Tuesday when Sheri and I left the hospital to face an uncomfortable and anxious evening anticipating my surgery scheduled for the following day, January 30. My previous experience included only two surgical procedures where general anesthesia was administered. The first occurred near the end of my first semester of law school in 1974. A rather large lump had developed under my right armpit, and my doctor was concerned that it could be a tumor. A biopsy was performed and the results were negative. To say I was relieved would be an understatement, and after a short healing period, I resumed the second semester of my law school career. My second surgical procedure was in December of 1997. After experiencing back pain for several months, it seemed to me that my left leg was dragging as I walked. An MRI confirmed the presence of a herniated disk in my lower back. The surgeon said he could repair the disk as well as the nerve impingement that affected my walk. Although the surgery was successful, the back pain has returned sporadically over the years, forcing me to seek out the services of physical therapists and chiropractors. My wife had to assist me in getting dressed at those times when it was hard for me to bend over sufficiently to pull on my socks. This was Sheri's primary experience as a caregiver for me, and we were both hoping that this most recent surgery would only require her to assist me for a short recuperative period.

On the night before my surgery, the first call was to my sister, Candy, in Minneapolis. I told her about my lung cancer diagnosis and we cried together on the phone. I asked her for a favor. Since it seemed too difficult for me to break this news to my 88-year-old father over the telephone, I asked if she would drive the 2 hours to La Crosse and tell him in person. She immediately agreed and said she would drive to La Crosse later that week. My sister has been a wonderful source of support to me throughout this health ordeal, and I'm sure she remembered a similar favor I had done for her about 5 years earlier. At 6:00 on a Monday morning, Candy called to say that Jerry, her husband of 33 years, had committed suicide on Sunday night. She asked me to drive to

Craig with his sister, Candy, who gave the bad news to his father.

La Crosse to break this tragic news to my father. I threw on some clothes, got in my car and arrived unannounced at my father's door around 10 a.m. After telling my father the terrible news, he insisted on coming with me to Minneapolis to comfort Candy. So, this protocol for delivering devastating news to my father was now repeating itself.

My surgery was scheduled for the afternoon. I have often wondered if it is better to have a surgeon operate on you right away in the morning when he or she is fresh or later in the day after they have "warmed up." Perhaps it depends upon whether your surgeon is a morning person or an afternoon person! There was no such personal information about my surgeon; instead, since my surgery had been scheduled on such short notice, I had to fit into the surgeon's schedule. Sheri and I arrived at the hospital a little before noon, and a nurse handed me the standard surgical gown with the opening in the back. It is difficult to maintain a sense of dignity in these gowns, and I felt like a flasher while moving from the changing room to a wheelchair. After being wheeled into a room where Sheri was allowed to stay with me, we waited for my surgery to begin. After an hour or so, a nurse came in to give me an IV. During the next 3 hours that Sheri and I spent in that room, our conversation was limited. Neither of us was in a particularly talkative mood. We only needed to look at each other to communicate out mutual fear and apprehension about my impending surgery. It felt surreal, but this was only the first of many surreal experiences arising from this ordeal.

At midafternoon, a nurse finally came in to wheel me into the operating room. I said goodbye to Sheri, neither of us knowing what to expect when we would see each other again. Our hope, of course, was that the surgeon would be able to remove the tumor and my body would soon be completely healed. We hoped. Once inside the operating room, I was transferred to the operating table and asked to lie on my left side since the incision for the lung surgery would be made on my right side. There were a number of people scurrying around preparing for the surgery. Several of them attempted to make a little conversation with me, but I was not terribly talkative. Utter fear tends to affect your conversational abilities. The anesthesiologist introduced himself and explained what he would be doing. For some odd reason, just before drifting off into my deep, drug induced slumber, I began thinking about "the things you don't want to hear when lying on the operating table" that I had recently read at a Web site. Here are some of my favorites:

- "OK, now take a picture from this angle. This is truly a freak of nature."
- "Come back with that. Bad dog!"
- "Oh, no. I just lost my Rolex."
- "Wait a minute, if this is his spleen, then what's that?"
- "Hand me that . . . that uh . . . thingie."
- "Damn, there go the lights again . . . "
- "What's this doing here?"

There are some credible anecdotal reports that surgical patients under general anesthesia can sometimes hear and recall comments that are made during their surgery. During my surgery, I cannot recall hearing anything, but after the surgery I was disturbed by the tone of the conversation with the surgeon. My first sentient moment came upon awakening in the recovery room. Although quite disoriented, I vaguely recall my surgeon appearing like an apparition before me, briefly commenting that he was unable to remove the tumor and that radiation and chemotherapy treatments would need to begin as soon as possible. Just before he left he made one attempt at encouragement: "We will get you through this." Without waiting for a response, he was gone, and I was left to mull over what he said and the lack of sensitivity in his bedside manner.

After a couple of hours in the recovery room, I was taken to a room in the Intensive Care Unit (ICU). Meanwhile, Sheri was waiting for the surgeon in a conference room, and when he finally entered the room, he was shaking his head and muttering, "It's not good, not good at all." Again, this does not seem to be an appropriate way for medical personnel to begin a conversation. The surgeon explained to Sheri that after he opened me up, he went into the lung and discovered that the cancer had spread to some lymph nodes in my right lung as well as behind my sternum, and since the cancer had already spread to other areas, he decided not to attempt to remove the tumor. Instead, he drained some fluid from my right lung and closed the incision. After getting such depressing news, Sheri raced around the hospital corridors trying to find me. She was feeling frantic. Finally, she went back to the room where we had waited prior to my surgery because it was the last place where we had some semblance of our former lives. There was no one in the room. All alone, Sheri cried for several minutes before gathering her composure and set off to find me again. Once she located my room, Sheri was able to provide me with a more complete account of the surgery, and now it was my turn to react to the devastating news.

After finally coming to grips with the cancer diagnosis, Sheri and I had hoped that surgery would remove the tumor and my cancer crisis would be over. Like most people, we wanted a "quick fix," but there would be no quick fix. This would be a battle, and hopefully it would be a long one, giving me a chance to beat the odds. The news of my unsuccessful surgery was hard to take. My world was breaking apart and my only thought was: "This is it. I'm going to die." My diagnostic category changed from IIIA to IIIB, dangerously close to the precipice of stage IV lung cancer. Sheri tried her best to comfort me, but no amount of consolation was going to work. Not now.

It was nearly 9:00 p.m. when Sheri finally left the hospital to go home; she was physically and emotionally exhausted. I was in a lot of pain after my surgery, despite the presence of a personal pain-medication administration machine. After initially pretending to be brave and able to endure the pain, I decided that this was not the way to go. At the push of a button, you could administer, within limits, painkilling medication as you needed it. I grew very attached to this machine. In the process of repeatedly using my pain-medication administration device over the next 2 days, it occurred to me what a wonderful resource it would be for all of those mind-numbing meetings I had attended over the years as a university administrator. Just a quick shot of some painkilling medication before a meeting and you could tolerate almost anyone or anything!

That first night after surgery, a nurse gave me water and a Popsicle because they had restricted me to a clear liquid diet. Since I had no appetite, that was more than enough. In addition to the discomfort from my surgery, it was impossible for me to sleep because I had to lie on my back when my normal routine is to sleep on my stomach, and being hooked up to an IV machine didn't help my comfort level. I did not sleep at all that first night. Lying alone in the hospital room, I tried to let the information sink in, tried to comprehend the situation. All of this life-altering bad news had occurred within a 2-week period of time. My life was like an airplane ride, climbing higher and higher by steadily achieving my goals, and then, without warning, I had fallen out of the plane and was in free fall, not knowing when I would hit bottom. Alone in my hospital room, with nothing else to do but mull over my cancer diagnosis and unsuccessful surgery, I began to weep uncontrollably. The night nurse heard me sobbing and came to my room. Dru wanted to know what was wrong—was I in pain, did I need anything? Trying to control my emotions, I explained that the psychological pain was greater than the physical pain, and the only "cure" for that was a different diagnosis. It was fortunate that Dru was my nurse that first night. She stayed with me and listened to all the fears, frustrations, and uncertainties in response to my new circumstance. She did not offer simplistic solutions or worn-out platitudes. She just tried to ease my pain by being there and listening. There is no way to adequately express my gratitude to Dru for her compassion and tender care. We even shared a few humorous moments. I needed that.

After my surgery, there was some concern about blood clots forming. To assist my circulation, both legs were encased in blood pressure leg cuffs (sequential compression devices) that covered each leg from ankle to thigh. Every few minutes I could hear the blood pressure cuffs inflate and feel them becoming tight around my legs; after a minute or so, the cuffs would deflate. The blood pressure cuffs were kept on my legs all night, and that was another factor in my inability to sleep. In the morning when a new nurse came on duty, she encouraged me to get out of bed and sit in a chair. When I returned to bed, the nurse slipped on the leg cuffs again. After a few minutes, it was obvious that something was wrong with the leg cuffs because the pressure was affecting more than my legs. Each time the leg cuffs inflated, I felt the inflation pressure in my penis. This was neither the time nor place to become aroused, and I nervously brought this misapplication of the technology to the nurse's attention. She immediately readjusted the cuffs and the dilemma was resolved.

I told this story to Dru when she came on duty the next day, and we shared a good laugh. It might seem strange to mix humor and tragedy together, but it felt good to laugh again. Laughter can be a powerful medicine for those who are ill, even with terminal diseases. Besides, laughter seemed like a good alternative since I was running low on tears. Later that day Dru and I had another laugh when my catheter was removed. The nurses wanted me to get up and use the bathroom as opposed to lying in bed and relying on the catheter. A few hours after the catheter was removed, I felt a lump on my penis and noted some dry blood. Feeling a momentary sense of panic, I called for Dru. She "looked me over" and declared all was normal, and then she washed off the dried blood. After this incident, I was forced to acknowledge that Dru and I had become intimate friends! When you are in a condition as vulnerable as mine was, you have no choice but to lose your normal inhibitions and modesty.

The second day in the ICU still felt surreal. My fantasy was that all of this was a dream, and that at any moment this awful dream would end and my normal life would resume once again. No such luck. In the afternoon, my daughter drove

Kent and Jan Koppelman, Craig's friends from La Crosse.

from La Crosse, where she attended college, to the hospital. To allay Lindsay's fears, my intent was to present a strong, positive demeanor. I am not sure my act was very convincing, but in any event, her presence was very beneficial for me. Later that same afternoon, Kent and Jan Koppelman also drove over from La Crosse. It was reassuring to have such good friends to talk with. It was easy to be more natural in their presence, and it allowed me to express some of my fears and apprehensions. Late in the afternoon, the medical oncologist who would be supervising my chemotherapy came to see me. Dr. Stephen Cooper (a fictitious name) looked to be in his late 30s. Although I was getting used to interacting with all kinds of professionals who were younger than me, he seemed awfully young to be entrusted with my life.

Dr. Cooper took out a blank piece of paper and outlined the treatment program that would begin on the following Monday. He was matter-of-fact and rather dispassionate in his discussion of the radiation and chemotherapy treatments. He recommended 35 sessions of radiation over a 7-week period. Simultaneously, I would receive chemotherapy in two 21-day cycles. That meant getting chemo for 6 days, then no chemo for 15 days, and then start a new 21-day cycle. I would be given two chemo drugs: cisplatin and etoposide. Dr. Cooper was very thorough in his description of my treatment plan, but there was nothing in his demeanor to inspire much optimism or hope. When he finished his explanation of my treatment plan, I asked him the $64,000 question: What are the chances for long-term survival with someone with my type of cancer? Without blinking an eye he said, "Oh, about 22.6 percent." I asked if we could round that number up to 23 percent. He smiled, the first indication that this interaction was occurring with a human being. This was the moment when I decided to work as diligently as possible to get medical personnel to treat me as a human being, not simply a patient. Dr. Cooper left saying he would see me again on Monday when we would begin my chemotherapy. After he left, Sheri, the Koppelman's, and I compared notes about our impressions of Dr. Cooper. The general consensus was that it would take a lot of hard work to develop the kind of relationship with him where the patient (me) would feel more like a person and less like a patient.

Later that same afternoon, Dr. Thomas Dalton (also a fictitious name) came to my room. Dr. Dalton is the radiation oncologist who would be supervising my radiation treatment. Although Dr. Dalton was located at St. Elizabeth's Hospital in Appleton, he was affiliated with the University of Wisconsin Cancer Clinic out of Madison. He was also an adjunct professor at the UW School of Medicine. His credentials inspired my instant confidence, but I knew that the quality of our relationship would be most critical. Dr. Dalton primarily just introduced himself and set up an appointment with me on the following Monday. The first order of business before actually beginning my radiation treatment was to "map out" my chest to precisely locate and mark the areas to be treated. Dr. Dalton seemed to be quite personable, and that helped me to feel more eager to start my treatment program.

On February 1, another Friday, I was finally discharged from the hospital. Shortly before my departure, Dru had given me a notebook to write down my thoughts. The notebook was entitled "Journaling Through the Storm: A Journal for Personal Reflections." In addition to her kind compassion and care, Dru had also given me a practical tool to use in my upcoming battle. That notebook has become my gratitude journal; writing in it at the end of each day forces me to recognize all the things I am grateful for. It was late morning when Sheri and the Koppelmans picked me up, and at my request we went to the university so I could meet with the dean of my college. By now, it was obvious that a medical leave of absence for the entire semester was required so that I could concentrate fully on my treatment program. The dean assured me of his complete support, saying that I could even work at home part-time if my health and stamina permitted that.

Walking to my office, my thoughts shifted to the faculty sabbatical that had been awarded to me for the spring semester of 2009 to write a book on supporting and empowering families of children with disabilities. A major publisher had sent me a contract, and last fall I had spent several weeks gathering articles as sources for this book. While at my office, I decided to retrieve all of those articles and bring them home. Understanding that the future was uncertain, it was important to me to pursue this book project, and it provided some comfort to bring these research materials home. They were a symbol of still being connected to my prior life and to my career. That connection was desperately important to me to for the sake of maintaining a significant aspect of my identity. Sheri and I were silent on the drive home. Walking into our living room was like stepping through the looking glass and encountering cancer world on the other side. It all looked the same, but it felt different, and I desperately hoped to find my way back. The journey would begin with those radiation and chemotherapy treatments next Monday, February 4. I was filled with a fear of the unknown. What now?

CHAPTER 3

The Cancer Journey and Detours Along the Way

The weekend before my cancer treatments began was filled with apprehension. I was grateful to be surrounded by family and friends. Lindsay stayed until Sunday afternoon when she and the Koppelmans both returned to La Crosse. My spirits were also buoyed by a Sunday visit from my good friend John Shaw. We have worked together for several years as facilitators of Parents in Partnership groups at many communities in Wisconsin. The companionship of family and friends was a good distraction while waiting for the treatment to start, but I couldn't stop worrying about possible nausea and vomiting from the chemotherapy. Because of the recent surgical stitches, the thought of retching my guts over the toilet was not terribly appealing. It reminded me of a scene from a movie Sheri and I had seen about a week before my diagnosis. Ironically, the movie was *The Bucket List,* starring Jack Nicholson and Morgan Freeman, where both actors played terminally ill cancer patients. In one scene, Nicholson's character is sick from his chemotherapy and violently vomits in the toilet of his hospital room. When he stands up looking weak and haggard and stares into the mirror, he says, "Just think, right now there is some lucky bastard who is having a heart attack." It seemed a real possibility that the side effects of my treatments might be worse than the symptoms of my disease.

Just before the cancer treatments began, the results of my gastroscopy examination were explained to me. The good news was that acid reflux was not the problem; the bad news was that I had celiac disease. Celiac disease is a digestive disease that damages the small intestine and interferes with the absorption of nutrients from food. With this disease, a person cannot tolerate gluten, a protein found in wheat, rye, and barley. Eating foods containing gluten would cause the body's immune system to respond by damaging or destroying the small, fingerlike protrusions called villi that line the small intestine. The villi allow nutrients from food to be absorbed into the bloodstream. Without healthy villi, a person becomes malnourished. Because it is the body's own immune system that causes the damage, celiac disease is considered an autoimmune disorder. The only treatment for celiac disease is to follow a gluten-free diet.

Although not nearly as daunting as my cancer diagnosis, it was still distressing to hear about this new problem. My treatment just became more complicated. Having already been told that chemotherapy would suppress my appetite, now I had to adapt to a diet that eliminated many of my favorite foods such as pizza, pasta, breads, and cakes. Because most processed foods contain wheat, my wife and I would have to become avid food label readers during grocery shopping trips. Eating and cooking would no longer be a pleasant activity; it would be a chore. Regardless, paying closer attention to food would have to be integrated into the overall battle with the cancer that threatened my life.

There are three standard methods of treating cancer: surgery, radiation therapy, and chemotherapy. The first option had already failed, so the remaining two methods would dictate the direction of my cancer journey. My first order of business was to meet with Dr. Dalton and the radiation therapy staff to discuss my treatment. The primary goal of cancer treatment is to cure the disease, but if that is not possible, the second goal is palliative care, which involves controlling or relieving problematic symptoms of the disease. During my first meeting with Dr. Cooper in the hospital, he referred to my treatment plan as having "curative intent." I kept repeating that statement in my mind as a kind of mantra before my treatment regimen began. Radiation therapy is a cancer treatment that uses high doses of radiation either to kill cancer cells or stop them from spreading. Radiation also attacks normal cells, which causes side effects such as fatigue and hair loss. There are two types of radiation therapy: external beam radiation and internal radiation or brachytherapy. My treatment involved external beam radiation therapy; this is called a local treatment because the radiation is aimed at a specific part of your body, the chest in my case. The radiation is delivered from a machine called a linear accelerator, which produces ionizing radiation such as high energy X-rays and electron beams. My treatment plan called for 35 sessions over seven weeks. It occurred to me that at the end of my treatment I might at least serve a useful function as a night-light. Perhaps that could become a part-time job to supplement my retirement income.

The first part of the radiation treatment process is called a simulation or "marking session," and the reason for that name soon became clear. While lying on the treatment table in a radiation therapy room, a radiation therapist took scans of my chest to identify the specific treatment area. The therapist put small marks (often referred to as tattoos) with a special kind of ink on locations of my chest where the radiation would be directed. The tattoos looked like green freckles and will remain on my skin for the rest of my life. These were the first "tattoos" that had ever appeared on my body. It was some kind of initiation into a gang identified by these common symbols, and I fantasized about joining a radiation treatment gang with an intimidating name such as "Cancerous Cell Mates" or "Lung Lunatics." My tattoos instantly gave me a new identity, but it was not one I was eager to have. After identifying the treatment fields on my chest, special blocks or beam shields are fabricated to protect nearby organs and tissue from direct radiation.

When the radiation treatment began, a therapist would put two different blocks in the linear accelerator to direct the radiation beams to my tumor and to my cancerous lymph nodes. In addition to the radiation treatment blocks, the therapists made a plastic mold of the back of my head. The purpose of the mold was to keep my head and body from moving during the radiation treatment. With each visit to the hospital for radiation treatment, the therapists would pull my personalized head mold from a shelf and place it on the treatment table. Having my own personalized piece of apparatus felt like being a valued customer, like being a regular at a restaurant and having your own coffee mug.

Another critical component of the simulation process was for the radiation oncologist to prescribe the appropriate radiation dose for each treatment session. The precise radiation dose is based upon body dimensions and the size of the area to be treated. There were new terms to be learned such as "rads" and "gray." Rads (radiation absorbed dose) are a measurement of the amount of radiation absorbed by the body, while gray is a newer international term—one gray equals 100 rads. The simulation procedure took about an hour. In a few more hours, my first radiation treatment would begin.

The treatment procedure that seemed so strange at first quickly became routine. It always began with me taking off my shirt in the waiting room and donning a hospital gown from a warming machine that reminded me of an oven. After slipping on a warm gown (which was welcome during cold Wisconsin winters), I waited for a radiation therapist to call me into the treatment room. Andrea, Kenny, and Barb were all wonderful therapists who treated me as a person and not just another "cancer case." They always engaged in friendly conversations and never failed to ask me how I was doing. Once in the radiation treatment room, I was lying on my back on the table with my head securely placed in the personalized mold. The gown was off so my bare chest was exposed to the radiation beam. That first time lying on the table looking up at the part of the linear accelerator that would deliver the radiation beam, I immediately noticed the Disney cartoon stickers plastered on the ceiling. To have Mickey Mouse, Donald Duck, Goofy, and Pluto staring down at me was oddly comforting, and at the same time surreal. I never asked about the reason for the ceiling stickers. It seemed logical to assume that it was for radiation patients who were children, and it was too painful to think about that sad reality.

The radiation treatment is painless because you cannot see, feel, or smell the radiation. The linear accelerator made a whirring noise as it circled around my head to direct the radiation beams to different locations on my chest. The radiation only lasts about 15–30 seconds for each treatment area, and each area receives four or five radiation doses for each treatment session. The radiation therapists left the room right before the treatment began, but they could see and hear me through a window to the control room. After a couple of radiation beams, a therapist would come in to place a block on the radiation machine and then leave the room to give me another dose.

The thought of being alone in the radiation treatment room never occurred to me until one day my daughter Lindsay accompanied me for a treatment session. Andrea gave Lindsay a detailed description of the treatment process and the equipment used. For the first time, I noticed the incredibly thick door through which we entered the treatment room, and I watched the therapists carefully close the door after they left the room to administer the radiation beams. Of course radiation has to be administered cautiously, but seeing that thick, bunker-type door to the treatment room made a powerful impression. In response to my question, the therapists assured me that my body would not be radioactive at the end of the 35 radiation treatment sessions. I asked if the treatments would at least help me to achieve a "glowing" personality.

After the radiation treatment simulation in the morning, Sheri and I went to the oncology clinic to meet with Dr. Cooper. The oncology waiting room was filled with patients, many of them carrying the obvious signs of their cancer identity—loss of hair on their heads, worried or pained facial expressions, and somber moods. My first thought upon seeing them was to wonder if they represented a mirror of my future. After a few minutes, one of the nurses called my name and we went to an examination room. The nurse had me step on a scale before she took my blood pressure, temperature, and pulse. She entered this data into the computer and always ended with a final question: Had I ever smoked cigarettes? With a slight smile I politely answered "No, never." As the months passed and oncology appointments continued, the nurse repeated this routine, asking me the same question. Finally, I complained to her about being asked about my smoking habits every time I came. It was like asking for my height—that information was not going to change so why did she insist on asking over and over when the answer would always be the same? She mumbled something about it being part of the routine she was supposed to follow. I asked if she would like me to start smoking on occasion so she could at least hear a different response some of the time. She did not appear to appreciate my attempt at humor.

After a few minutes, Dr. Cooper entered the examination room. He reviewed my chemotherapy treatment and said the treatment would be aggressive with a curative goal. So far, so good. Remembering the Jack Nicholson character from *The Bucket List,* I asked Dr. Cooper about the likelihood of experiencing nausea and vomiting. He assured me that there had been real improvements in anti-nausea medications, and with these he thought I would tolerate the chemo quite well. Then he reviewed typical chemotherapy side effects: hair loss, appetite suppression, fatigue, and suppressed immune system. Having done my research, none of these side effects were new to me, but listening to the doctor state them made them seem more real, not just a speculation but a prediction. It would not be long before my treatments caused me to exhibit the same signs of my new cancer identity as could be observed in the oncology waiting room. When that began to happen, it made me wonder if becoming a member of this group would involve a special initiation or handshake. As you may have noticed, one of my primary coping strategies is to look for the absurdity in situations and to appreciate the humor. I was hoping that my iconoclastic attitude would help sustain me during the tribulations that would have to be endured in the coming months.

On the first day of treatment, I was asked to sign a consent form for my chemotherapy with a treatment regimen consisting of cisplatin and etoposide. Cisplatin is a platinum-based chemotherapy drug used in treating a number of cancers, including non-small cell lung cancer. Cancerous tumors are characterized by rapid cell division, which is no longer controlled as it is in normal cells. Cancer cells do not have the cellular check-and-balance mechanism that controls and limits cell division. Chemotherapy drugs kill cancer cells by halting cell division, typically by damaging the DNA that tells the cell how to copy itself in division. If cells are unable to divide, they die. Unfortunately, chemotherapy drugs do not know the difference between cancerous cells and normal cells.

The destruction of normal cells causes side effects. The side effects from cisplatin can be severe; for example, kidney damage. Cisplatin can also lower your white blood cell count, increasing chances of infection, and it can reduce your blood platelets, which are necessary for blood clotting. To monitor these side effects, a patient is regularly checked by drawing blood and analyzing it. The level of blood creatinine can indicate whether there is any kidney failure. Similarly, white blood cell counts and platelets are monitored through blood analyses. On a couple of occasions during my treatment, my white blood cell count became rather low. At those times, I was given a neulasta shot to increase my white blood cell count. The other drug, etoposide, is classified as a plant alkaloid and is often administered in conjunction with cisplatin. Etoposide works in a similar fashion as cisplatin by disrupting cancerous cell division, and the side effects are similar. Both chemotherapy drugs are administered intravenously through an infusion pump.

Walking into the chemotherapy infusion room at the oncology clinic for the first time felt a bit intimidating, but it also piqued my curiosity. The large room had about 15 reclining chairs placed along the walls with an infusion pump next to each chair. The reclining chairs were placed fairly close to each other with no curtains between them. On most of my chemotherapy days, a majority of the chairs were filled. Cancer was clearly a booming business! Observing the patients in the chemotherapy infusion room, I realized that most of them seemed several years older than me. There was not much comfort from that discovery. I was also curious about how people behaved during their chemotherapy sessions. Some individuals seemed extremely talkative and willing to relate their entire medical history to anyone and everyone. Some patients appeared to have established relationships with each other as a result of going through chemotherapy together. It was easy to identify the "veterans" among the patients. These individuals would get their own pillows and blankets from the cabinet and quickly settle into their chemotherapy routine. The nurses and technicians knew them by name and often had animated conversations with them. The veterans skillfully maneuvered their infusion pumps when they needed to use the restroom. In my first attempt to use the restroom, I almost tripped over the cord and ran into a chair. An obvious rookie.

Everyone copes with cancer differently. Since I was not looking for a support group, I did not discuss my medical history with the other patients. Instead of being talkative during chemotherapy, my coping strategy was to withdraw, not even making eye contact with any of the patients. If I did not feel like reading a book, I would shut my eyes and try to sleep. Avoidance and withdrawal were a feeble attempt to deny the reality of my situation. Failing to acknowledge and interact with the other cancer patients was my way of not having to admit that I was one of them—that I had cancer. My goal was simply to complete my treatment and get out of that room as quickly as possible.

The chemo sessions usually lasted 2 to 3 hours; the longest session went more than 4 hours. The length of time varied depending upon whether both chemo drugs were given to me that day and on the rate at which the drugs were dripped into my body. A nurse or lab technician would first find a vein and stick a needle in me to attach an IV for the infusion of the drugs. In previous experiences of drawing blood, nurses and lab technicians often had to stick me multiple times before finding a suitable vein. One of my standard jokes was to say I wasn't "vein enough." Fortunately, for my chemo infusions the nurse always found a good vein on the first needle stick, then she would give me an infusion of anti-nausea medication first, followed by a saline solution. After that, the chemo drugs would be hooked up to the infusion pump and slowly dripped into me. Cisplatin is so toxic that the nurses and lab technicians wear plastic gloves when hooking up the bag of clear liquid to the IV machine. Watching them compelled me to think: "So, you're telling me this poison is supposed to be good for me. Really?"

While sitting in the chemotherapy infusion room, there were constant beeping sounds that alerted nurses or technicians as each bag of medicine got near the end on the infusion pump. The nurse or technician would remove the completed bag and hook up the next bag of medicine. On busy days, the nurses and technicians were constantly running from one IV machine to the next exchanging medications. It was a strange symphony of sound and movement. A couple of times, my infusion pump beeped because there was an air bubble in the IV tube. The first time it happened, a patient seated in a nearby reclining chair assured me that the air bubble would not kill me. Until he made that comment, I had never even thought of that possibility! It is true—ignorance can be bliss.

Sheri would typically stay with me during the chemo session, and she often brought something for me to eat. Although the oncology waiting room had muffins and cookies for patients, that wasn't an option because of my celiac disease. Sheri usually brought smoothies to keep up my daily caloric intake. Each chemo session ended with a saline flush. With all of this liquid dripping into my vein over the course of each chemo session, I had to use the restroom once or twice each time. Eventually I became more skilled at navigating the room with my IV machine, and before long negotiated that task as well as any of the skilled veterans.

Since I was going to have blood drawn regularly and chemotherapy for a considerable period of time, Dr. Cooper recommended that a port be inserted into my chest. The port allowed for a simple and painless method of drawing blood and infusing the chemo drugs. The outpatient surgery to install the port took place shortly after my second chemo sessions. The surgery was over in about 30 minutes and only required a local anesthesia. The port was inserted under the skin in the fat layer. There is a tiny catheter that goes from the port to the jugular vein in the neck. The port was clearly visible as a hump on the right side of my chest below the collarbone. My daughter Lindsay teased me by calling it a third nipple. The catheter in my neck was also plainly visible because there was a rippling of the skin at that location. These are some of the visible markers of my identity as a cancer patient.

My wife has often noted my tendency to engage in compulsive behaviors. When leaving the house, it is part of my routine to always check to see if the door is locked and the coffee pot unplugged, and I'm constantly checking my watch for the time. Now I am conscious of the port and touch that area of my chest repeatedly throughout the day—a new compulsive behavior to contend with. But it is clear to me that installing the port was a good decision, as long as it is taken care of properly. After accessing the port with a blood draw or chemo infusion, it is flushed with heparin. The port must be flushed with heparin at least once a month. The surgeon who installed my port told me that it could stay in my chest for up to 5 years. I asked if he would guarantee that my life would last for at least that long. He was noncommittal.

The anti-nausea medication worked well. There was a minimal sensation of nausea and no vomiting, but when first trying to mow my lawn, I got breathless and experienced dry heaves for several minutes. Although unpleasant, this was tolerable, and I was simply thankful that the medication was working to minimize at least one of the side effects of treatment. After my first week of chemotherapy, my taste buds seemed to stop functioning, so eating became a tedious task. With no appetite and no energy, I lost 25 pounds in 1 week. Several years earlier, during an annual physical examination, my primary-care physician announced that my excessive weight was becoming a health hazard. He referred to my weight condition as "creeping obesity," referring to my gain of four to five pounds per year over several years. Being known as slightly overweight is one thing, but having "creeping obesity" is quite another matter. It sounds like something contagious with distinct possibilities for social shunning. After radiation and chemo, my creeping obesity problem was resolved. Just think of the marketing possibilities for my treatment regimen as a new diet plan! But most people would likely perceive such a diet program as a bit drastic. The South Beach diet seemed safe for now.

Although losing some weight was acceptable, it was important to maintain a stable weight while going through my treatment program. At a meeting with a dietitian, she recommended eating five or six small meals during the day as well as drinking high caloric diet supplements like Ensure or Boost. Unfortunately, those high calorie drinks made me almost gag because of their extremely sweet taste. Eating fruits and vegetables was much more appealing, and I hoped this would also be more beneficial to my immune system and enhance my cancer fight. Eventually my weight seemed to have stabilized, and after a few more weeks, my appetite slowly returned.

By receiving radiation therapy and chemotherapy simultaneously, I was hit with a double whammy of exhaustion. The fatigue was ever-present, leaving me with no energy for anything. My life consisted of sleeping or lying on our bed or sofa most of the day. Walking felt like moving in slow motion as if I was walking in deep water. My exercise consisted of walking from the bed to the sofa, then from the sofa to the bathroom and back throughout the day. This new level of exhaustion was difficult to accept as part of my new identity because I had always been an energetic person, working long hours each week. For the past few years, my usual routine was to wake up at 5:00 a.m. and go to the local YMCA for an hour of aerobics and weight lifting exercises, arriving at my office by 7:30. But now, for the first week or so after my treatments began, it was not even possible for me to focus or concentrate enough to read. From this experience it was obvious that it had been the right decision to request a medical leave for the semester. There was no way I could have taught or performed the various responsibilities of a faculty member, but this was another significant identity change that was difficult to accept.

Although my hair had turned increasingly gray in the past 5 years, I still wore it at the same length and style as during my college days more than 30 years earlier. My wife would sometimes chastise me about my unchanging hairstyle by referring to me as the fifth Beatle, circa their 1964 appearances on *The Ed Sullivan Show*. It has never been one of my strengths to deal effectively with change, so when "something works for me," whether it be my personal appearance or a menu item at a favorite restaurant, I tend to stick with those tried and true choices. I pride myself on not being a slave to popular styles or trends. The most skilled teacher in my college experience wore the same style of clothes every day—blue jeans and a light blue shirt. When a student finally asked him about his singular choice of clothes, he simply responded, "I prefer to spend my time thinking about matters other than what I am going to wear each day."

As soon as the cancer treatments began, I expected to start losing my hair, but after the initial 2 weeks of treatment, I still had a lot left. To preserve that hair, I shampooed very gently, not wanting to agitate any embattled hair follicles. Worrying about losing my hair was not really a vanity issue; my purpose was to delay acquiring this aspect of the distinct appearance of a cancer patient. For as long as possible I wanted to hold on to my stolen identity by resisting the new one. Finally, the hair loss started to happen. After getting out of bed one morning, I noticed an excessive amount of hair on my pillow, and running my fingers through my hair resulted in large clumps of it coming out in my hand. Immediately feeling a sense of panic, I became calmer after realizing that, in the larger scheme of things, losing my hair was not the most challenging problem in my life right now. Instead of watching my hair fall out over the next several days, my preference was to exert some control over my situation. Heading off to see my barber, I asked for a buzz cut and that was the end of my hair debacle. Trying to gain some control over my situation would be a frequent goal during the upcoming months of my cancer battle. It was a couple of weeks after my buzz cut when I noticed that my mustache was shedding. Having worn a mustache for 35 years, it was difficult to let it go, but eventually I put the mustache out of its misery by cutting the few remaining hairs. The hair loss continued over most of my body including eyebrows, eyelashes, chest; well, you get the picture. On the positive side, I could now take up competitive swimming.

In early February, shortly after my radiation and chemotherapy began, Stu Robertshaw visited me. As always, it was a pleasure talking with Stu, but he also came with a gift—a laughter CD that he encouraged me to listen to every day. The CD is about 10 minutes of nothing but hysterical laughter from a group of people. Stu advised me to sit in a relaxed position, listen to the laughter CD, laugh along with it for several minutes, and then finish with some deep breathing relaxation exercises. Although I have not listened to this CD every day as Stu recommended, when I do listen it seems to relax me and to buoy my spirits. I

Craig removing the remaining hairs of his mustache.

wondered what my cancer cells thought about this coping strategy. Frankly, if they don't like it, they should go somewhere else!

A couple of weeks after my cancer diagnosis, get-well cards and other messages of support and encouragement began showing up in my mailbox. Many of the cards and well wishes came from my college colleagues. To express my appreciation for their support, I wrote the following e-mail, addressed to all my colleagues and friends at the College of Education and Human Services (COEHS):

> I wish I had the energy to write each of you an individual thank you note for your kind expressions of support and encouragement as I battle this lung cancer. Please accept this mass email as my acknowledgement and show of appreciation for the many cards, emails, phone calls, and personal visits I have received from college colleagues. The COEHS has been my intellectual home for 21 years. After receiving this outpouring of support, I now know that the college has been much more than merely an intellectual home for me.
>
> I am sporting a new look these days—a bald head. I call it my "chemo cut." . . . My treatments are going reasonably well but the chemo and radiation leave me with little energy and even less appetite. I realized early on that I needed to take some affirmative actions to feel a sense of empowerment as opposed to simply passively receiving the chemo and radiation. To that goal I am trying to eat a more nutritious and balanced diet. There is one piece of bad news as a result of my better food choices. For those of you who own stock in the Frito Lay Company, expect a decline in that stock price as the company experiences a precipitous drop in sales!
>
> I have also added two rituals to my daily routine. First, I practice "laughter meditation" every day. A friend gave me a CD with several minutes of nothing but the sound of a group of people laughing; hysterical laughter. I listen to that CD and laugh along for several minutes. Then I shut my eyes, practice deep breathing, and let my mind wander. As he witnesses this event, my dog thinks I am pretty strange but it feels good. Second, I am keeping a gratitude journal. Every night before going to bed I make a list of three things I am grateful for from that day. I feel fortunate in that it is not a challenge to come up with a list each night.
>
> I have always thought of myself as a decent writer but words fail me now. I cannot adequately express what it has meant to me to receive this wonderful outpouring of support from my college and university family. A thank you is simply not enough.
>
> I would like to close this thank you note with a presumptuous offer of advice. Please allow me this indulgence. Cancer has a way of bringing greater clarity to your life. It quickly establishes priorities. I do not know how much time I have left on this earth. In that regard, we are all the same. None of us has the answer to that mystery. The difference is that in my situation, I feel a greater sense of urgency related to that issue. I encourage each of you to bring some urgency to your loving relationships. Here is my simple piece of advice: Hug the ones you love with greater conviction and firmness. NOTHING is more important.
>
> Thanks to all of you who have kept me in your thoughts and prayers.

My new life was falling into a routine. Resting, reading, resting, going to doctors' appointments and therapies, resting, trying to stay out of my wife's way, resting; well, you get the picture. I was also trying to consume at least 2,500 calories per day to maintain my weight. This was quite a different daily routine for someone who had been a workaholic. It is a clear sign that you have too many health problems when you have explored every nook and cranny of a hospital and the hospital volunteers address you by your name. The route to the hospital for my appointments and treatments was now etched in my memory because that drive was becoming almost a daily occurrence. And as the saying goes, this kind of familiarity was starting to breed contempt.

It was a slow process for me to reluctantly acknowledge some of the "gifts" that cancer had provided. For instance, all of the people who reached out and offered their support to me and my family were instant sources of inspiration. I felt embraced by a loving and caring community of family members, friends, and colleagues. Recognizing how overly judgmental and petty I had often been in interactions and relationships with people, I resolved to make amends with some individuals I had hurt or neglected over the years. After Sheri had e-mailed

After his hair grew back, Craig posed for a photograph with some of his Special Education colleagues at UW-Oshkosh.
From left to right: Dr. Thomas Fischer, Mrs. Becky Thorson-Randall, Craig, Dr. Denise Clark, Dr. Loretta Mason-Williams, and Dr. Wayne Swanger.

some of my old friends to let them know about my cancer, one of my best childhood friends, Bruce Javenkoski, contacted me. As often happens with childhood friends, we had slowly drifted apart over the years and were not involved in each other's lives anymore. Bruce began to visit me on several occasions throughout my treatment and has been a great support person to lean on. Another childhood friend, Lou George, has maintained regular communication since my cancer diagnosis. I am grateful for the restoration of these old friendships.

By March 2, about one month after treatment began, I started to eat more, and my energy improved. Lindsay came home from college that weekend, making it even more enjoyable. On Sunday, Sheri fixed a nice breakfast for the family, but I was not able to finish it. My breathing became difficult and extremely labored. For 20 minutes I simply sat in the living room trying to engage in deep breathing and relaxation. This did not help my breathing. Sheri finally decided we should go to the emergency center at the hospital. She drove me there, and Lindsay drove separately, because as soon as she could, Lindsay needed to leave for the 3-hour drive back to college. The emergency staff hooked me up immediately to oxygen and then took an EKG and a chest X-ray. Both results were normal. After examining me, the doctor thought my esophagus might be swollen from the radiation treatments, thus causing my breathing problems. I was given a liquid to swallow consisting of lidocaine and Benadryl. Since the crisis seemed under control, Sheri and I encouraged Lindsay to leave for La Crosse. While waiting to determine if the lidocaine and Benadryl concoction was working, a hospital chaplain stopped in. St. Elizabeth's Hospital is a Catholic facility, so the chaplain was Sister Margaret. She was in her 70s and had been a Catholic school teacher for more than 40 years. We had met previously when she stopped by before my surgery and offered a prayer. Prior to entering the examination room on this day, Sister Margaret obviously was told of my lung cancer diagnosis. She knew the challenge ahead for me.

When she entered the examination room, Sister Margaret asked if she could spend a few minutes with Sheri and me. Since I was not going anywhere soon, I agreed. She ended up talking with us for about 45 minutes. Honesty compelled me to tell Sister Margaret that while not a particularly religious person, I was a spiritual individual. As for organized religion, I had become increasingly negative toward it, especially the religious right's intrusion into politics and public-policy making. What had always mattered most to me was that our government was based upon that ingenious document called the Constitution, and that the First Amendment's protection of religious freedom and at the same time its prohibition of a state-sanctioned religion was a critical component of our rights as citizens of the United States. I admired Thomas Jefferson for his wisdom and foresight in articulating the concept of separation of church and state, but this wall of separation was increasingly under attack from the religious right and from the current Bush administration. Sister Margaret did not choose to debate my religious views nor defend organized religion; instead, she simply talked about faith and facing difficult circumstances. She said that a couple of her siblings had dealt with terminal illnesses. She shared a recent tragedy where an emergency room physician at St. Elizabeth's Hospital was found dead from a massive heart attack at his home. He was only in his 40s. She encouraged me not to become obsessed with why this terrible illness struck me because there would never be a clear answer, especially in my situation, where the doctors could provide no obvious medical explanation for my lung cancer.

Sister Margaret listened intently as I discussed my career and work history and admitted my struggles with an issue that would require a decision in the coming weeks: whether to retire or try to return to teaching. I did not know what would be best for my mental and physical well-being. I have known terminally ill individuals who chose to work until it was no longer physically possible. For example, a local school district superintendent battling several types of cancer continued to work for 3 years until the last week of his life. Sister Margaret responded with some of the most valuable advice that had been offered over the past several months. She said all people struggle with the conflict between doing and being. From listening to me, she concluded that most of my life had been based on doing—focusing on my career, raising a family, accomplishing professional goals and receiving accolades. She suggested that, perhaps, it was time to focus on simply being—taking time to enjoy family and friends, to travel, and to relish simple daily experiences. Thinking about her description of the tension between doing and being, it made sense that the time had come for me to concentrate on being. My remaining time could best be spent showing appreciation for the people I cared about, and just possibly learning more about myself.

As the conversation with Sister Margaret was ending, I asked her a final question. Did she believe in miracles? This was an important issue because of my growing skepticism that medical science alone could cure my cancer. She admitted that she absolutely believed in miracles. I asked if she would lead me in a prayer to a saint who might grant me a medical miracle. She asked if I had a specific saint in mind, and my pragmatic response was: "Which saint has the best track record for miracles?" She thought for a few seconds and then mentioned Our Lady of Lourdes. Although vaguely aware that people had made medical pilgrimages to this religious sanctuary in southern France and that many claimed to have experienced miraculous cures for various afflictions, I was not aware of how Lourdes gained its religious significance for the millions of people who flock to this site every year. Sister Margaret related the story of the apparitions of the Blessed Virgin that appeared to a peasant girl named Bernadette Soubiroux.

The first apparition appeared to Bernadette in February of 1858, and she was the only one who saw and heard the apparition. This young girl would see the apparition several times, and during one of these visits, the apparition told Bernadette to drink the water from a mysterious fountain in a grotto. It is this water that many people claim has cured a multitude of ills and diseases. Catholics consider Bernadette to be a saint, so it was to her that Sister Margaret prayed for my medical miracle. Although my professional life has focused on empirical observations that can be quantified, faith and hope for a medical miracle would become an aspect of my day-to-day coping with this terminal disease. Sheri and I thanked Sister Margaret for the time she spent with us, and as she was leaving, she wished me peace of mind. Her wish apparently came true. I felt more calm and at peace after her visit. But I am still waiting for a miracle.

Since the mixture of lidocaine and Benadryl seemed to ease my breathing difficulties, I was released from the emergency center. Yet a few days later, Sheri and I had just left the radiation therapy center of St. Elizabeth's Hospital after a treatment session when I experienced trouble breathing again as we were walking to the car. After complaining about my distress, I got in the car and told Sheri to give me a few minutes to catch my breath. The breathing problem persisted even after my attempt to engage in slow, deep breathing exercises. At my request, Sheri went back to the radiation therapy center to get a nurse, and within minutes a nurse and several other medical personnel came through the center's entrance with a wheelchair. Apparently, a code blue was issued for my medical emergency. Although this breathing difficulty concerned me prior to the appearance of the medical SWAT team, seeing their anxious faces when they reached the car made me really nervous. They wheeled me into an examination room and immediately gave me oxygen. Within minutes my breathing returned to normal, and yet my blood oxygen level remained low.

When Dr. Dalton came to see me, he was concerned that a pulmonary embolism could possibly be the cause of my labored breathing. A pulmonary embolism is a blockage of the pulmonary artery or one of its branches, usually occurring when a blood clot becomes dislodged from its location of formation and embolizes to the arterial blood supply of one of the lungs. For the first time, the doctor informed me that pulmonary embolisms are quite common with lung cancer, and that a pulmonary embolism could kill you. I wish this subject had been brought to my attention earlier. Dr. Dalton made arrangements for a chest CT scan and scheduled an appointment with Dr. Cooper to discuss my scan.

During the meeting with Dr. Cooper, he recommended hospitalization for close monitoring overnight along with an ultrasound examination to determine if I had any blood clots, and if clots were detected, where they had originated. The results from the chest CT scan would take a couple of days. My initial response was to resist the doctor's recommendation of being hospitalized based on my certainty that I would feel better at home. In *Anatomy of an Illness*, Norman Cousins (1981) concluded that hospitals were not conducive environments to getting better, and I concur with him. But just hearing the words pulmonary embolism scared me, so I agreed to be hospitalized overnight.

After being transported in a wheelchair to the hospital and admitted, my hope was that it would only be for 1 night. Nurses gave me an IV drip and placed me on a heart monitor. When they attached several electrodes to my chest, it was not painful, but when those patches were removed, the pain told me that there would be even less chest hair than the little that had managed to survive the chemotherapy. That evening they gave me an ultrasound procedure to determine the origination of my blood clots. I shared the sordid details of my recent medical travails with the ultrasound technician who was friendly and very sympathetic to my medical history. I was lying on my back when the technician applied a cold jelly to my legs and then began the scan looking for blood clots. As she watched the monitor during the scanning, the technician was making an audio tape of her observations and impressions. It is always interesting to listen to medical personnel describing their observations and impressions of your physical condition in your presence. Based upon the ultrasound, the technician concluded that the sources of my blood clots were in both calves; from there they moved to my lung and caused the pulmonary embolism. Someone wheeled me back to my hospital room with tubes and electrodes stuck all over me, and that meant that my overnight stay would inevitably be a sleepless experience.

Early the next morning, Dr. Cooper stopped by my hospital room. After reviewing the chart, he indicated that my heart rate was normal, my blood oxygen level was better, and my breathing had improved. The best news was that he would release me from the hospital later that morning. The bad news was that he prescribed some blood thinning medication to control further blood clots. The medication was warfarin, also known as coumadin, and he said it might be necessary for me to continue taking the medication for at least a year. My immediate thought was, "Is that a guarantee that I will still be around for at least another year?" I didn't ask the question (because no one ever answered it), but I pretended the answer was "yes." Taking warfarin also required weekly or biweekly blood testing to determine the international normalized ratio (INR) level for the safe and therapeutic dosage amount. It was becoming clear that having cancer required learning about more technical terms than I ever wanted to know, but there is no substitute for being an informed consumer.

The other surprise related to taking a blood thinning medication was that it would necessitate twice daily injections of lovenox for a week or so to control for pulmonary embolisms. A nurse showed Sheri and me how to administer the lovenox shot in my belly. Being skittish about giving myself the lovenox shots, I pleaded with Sheri to administer them. Every day, right after breakfast and dinner, Sheri and I would go to the bathroom, and while I grabbed some skin on my belly, she stuck me with a needle and injected the medication. We rotated injection sites between the right and left sides of my belly so that the bruising was more uniform. Although I'm not certain, Sheri seemed to relish the prospect of plunging a sharp object into my body two times a day. Actually, it was not particularly painful, and eventually I was even able to watch her injections. Even so, I was happy when Dr. Cooper indicated my INR levels had stabilized and the lovenox shots could end. A final issue related to taking warfarin was that it would require me to restrict my consumption of green vegetables that contained high amounts of vitamin K. Oh good, more food restrictions! Sheri knew that a significant weight loss during cancer treatment decreases long-term survival. When she heard this latest dietary restriction, she was almost in tears trying to figure out what to cook for me.

A couple of days after my hospital release, Sheri and I met with Dr. Cooper to discuss the chest CT scan results. He showed us where the pulmonary embolism was located in my right lung, but he seemed confident that the warfarin would control and eliminate the embolisms over time. We received more good news: the radiation and chemotherapy treatments had shrunk my tumor by about 30% and there was additional shrinkage of the cancer in my lymph nodes. Finally, a ray of optimism. But, as I would learn later, cancer patients typically travel a bumpy road with many ups and downs, and it is important to maintain an emotional equilibrium, if possible.

The goal of my cancer treatment was to shrink the cancer in my lung so they could try another surgery to remove the tumor and cancerous lymph nodes. I knew that the original surgeon did not see me as a viable candidate for a second surgery, so I asked Dr. Cooper if he thought a second surgery should be considered. Because of my good initial response to treatment, he thought that surgery was an option to explore. Wanting to get a second opinion on the surgical option, I requested a referral to a physician at the Carbone Cancer Clinic at the University of Wisconsin in Madison. This clinic is a nationally recognized cancer research and treatment facility. Dr. Cooper said he would set up an appointment with a medical oncologist in Madison. Sheri and I were feeling more optimistic at this point than at any time since my cancer treatment began.

My reading of cancer research suggested that when lung cancer spreads it typically attacks the brain first. This daunting piece of information challenged my optimism about a second surgery. Prior to visiting the Carbone Cancer Clinic in Madison, I had already been scheduled for an MRI scan. Having had an MRI scan 10 years earlier to diagnose my herniated disk, I knew that feeling claustrophobic would be an issue for me. The MRI scanner makes use of radio waves in detecting benign and malignant tissue. You lie on a narrow table that slides into a large tunnel-like tube within the scanner. In preparation for the MRI scan, I took a sedative and kept repeating over and over, "This cannot be as bad as my cancer; this cannot be as bad as my cancer." Since the MRI scanner produces loud thumping and humming noises when it is in operation, the patient is given earplugs prior to sliding into the dark tunnel. The noise was a bit like standing right next to a member of a road construction crew using a jackhammer to break up concrete. The technician had thoughtfully placed a cloth over my eyes to ease my claustrophobia, but my body was squeezed into the MRI tube like a sausage going into its casing. Emerging from that tunnel of darkness after about 20 minutes felt like being a gopher emerging from its underground hole. It was a brief respite. The technician inserted a contrast dye into a vein on my hand and sucked me back into the dark oblivion for another 20 minutes of noises sounding like a jackhammer. At one point during the scan, I peeked around the cloth that covered my eyes and discovered that the top of the MRI tube was about an inch from my nose. That was the last time I peeked at my predicament.

If you believe Nietzsche, surviving the MRI scan should have made me a stronger person. Perhaps, but I waited anxiously for the results, and in a few days met with Dr. Dalton to review them. Most people have heard the old joke: "They did a scan of my brain and found nothing there." Well, I was ecstatic to learn that my brain MRI scan produced such a result—the cancer had not spread to my brain. With renewed optimism that a second surgery might be a viable option, Sheri and I set off for Madison to meet with the medical oncologist at the Carbone Cancer Clinic.

The University of Wisconsin Hospital and Clinic is a huge facility, but Sheri knew her way around from previous appointments with a pediatric endocrinologist who has treated Lindsay since she was about 10 years old. The clinic was full of people waiting for medical appointments and tests. It was easy to see that the health care industry is a booming business, but it made me think about the people in this country without adequate health insurance. It has always been my belief that adequate health care should be a basic human right for everyone, not a commodity available only to those who can afford it. I was fortunate to have good health insurance from my university employment. Since my cancer treatment began, regular insurance statements had been mailed to me detailing the medical costs and how much the insurance paid. To date, my financial responsibility has been limited to small co-payments for prescribed medications and a $60 deductible for my emergency center visit. That was it; yet my medical expenses were well over several hundred thousand dollars. For example, one CT scan costs over $1,500. It is a national disgrace that the richest country on the planet does not provide for universal health coverage for all of its citizens. Since it is a presidential election year and this issue continues to be raised, perhaps Americans will finally give the new president and Congress a mandate to address this problem.

We waited in an examination room for the medical oncologist. She had previously been sent my medical files, including my most recent CT scan. When the oncologist entered the room, she was strictly business right away. No idle chitchat here. When will more doctors realize that interpersonal communication is an important aspect of the doctor-patient relationship and the entire healing process? Since she got right down to business, I immediately asked the critical question: "Am I a candidate for a second surgery to remove the cancerous tumor from my right lung?" She emphatically answered, "No." Her response rattled me, but after regaining my composure, I asked her for an explanation. The oncologist said the main problem was the location of the cancer. Since the cancer had spread to my lymph nodes and behind my sternum, even if a surgeon were to remove my entire right lung there would be no guarantee that all of the cancer was gone. She said there would be considerable post-surgical pain without a clear positive outcome. If this scene was depicted as a cartoon frame, you could see the bubble bursting right above my head. Apparently, the surgical door had just been closed. What's next?

The oncologist took out a prescription pad and began writing her recommendations. She had four of them. First, with only a few more sessions remaining, complete the 35 sessions of radiation. Second, continue chemotherapy with cisplatin and etoposide for two more cycles. The final two recommendations were much more experimental and preventive. She suggested a test that would determine if I had the epidermal growth factor receptor (EGFR) genetic marker. She explained that the EGFR can result in uncontrolled cell division causing a predisposition for cancer. The testing for EGFR is only done at a private lab and the oncologist estimated that the cost was about $1,000; she also said my insurance might not cover it. If a cancer patient is found to have the EGFR genetic marker, a drug called tarceva can be administered that, in essence, turns off the EGFR cancer predisposition switch, enhancing long-term survival. Tarceva is a pill that must be taken every day for up to 2 years. Typical side effects of this medication are diarrhea and a skin rash or acne. The oncologist warned that terceva was a very expensive drug, costing over $5,000 per month. If I needed this drug, it would represent a test of how good my insurance coverage was. The final recommendation from the oncologist was to consider the option of having preventive brain radiation. The potential side effects of this treatment ranged from short-term memory loss to some permanent cognitive impairment.

Despite her coldly professional demeanor, the Madison oncologist provided some peace of mind by assuring me that if I were a patient at the Carbone Cancer Clinic, I would be receiving the same cancer treatment as I was getting at St. Elizabeth's Hospital. If for no other reason than this, there is value in seeking a second medical opinion. After discussing both of her preventive recommendations with Drs. Cooper and Dalton, Dr. Cooper sent the required tissue sample into the private laboratory to test me for the EGFR genetic marker. It was a pleasant surprise to find out that my insurance would cover the cost of this test. A week later the results came back negative. I did not have the EGFR genetic marker. This result was ironic since my hope was for an abnormality that would mean I could take the preventive tarceva medication and control my cancer. No such luck here. On this issue, I was normal. Why normal on this and abnormal on lung cancer? Sister Margaret's admonition came to mind, reminding me not to continually chase my tail with "why" questions. As I had learned from parenting a child with a disability, you do not get clear answers by questioning the injustice of a tragedy that has befallen you or a loved one. It is not about justice or injustice. It's just a roll of the dice for all of us.

Lindsay joined Sheri and me when we met with Dr. Cooper to ask for his opinion of the Madison oncologist's recommendation for preventive brain radiation. He was generally supportive of that option, but even more than the

Madison oncologist, he stressed that there was very likely to be some loss of permanent cognitive functioning. But he quickly added, "I think you have a few IQ points to spare." Having her father's sense of humor, Lindsay rolled her eyes and said, "I'm not so sure of that." For a person who had spent his entire career in "intellectual pursuits," the loss of even some cognitive ability was a daunting proposition. Dr. Cooper assured me that it was not necessary to make an immediate decision on this treatment recommendation.

After completing my 35 radiation sessions in mid-March, Sheri and I left for a week's vacation in Arizona. Because my university's spring break is in March, we had planned to take this trip prior to my cancer diagnosis, and now we were both feeling a desperate need to escape the Wisconsin winter and the routine medical drudgery forced upon us over the past 2 months. This was our third March trip to Arizona where I could watch the spring training games of the Chicago White Sox and Arizona Diamondbacks, since both teams have spring training sites in Tucson. I have been a lifelong White Sox fan and realized a long-time dream when they won the World Series in 2005. On this trip, we went to three spring training baseball games and discovered a Mexican restaurant at the ballpark that served great nachos. As long as there were no flour tortillas, I could eat most Mexican foods on my gluten-free diet. It was a pleasant vacation, and much of my time was spent reading at poolside or on our back patio. It was still necessary for me to take daily naps, and our hiking was limited since I could only walk for short distances before having to rest and catch my breath. But this trip allowed for an escape from the recent medical realities, and that was a welcome respite. Fortunately, there were no medical complications at any time during our 1-week vacation in Arizona.

After returning to Wisconsin, I continued chemotherapy until late April when the four chemo cycles were finally completed. At this point, the plan was to monitor my cancer through MRI and CT scans every 2 to 3 months. It felt so good to be done with chemo, and gradually my appetite and energy began to return. Meanwhile I was voraciously reading books. This was a real luxury. I generally read nonfiction, so in addition to books about the immune system, healthy nutrition, cancer and medical miracles, my reading also included spirituality, biographies, American history, and of course, baseball. I visited my campus on a couple of occasions, mainly to see colleagues, but it was painful to be in that familiar environment and not be an active participant. No one is irreplaceable, we all know that, but couldn't the college and my department have experienced at least a little difficulty due to my absence? Apparently not; life moves on, with or without you.

Feeling better in late April inspired me to make a "bucket list" with Sheri of things we (primarily me) had talked about doing but had postponed for later during my retirement. Obviously I was retired now, so our motto became: "there is no time like the present." We began planning trips during those times when I was not tied to a treatment schedule. These trips represented detours from the cancer journey, a little time off that well-beaten path to explore some other sights that would be much more enjoyable. Our first trip was in early June, taking Amtrak from Milwaukee to Seattle, a train ride lasting 42 hours. We had a sleeper compartment and plenty of books to read. My paternal grandfather worked for many years for the Burlington Northwestern Railroad Company, and perhaps part of my genetic inheritance was to share his fascination for trains. The train trip was a bit more enjoyable for me than for Sheri because she had to sleep on the top bunk, requiring her to scramble up to the top of the compartment and lie down in a very cramped space. Daytime was better for her as we spent time in the observation car watching beautiful landscapes, especially as the train entered Glacier National Park. A couple of hours after the train arrived in Seattle, we were boarding the cruise ship for a 7-day trip up and back down the Alaskan inside passage.

Sheri and I both wanted this trip for our first bucket list adventure because we had always wanted to take a cruise, and I was especially interested in visiting Alaska. Although Alaska is a beautiful state, the weather was still cold in mid-June, with daytime high temperatures only in the low 50s. Naturally I caught a cold on the trip, and with my compromised immune system, I was worried about contracting pneumonia. Nevertheless, Sheri and I enjoyed the fantastic entertainment that the cruise ship provided, and when we weren't being entertained, we relaxed and read on the ship. The main problem was that my appetite waned as the trip went on, in part because of the struggle to find foods that fit into my gluten-free diet. I am probably one of the few people who lost weight during a cruise ship vacation. When the ship returned to Seattle, we spent the weekend with my aunt and uncle and my cousin, Rick, who flew in from Honolulu just to see us. It was nice seeing family that we seldom get to visit.

We flew back to Wisconsin to get ready for our next bucket list adventure—a week's vacation to New York and Pennsylvania. The two main destinations were once again my choices: to visit the Baseball Hall of Fame and Museum at Cooperstown, New York, and the Civil War battle site at Gettysburg, Pennsylvania. We coordinated our trip to meet up with Kent and Jan Koppelman for the 3 days at Cooperstown. As a surprise, Kent and Jan presented me with a year's membership to the Baseball Hall of Fame. It made me feel like a little leaguer again as we toured the wonderful exhibits at the Hall of Fame. As an extra surprise, on our second day, the Hall was rededicating its Jackie Robinson plaque with a special ceremony that included Jackie's widow, Rachel, and their only daughter, Sharon. The new plaque added language honoring Jackie Robinson's unique contribution of breaking the color barrier in the major leagues in 1947.

Watching the ceremony, it almost brought me to tears that I had stumbled upon this opportunity to witness a part of baseball history. Thinking about Jackie Robinson and his courageous battle to integrate major league baseball

Craig finally achieved his lifelong goal of spending several days at the Baseball Hall of Fame in Cooperstown, New York.

made me wonder how old he was when he died. Since my cancer diagnosis, it has become almost an obsession for me to find out the ages and causes of death of famous baseball players and historical figures. For example, as a child, my favorite baseball player was Nellie Fox of the Chicago White Sox, and it turned out that he died at 48 from cancer. Perhaps this was a morbid curiosity, but it was as if I needed to establish a baseline of how long certain famous individuals lived to see if I had already beaten their marks or not. To know that my life was already as long or longer than some of these people should have made me more reconciled to my own mortality. But if that was my intent, it didn't work. According to a reliable source, Jackie Robinson died in 1972; he was 53 years old. Abraham Lincoln was 56 years old when he was assassinated. I am 56 years old, and no more ready to leave this life than either of these men.

When the Koppelmans and Fiedlers left Cooperstown, we caravanned to the Catskills and spent a night in that beautiful part of New York State. The next day

Craig indulging in a baseball fan's fantasy by pretending to be at bat in front of statue of Hall of Fame catcher, Roy Campanella.

we drove to Bethel to tour the Woodstock Museum. We were instantly transported back to 1969 and the counter-cultural revolution of the baby boomer generation. The museum was very entertaining and informative, and we were glad we added this stop to our itinerary. At this point, we parted company as Sheri and I drove to Gettysburg and the Koppelmans drove to New York City to attend the high school graduation festivities for Kent's niece. When we took the tour of the Gettysburg battlefield, I had lots of questions for our tour guide, having just finished reading a 600-page book on that battle. Because Sheri was so patient and tolerant during our 2 days at Gettysburg, I promised her that the next trip would involve a destination of her choice.

Just prior to departing for the New York and Pennsylvania trip, I had a follow-up chest CT scan, so when Sheri and I returned to Wisconsin, we met with Dr. Cooper to review the results. It was not good news. The CT scan revealed that my original tumor had now regained some of its initial size that had been shrunken by my treatments. Worse yet, the cancer in my right lung had metastasized to four new tumors in my lung, and the existing cancerous lymph nodes had remained the same size since the previous scan. My cancer diagnosis now went from IIIB to IV. Is this change in designation referred to as an upgrade or a downgrade? (Mental note: find out the correct term!) In any event, I had now reached the pinnacle of the cancer diagnostic scale. Unfortunately, this scale is like golf, where the lower score is better. It is easier to joke about it now as I'm writing this, but at the time the news rocked me, my eyes filling with tears. Sheri tried to comfort me, and Dr. Cooper suggested reading *Tuesdays with Morrie* (1997) by Mitch Albom. I had read this book several years earlier, and it seemed inspirational at the time. Dr. Cooper thought that reading it might help me to "refocus" and face my new treatment regimen. I did not say anything, but as my oncologist gave me this pep talk, I was thinking about the book. Morrie was Albom's former college professor who had been retired for several years prior to being diagnosed with amyotrophic lateral sclerosis (also known as Lou Gehrig's disease). The inspirational message about living each moment of your life to the fullest was certainly relevant, but there were two important differences between Morrie and me: he had not been forced to take an early retirement, and his physical deterioration and death were happening when he was considerably older than me. Because of these differences, it didn't seem likely that the book could offer me much comfort now.

Based on this latest CT scan, Dr. Cooper recommended a new chemotherapy regimen of three drugs: avastin, carboplatin, and paciltaxel. To reduce the side effects, this new treatment regimen would involve a day a week of chemo for 3 weeks and then a week off for 3 to 4 months. Avastin is classified as a monoclonal antibody drug; it creates new antibodies to enhance the body's immune system as it destroys cancer cells. Carboplatin and paciltaxel are typical chemotherapy drugs in that both are designed to halt cancerous cell division by killing the cancerous cells. As with any chemo drug, there would be typical side effects, meaning that each one had the potential of causing its own unique type of debilitating consequences. I needed some time to process all of this bad news, so I asked Dr. Cooper to give me some time to consider the prospect of further treatments. It seemed that we had now entered the realm of weighing quality of life issues against buying a little more time to live. In the back of my mind, I kept hearing the words that express the fundamental principle of the Hippocratic Oath: to do no harm. Perhaps the chemotherapy would reduce my quality of my life so significantly that more harm than good would come from the treatment. It was a decision I was dreading to make.

There were two additional complications during my treatment program. First, a chest CT scan in April revealed a cloudy infiltrate in my right lung. It was described by the radiologist as having the consistency of "ground glass." Dr. Cooper was concerned that this might indicate a further malignancy in my lung, so he referred me back to Dr. Avery for additional diagnostic work. Dr. Avery thought this cloudy infiltrate was caused by one of three conditions:

radiation scarring, an infection, or more cancer. He said his gut reaction was that it was not additional cancer. Dr. Avery suggested conducting another bronchoscopy, but he did not want to do a biopsy. A biopsy would require me to go off the blood thinning medication for a couple of days, and he did not want to risk another pulmonary embolism. Instead, he would collect some fluid in my lung and test that for infection or cancer. The bronchoscopy was performed and the results indicated that the infiltrate was neither an infection nor cancer. Dr. Avery suggested draining the fluid build-up in my lung, and a few days later he did that. When he checked the fluid there was nothing abnormal about it. Apparently, I had dodged a bullet.

The second complication involved my January surgical incision. It had been weeping fluid for a few weeks. The incision site looked red and swollen, and it was slightly sore. Both Drs. Cooper and Dalton were worried that the inflammation and hardness under my skin near that incision could be a tumor. They referred me to a surgeon for outpatient surgery, and a few days later the surgeon performed a needle biopsy. The following week Dr. Dalton met with me to discuss the biopsy results and my latest brain MRI. It was one of my better visits in the past few months because both the MRI and the needle biopsy were negative. This news came on top of a negative abdomen and pelvic CT scan a few days earlier. At least to this point, the cancer had not spread beyond my right lung. Another chest CT scan was scheduled for next week to monitor my cancer.

On Monday, August 11, Sheri and I met with Drs. Avery and Cooper to discuss the CT scan, and we were provided with another slight ray of hope. Although the amount of radiation scarring in my lungs made reading CT scans a challenge, the latest CT scan revealed that what was thought to be four new cancerous tumors in my right lung were more likely to be non-cancerous nodes that had calcified due to the treatment. Another node in my left lung looked suspicious to Dr. Cooper, but he was not willing to call it a cancerous tumor yet. The original tumor in the lower lobe of my right lung was still there and the cancer was still in my lymph nodes, but at this point, the goal was to stabilize the cancer and stop it from spreading. Although it wasn't quite a good enough reason to throw a party, Sheri and I were grateful for this information. When you are battling cancer, you look for any kind of good news to feel a sense of optimism and to strengthen your continued willingness to fight. I was still willing to fight, at least for the moment.

The best news was that these latest CT and MRI scans meant several more weeks without chemotherapy. My treatment plan called for scans every 2 months, and the next CT and MRI scans would not happen until the fall. Once we had those findings, we could determine future treatments. At least for now I had been given a brief reprieve, so Sheri and I began planning a Caribbean vacation in August to the Dominican Republic. We just wanted to enjoy each other and have a relaxing time without having to deal with the specter of imminent death. As Sheri put it, "It will be nice to get away from all of the medical tests and appointments and not think about death and dying for a few days."

References

Albom, M. (1997). *Tuesdays with Morrie*. New York: Doubleday.

Cousins, N. (1981). *Anatomy of an illness as perceived by the patient*. New York: Bantam Books.

CHAPTER 4

Resolving to Battle the Bully

My body had betrayed me. Big time. Not just once, but twice. First, with lung cancer and, second, by getting celiac disease. If the goal was to suggest the need for me to make some lifestyle changes, the cancer got my full attention, but threatening my life seemed like a rather extreme way to make such a demand. Perhaps this could be the premise for a new reality TV program called "Extreme Terminal Illness Makeover." Or is it redundant to use the words "extreme" and "terminal" in the same title?

In the waiting room at the oncology clinic was a plaque prominently displayed that was obviously intended to offer inspiration to all cancer patients. The message on the plaque was the following:

What Cancer Cannot Do
Cancer is so limited.
It cannot shatter hope.
It cannot corrode faith.
It cannot destroy peace.
It cannot kill friendship.
It cannot suppress memories.
It cannot silence courage.
It cannot invade the soul.
It cannot steal eternal life.
It cannot conquer the spirit.

I appreciated the inspirational intent of the message, but for many patients, cancer can and does rob you of all that and more. When cancer commits its identity theft, it steals your future. For most of my adult life I had tried to do all the right things, such as exercising regularly, eating a balanced diet, and taking vitamin supplements. Aware of my tendency to be a workaholic, I made a conscious effort to have a balance in my life between work and leisure. I never smoked. And yet I had lung cancer.

How do you respond to what is essentially a death sentence? Well, you pick yourself up from the floor and fight back. Everyone copes differently with disaster and tragedy. Lance Armstrong, the 7-time champion of the Tour de France bicycle race and also a survivor of testicular, lung, and brain cancer, embodied that fighting spirit in his book, *It's Not About the Bike: My Journey Back to Life*. He described how he battled cancer: "I decided to get personal right back, and I began to talk to it, engaging in an inner conversation with cancer. I tried to be firm in my discussions. 'You picked the wrong guy,' I told it. 'When you looked around for a body to try to live in, you made a big mistake when you chose mine'" (2000, p. 97). On my good days, I attempted to emulate Lance Armstrong as my fighting spirit role model. On my bad days, I struggled with thoughts such as "Why bother, nobody beats lung cancer" or "Just let me die now" or "I don't have the strength to go through this ordeal."

In one of my attempts to display a fighting spirit, I had the opportunity to address the graduating seniors during commencement at my alma mater, La Crosse Central High School. It all started back in February with a phone call from Tom Barth, the principal at Central High School, who informed me that the High School Alumni Association had voted for my induction into the school's Hall of Excellence. The Alumni Association had started this Hall of Excellence in 1999 to honor graduates of Central High School for their post-graduation achievements. Every year since then, the Alumni Association had inducted up to three Central High School graduates. My nomination was submitted by two parents from a Parents in Partnership group that I had co-facilitated. My nomination and induction came as a complete surprise, and I told the principal that this honor came at a good time to bolster my spirits and my resolve to battle the cancer.

The Central Alumni Association held a reception for me and the other two inductees at the high school on Saturday, May 31. Our plaques would be installed on a wall outside the school's auditorium. In reviewing the plaques of the previously inducted members of the Hall of Excellence, one of the inductees that caught my eye was Don Herbert, a 1937 Central graduate. Don Herbert is better known as Mr. Wizard of the television science program for children in the 1950s and early '60s. Like most baby boomers, I remembered watching Mr. Wizard. A few days after the induction ceremony, my Google search of Don Herbert revealed that he died in 2007 at the age of 89 from bone cancer. The Hall of Excellence inductees were asked to address the graduating seniors at commencement the next day, June 1. Here is what I said to them:

> I have recently been reminded of an important life lesson. That lesson is this: We cannot often control external events that happen to us but we can control how we respond to those events. I have relearned this lesson since January 28, 2008, when I was diagnosed with terminal lung cancer. This diagnosis came as a total shock since I have never smoked and there is no history of cancer in my family. My initial thought was "why me"? But I quickly resolved not to focus my attention on this issue as I realized that bad things happen to people all the time and often for no apparent reason.

> Instead, I decided that I would face this cancer as I have tried to live my life—with purpose, passion, and hope. My special education career has been enriched by a clear purpose in what I do for a profession. I owe that sense of purpose to my oldest daughter, Jennifer, who was born with severe and multiple disabilities. Similarly, in responding to my cancer diagnosis, I have a clear purpose to educate myself on this disease and all treatment options so that I can be an active partner with my medical team in fighting my cancer.
>
> My passion for my profession has always been fueled by my love of teaching. As a teacher, I learned long ago that I did not need to know all of the answers to engage my students. In fact, I believe the best definition of a well-educated person is an individual who has more questions than answers. My passion is now focused on wanting to live as long as possible. And I know that my long term survival chances are better if I am educated on my condition and treatment options so that I can ask lots of questions to the physicians treating me.
>
> Finally, as a teacher, I always hope and strive to get better. Now, I hope that I will beat the odds and experience a medical miracle by conquering this lung cancer. My hope and optimism are bolstered by a firm belief in the mind-body connection. That is, I believe that our attitudes and emotions significantly impact our health and how our immune system fights off diseases. Hope is essential to any patient facing a terminal diagnosis.
>
> As you complete your high school education and go forward from this day, I urge you to lead your lives with a strong sense of purpose, passion, and hope. If 20, 30, or 50 years from now you can truthfully say that your life has purpose, passion, and hope, you will have clearly led a good life. My congratulations to all of the graduates and I wish you well in all of your future endeavors.

Giving this address at commencement caused me to reflect on the current high school graduates and my own K–12 school years. In an introspective mood, I began to see a connection between my cancer and the scourge of many adolescents—the school bully. Bullying and student harassment have become a major problem in schools across this country. Bullies have even gone high tech by engaging in a new tactic called cyber bullying. What bullies and cancer have in common is that both of them attack you for no reason and make your life miserable. Thinking about this comparison stimulated me to pursue the metaphor a bit more.

Cancer as a bully: until now, the biggest bully I ever knew was Paul Leonard. Paul terrorized his fellow students during his junior high school reign. Sometimes he would simply extort lunch money from fellow students, other times he would get physically aggressive and even violent. There was a small, family-run candy store across the street from Longfellow Junior High School, which I attended. Longfellow students frequently hung out at Sweeney's candy store during lunch break. One of the main attractions in the alley alongside Sweeney's store was an almost daily fighting bout between some of the more hardened students in school.

Craig is presented with his plaque for inclusion in the
Hall of Excellence at La Crosse (WI) Central High School.

Paul was a frequent combatant during these noon-hour fisticuffs. His boxing skills solidified his reputation as a bully and made him appear even more intimidating. My friends and I knew nothing about Paul's home life; all we knew was that it was best to stay out of his way. In that regard, most of us sought a low profile and tried to avoid crossing paths with Paul during school days.

Unfortunately, while hanging out with a couple of my friends, we happened to cross paths with Paul and a buddy of his on a Saturday afternoon. We ran into this terroristic duo in downtown La Crosse during an annual celebration called Oktoberfest. Paul and his fellow bully came up to us, acting tough. At one point, Paul grabbed my shirt and made a fist. He asked his buddy, whose name I cannot remember, if he wanted to slug me. Without any warning, his friend's fist struck my chin with speed and precision. And by the way, just so the point is not lost, it hurt. I was stunned, and before it was possible for me to muster any kind of a masculine response like, "Please don't hit me again," Paul and my tormentor had moved on to look for other victims.

This was my closest encounter to getting into a fight during my entire school career. But perhaps you cannot really call it a fight when my participation was limited to lending my face as a punching bag. I was a pacifist, not for any philosophical reasons but strictly out of practical necessity. That encounter with Paul and his friend informed my thinking about just how much damage and pain could be caused by a fist wielded by a skilled individual. Clearly my strengths were in different areas of human endeavor.

That was the first sucker punch I ever received, but the second one was delivered by that unexpected diagnosis of lung cancer on January 28, 2008. The first caused mainly physical pain, the second primarily psychic pain. Which one was worse? In terms of recuperation, it didn't take long to recover from the physically painful sucker punch, but with the psychically damaging second blow, recuperation was taking a lot longer.

Like most bullies, cancer is aggressive and unpredictable. It can raise your hopes for a recovery and then dash those hopes with an MRI or CT scan that shows the cancer has returned or spread. My friend Lisa has been battling breast cancer for over 10 years. She has gone into remission twice, only to have the cancer return each time with even more vengeance. Lisa has lost and regrown her hair three times. The last time she started losing her hair, the entire family, including her husband and three children, participated in a sort of celebration. They dyed Lisa's hair several colors and styled it in a punk fashion. After several memorable photos and some family laughter, Lisa's husband, Brian, shaved her head. Lisa and her family illustrated the old adage that when life gives you lemons you make lemonade. In response to my question about what helped her to maintain her fighting spirit in such a long cancer battle, Lisa's immediate response was that her initial cancer diagnosis came when all three of her children were quite young. She was determined that she was going to fight to live long enough to see her children grow up. And the good news is that Lisa is still alive, fighting the bully with every ounce of her strength and winning her cancer battle. Her second-oldest child will graduate from high school in 2009. Lisa's story is a story of hope.

Cancer and bullies are an apt comparison because both are malevolent and vindictive. They both sense fear and strike out at the weakest. There is plenty of medical research on cancer that shows the connection between a weakened immune system and the onset of disease. In my case, it is possible that my immune system had been systematically compromised over time, making my body unable to effectively destroy the cancerous cells that exist in all human beings. I have always had a tendency to wear "my emotions on my sleeve," meaning it is difficult for me to restrain my emotions, especially negative emotions in response to my perceptions of problematic students, recalcitrant co-workers, ungrateful friends, and irresponsible family members. If this makes me sound like a very judgmental person, I plead guilty. That human flaw caused me much pain and caused me to inflict pain on other people whom I ultimately cared about. In addition, another lifelong tendency for me is to be a world-class worrier and obsessive contemplator of every perceived slight, real or imagined. On occasion, strong negative feelings about particular incidents have affected me for unhealthy periods of time. It seems probable that these bad emotional habits eventually led to the impairment of my immune system.

As an example, shortly before my cancer diagnosis, I had endured several highly stressful years at my university. From 2003–2005, I served my college as interim dean, not because any desire for the appointment but out of a strong sense of loyalty to my institution. After the first week of my new administrative assignment, it became clear that I had inherited a sizeable college deficit from the preceding dean, forcing me to make several painful and controversial decisions about staff and course reductions. Many faculty members blamed me for the problems and criticized my decisions. In 2005, I gratefully returned to my faculty position, but then agreed to serve as department chair for 3 years because once again, no other faculty member was willing to assume this responsibility. The additional stress that accompanied these administrative appointments, along with my constitutional inability to handle work and life stressors effectively, in my mind has contributed significantly to my weakened immune system. I was a sitting duck for a bully like cancer.

Another similarity: cancer and bullies are incapable of compassion or empathy for their victims because a major part of the attraction of being a bully is the feeling of power, of being in control of another person. Cancer feeds on a similar need for power and control as cancerous cells multiply to achieve the ultimate goal of taking over a person's body. Although still trailing heart disease, cancer is now the number two killer in the United States, and it is gaining ground fast. In the near future, it should not surprise anyone to find that cancer has overtaken heart disease as the number one cause of death. The final similarity that occurred to me between cancer and bullies is that cancer does not care if the victim is a good person, a kind person, or a cruel person, nor does cancer factor such human traits into the equation to determine the next victim it attacks. Cancer and bullies are ruthless in their pursuit of mayhem and destruction.

Can either cancer or bullies be rehabilitated? Unfortunately, in this country we devote more resources to punishment than rehabilitation, even for children. We punish not only juvenile delinquents, but children with severe emotional and behavioral problems rather than provide them with preventive therapies and supportive special educational services. As a consequence, the numbers of such troubled youth continue to grow. Similarly, in the 1970s during the Nixon administration, the United States launched a war on cancer, and although progress has been made in understanding the disease and improving treatments, the nation continues to fight a losing battle as the number of cancer deaths persistently increases each year. Yet Americans appear to be unwilling to make a sufficient societal commitment to provide funding for cancer research. We seem to be more committed to fighting conventional wars against other countries with real armies than fighting against faceless opponents such as cancer and poverty.

How can you cope with this bully, this killer called cancer? As I said before, coping with cancer and battling this disease is highly individual; what works for one person may not be the best strategy for another. In addition, coping with cancer always occurs on an uneven battlefield; some days there is optimism and renewed commitment to fight, and other days you just want it all to end. Living with cancer is like being sentenced to death by the so-called Chinese water torture method. Every day, hour after hour, the dreadful prognosis continues to trickle into your conscious mind, and the drip, drip, drip of it persists throughout your daily activities. It wears you down mentally and physically. It can break your spirit and your will to live. I have tried to approach my cancer crisis in the best way I know how—intellectually.

Cancer causes stress because its devastating demands can overwhelm or exceed an individual's resources for managing that stress. My initial intellectual attempt to determine strategies for coping with my cancer diagnosis evolved from reflecting on my work with two colleagues for an academic book (2007). The book described how school professionals could support and empower families of children with disabilities. One chapter discussed stress and the need for coping strategies for families and presented several theoretical models. The basic coping model, developed in the 1950s, was called Hill's ABCX family crisis model. In Hill's model, characteristics of the stressor event (A), interacting with the family's crisis-meeting resources (B), then interacting with the definition the family makes of the event (C), produces the crisis (X).

Applying this model of coping to my cancer situation provided some solace by offering a better understanding of how my cancer crisis was developing. The stressor event (A) was finding out about my life-threatening disease. The family resources (B) included having good health insurance and my university's excellent retirement program, which created the possibility of taking an early disability retirement. Such resources were significant in addressing my cancer crisis. In terms of family perceptions and reactions to the cancer diagnosis (C), after the initial shock and denial, my family was determined to fight this battle, and they encouraged me to use all of my available resources: intellectual, physical, emotional, and spiritual. Family resources (B) and how my family and I defined this health crisis (C) did not eliminate the crisis (X) because the cancer was still in my body, but it gave us the strength to get past the initial panic and to start addressing our new reality. So now the question was, how could I use my intellectual, physical, emotional, and spiritual resources to cope with cancer?

Intellectual Resources

As stated previously, my entire life has been devoted to intellectual pursuits, first as a student, all those years spent accumulating four college degrees, and then as a professor. This lifelong intellectual perspective compelled me to gather information and resources to become an informed partner with the medical personnel treating me. But don't get the wrong idea about this focus on intellectual resources, I still believe there are phenomena that defy explanations (e.g., miracles) and have often been quite superstitious. Growing up with an interest in sports exposed me to the quirks of many athletes and their strange superstitions. For example, baseball Hall of Famer Wade Boggs would always eat chicken before every game. The Louisiana State University and National Basketball Association star Pete Maravich wore the same dirty and droopy socks for each game he played in college. A recent event illustrated my own susceptibility to superstition.

Having obtained my PhD degree in special education from the University of Kansas caused me to become an ardent Kansas basketball fan. Although Kansas usually has a good men's basketball team, for several years in a row they had been eliminated early during the NCAA basketball championship tournament. The spring of 2008 was different as Kansas made it to the championship game against Memphis University on April 7. All day I kept thinking that if Kansas won this game it would be an omen that my cancer would miraculously go into remission and I would be cured. If my alma mater lost, the initial grim prognosis would be confirmed. Watching Kansas play in the championship game that night, I rooted for the Jayhawks with all my strength, as if my life depended upon it. Yet with about 2 minutes left in the game, Kansas trailed Memphis by nine points, and it seemed certain that my alma mater would lose. Not willing to watch what seemed like an inevitable outcome, I turned off the television and went to bed, muttering "I'm a dead man" as I shuffled off to my bedroom. In the morning, I turned on ESPN and was stunned to hear that Kansas had won the game. Mario Chalmers hit a last second three-point shot to send the game into overtime where Kansas prevailed 75-68. Of course the joy I felt was not simply for my alma mater, but stemmed from my belief that this meant my life was saved. This is just one example of the mind games that help to foster hope by providing a distraction from this bleak reality. Such distractions are essential to escape the day-to-day grind that is cancer.

There are also some superstitious artifacts that bolster my spirits when needed. In July, Sheri drove me to La Crosse, where I was to be honored with an outstanding service award from the La Crosse County ARC (which used to stand

five areas of motivation (self-efficacy, perceived control, hope, energy, and persistence) and four knowledge and skill components (relevant information, problem solving, coping skills, and communication skills). With this cancer crisis, one of my challenges was to determine how to live in a way consistent with my own theoretical beliefs and teachings by striving to become empowered in this battle with lung cancer. It would require an active commitment to equip myself with the motivational elements and the knowledge and skills of the empowerment model delineated above.

A key motivational element is hope. Hope is the belief that individuals will get what they want and need. There are thousands of documented medical cases where seriously ill patients who lost all possibility of hope succumbed quickly to their illnesses. Sometime in March I resolved to put my teaching philosophy into practice by actively seeking to become empowered in my cancer battle and by maintaining a strong sense of hope during this ordeal. It is a daily struggle to maintain this perspective, and some days I am more successful than others, but the goal of empowering myself has provided the fuel that generates a belief in the possibility of a long and healthy future. I am trying to cling to that belief with all of my strength.

Life does not stop just because you have cancer. If you allow it, cancer can take over your entire life by forcing you to focus only on your illness and draining you of energy. You are certainly jolted by this diagnosis, and it is common for people to stop thinking about the future and stop living their life to the fullest, but that is a defeatist perspective that only leads to misery and despair. None of us knows how many days we have in this world, yet people facing a terminal or serious illness often conclude that their lives have ground to a complete halt. Instead of sitting around waiting to die, people must try each day to live a purposeful life by finding joyful and meaningful activities. Developing this insight also came from my work with future special educators.

In an article published earlier in her career, Ann Turnbull (1988) coined the phrase "marathon skills" in discussing some common traits and competencies of parents of children with disabilities who have managed to remain healthy, functional, and hopeful over the long haul (marathon) of parenting. Since I get tired just riding in a car for 26 miles, the thought of running a marathon has never appealed to me. However, it is a good metaphor for the challenges faced when parenting children with disabilities, even though this responsibility is even longer than a marathon—it is a lifelong race. There are specific skills that help families of children with disabilities to become resilient and functional participants in the disability marathon, including knowing community resources, loving family members unconditionally, finding humor in daily life, being able to take charge of your life, striking a balance in meeting the demands and needs of all family members, understanding and benefiting from grief, relying upon support from others, and planning for the future. These marathon skills are also needed in the battle with cancer.

A great example of employing marathon skills in coping with cancer is the *My Cancer* blog (now *Our Cancer*; www.npr.org/blogs/mycancer) created by television journalist Leroy Sievers, who was diagnosed with brain cancer in late 2005. This diagnosis came after a skirmish with colon cancer almost 5 years earlier. The surgery for his colon cancer was successful and he was cancer free for those 5 years. After the initial diagnosis of brain cancer, it quickly spread to his lungs and spine. Sievers maintained his daily blog on the Web site of National Public Radio (NPR) for 33 months as he courageously lived his life while confronting the cancer and his terminal diagnosis. Leroy Sievers epitomized an individual with marathon skills seeking to live his life as fully and as long as possible. Unfortunately, Leroy lost his cancer battle in August of 2008 (since his death, Laurie Singer has take over his blog). The bully had beaten another victim. But Leroy left a lasting legacy in his sterling example of how marathon skills can be used to find joy and meaning in life even when confronted with a terminal illness.

While observing people in the oncology waiting area and the chemotherapy infusion room, it seemed like cancer patients had a tendency to size each other up by speculating about who is better or worse off than themselves. This does not seem to be done in a mean-spirited manner but as a normal response, and most likely a useful coping strategy. One man who must have been receiving chemotherapy on a schedule similar to mine looked emaciated and struggled to walk. He was pale and his head was mostly bald with a few splotches of thin hair. His wife told me that his esophageal cancer had spread to his lungs and liver. It was a chore for him to talk. I must confess that my first thought was, "I guess I'm better off than that poor guy." This is an example of a cognitive coping strategy known as downward social comparisons; many parents of children with disabilities also use this strategy. The strategy involves comparing your situation to the circumstances of someone perceived to be less fortunate in order to be comforted by the thought that no matter how bad it is for you, it could always be worse. I assumed my life expectancy was much longer than this other cancer patient, and that thought was a useful coping mechanism. When you are a terminally ill person, you are looking for any ray of optimism to help you deal with your current predicament.

In his blog, Leroy Sievers wrote often about being stuck in cancer world because he was so easily identified as a cancer patient by the typical outward markers such as hair loss, pale complexion, fearful eyes, depressed affect, and general lethargic appearance. He longed to slip back into blissful anonymity. His desire reminded me of my parental experiences with a child who had an obvious disability. Jennifer gets around by being pushed in a wheelchair, and she verbalizes not by words but by high pitched squeals. She often flaps her ears with her hands in an excited fashion, and at times you swear she is getting close to "liftoff" from her chair. Whenever Sheri and I have taken Jennifer into a public setting, our family quickly loses any semblance of anonymity by these behaviors that cause Jennifer to stand out in any crowd. Over the years, a number of total strangers have approached us to ask very personal questions about Jennifer and our family. It is natural to be curious about someone with such stark human differences, and we usually tried to patiently and politely respond to the questions of these strangers. But sometimes we were exhausted and simply wanted to blend into the crowd; we were tired of giving lectures on mental retardation. As with many parents of children with disabilities, the individuals with cancer want to return to a normal existence, and primarily that means going through daily life in an anonymous fashion like other people.

In my new world, and against my will, cancer was becoming my all-defining identity. As a professional in the field of special education, I have long been acutely aware of the power and impact of labels we employ for individuals with disabilities, and this enabled me to recognize the similarities of labels for those with serious or chronic illnesses. Disability or illness labels are merely shorthand descriptors of a person who fits a particular diagnostic category. The problem is that labels are incapable of capturing the complexity and wholeness of a person. Labels tend to dehumanize people because they cannot convey anything about the personality or the dreams of the person behind the diagnostic term. Any human being will always be more complicated than the simplistic perception and information that a label provides. The two most important motivations for me to write about my experience with cancer were to leave a diary for my family and close friends and to describe my circumstances to others so that I am not simply viewed or remembered as a "cancer patient." Cancer is not my primary identity.

One of the kindest acts of friendship bestowed upon me came from my close friend and colleague Becky Thorson-Randall. After my radiation and chemotherapy treatments began and my hair had finally fallen out, Becky came to visit me one day at my house. Being quite self-conscious of my changed appearance, one of my first comments was to state the obvious: that the person she was seeing today certainly didn't look like the same person she knew 2 months earlier. Without a moment's hesitation, Becky assured me that I was still the same person inside, and this was what was most important to her. Everyone who is confronted with a terminal illness needs close and caring friends like Becky to remind them of their true identity.

Facing a terminal cancer diagnosis is a fearful proposition for lots of rather obvious reasons, but one of the strongest fears is the fear of the unknown. After first being told of my lung cancer diagnosis, it was impossible for me to understand what that involved or what kind of future was in store for me, other than that it was sure to be bleak. To deal with the uncertainty required me to begin immediately reading books and articles on lung cancer and treatments. Gathering information on lung cancer while living in cancer world over a period of time, the mystery and eventually the fear of my situation slowly started to dissipate. One of my first conclusions was that coping with the fear of the unknown was directly related to the family systems theory that I had taught to prospective special education teachers. Employing family systems theory allows professionals to better understand families of children with disabilities so that they are attuned to a family's strengths, expectations, priorities, and needs. The family systems approach assists professionals in working more effectively and collaboratively with family members, and it seemed clear to me that the sensitivity involved in this perspective could facilitate my efforts to establish collaborative physician-patient partnerships.

Family systems theory consists of four major components to aid in understanding families of children with disabilities: family characteristics (e.g., descriptive elements of the family including size and form, racial and ethnic background, socioeconomic status, geographical location, personal coping styles, and special challenges), family interaction (e.g., how individuals in a family interact and the various subgroups of family members—marital, parental, sibling, and extrafamilial), family functions (e.g., categories of needs the family must address to remain a viable unit), and family life cycle (e.g., sequence of developmental and nondevelopmental changes that affect families). It is the family life-cycle component that is most directly related to this issue of the fear of the unknown. Change or transition usually causes stress for people. This stress is the fear of the unknown, not knowing what will happen given this new life change and wondering how you will cope with the new challenges wrought by this life change. Professionals working with either families of children with disabilities or individuals with terminal illnesses must react sensitively to changes in the life of that family or in the lives of individual members of that family so that appropriate support can be generated to cope with the increased stress.

A common reaction of people just given a cancer diagnosis is "why me?" This question is related to the grief process first discussed by Elisabeth Kübler-Ross (1969) in her work with terminally ill people (denial, anger, bargaining, depression, and acceptance). Kübler-Ross's grief process has been applied to parents of children with disabilities because some parents may experience their child's disability as a loss since their dreams and hopes for this child have been shattered, or at least altered. Many professionals working with families of children with disabilities or with individuals facing death maintain that the emotions associated with the grief process (including fear, guilt, and anxiety) are a natural and adaptive response to such devastating information.

All of the grief emotions assailed me after the initial diagnosis of my lung cancer condition. For a time, I was critical of myself for having these emotions, viewing them as an indication of my weakness and inability to rally to my new situation. During several weeks of grappling with these grief feelings, I did not apply my knowledge of the grief process as applied to families of children with disabilities. I failed to remember what I had learned about how grief emotions can be very adaptive and healthy if you do not fight those feelings or think negatively of yourself for having them. It took a long time before this insight came to me, but once it did, it became easier for me to start coping more effectively with my cancer diagnosis. That is not to say that my struggle with feelings of denial, guilt, depression, anger, or anxiety have ended, because they have not. What is different now is my realization that these emotions are part of a natural process of healing. That offers me some peace of mind.

In a book co-authored with Richard Simpson and Denise Clark entitled *Parents and Families of Children with Disabilities: Effective School-Based Support Services* (2007), one of my chapters focused on coping with stress and discussed the grief process. The chapter described five typical feelings that occur during grief and the adaptive functions and supportive professional responses for each emotion. Table 1 is a summary. When reviewing this information on stages of the grief process and feelings associated with grief, it is apparent that supportive professionals can serve an essential function by being present, listening, and showing empathy to those individuals struggling with devastating life situations. There are no simple panaceas, only caring and compassionate human connections.

Another important cognitive coping strategy is to focus on the positives of any challenging situation, and having a terminal cancer diagnosis represents an extreme challenge physically, mentally, emotionally, and spiritually. As a parent of a child with severe and multiple disabilities, focusing on positives has been a cognitive strategy I have used for many years. It would be easy to dwell on all of the negatives stemming from Jennifer's disability: she is not toilet trained, she cannot feed or dress herself, she has no communication skills, she does not walk, and all the other deficiencies that professionals over the years have identified. Yet it has been more helpful for me to focus on Jennifer's positive attributes: she is very healthy, she has given me a deep appreciation for the wonder of child development, she has taught me more about individuals with disabilities than any course or instructor I have ever had, and perhaps most importantly, as an adolescent she has never argued with me about having to wear Guess jeans as opposed to some off-brand pair of jeans!

Now anybody in his or her right mind would prefer to avoid a cancer diagnosis, but in my reading there have been many articles written by people with cancer who describe it as a gift in terms of providing new perspectives and insights. It has taken time for me to develop an appreciation of the positives that cancer has brought to my life, but it has enhanced my appreciation for everyday activities and events, and it has taught me to be much less judgmental of other people. Another positive is that my wife and I have taken a new attitude about traveling to places we have always wanted to visit—there is no time like the present. Because of my forced early retirement, there has been the luxury of time to read lots of books. My response to this health crisis has taught me much more about myself, and has brought me closer to family members and friends than ever before. These are truly gifts to be grateful for. It is sad that most of us have to experience a life crisis to understand and enjoy these simple pleasures.

Table 1. Five Typical Feelings That Occur During Grief and the Adaptive Functions and Supportive Professional Responses for Each Emotion

Feeling	Adaptive function	Supportive professional responses
Denial	Buys time to deal with difficult news	Do not pressure the person; let them come to their understanding at their own pace
Guilt	Helps locate resources and develop supports	Connect the person with other individuals in similar circumstances
	Assesses reality of what you are and are not responsible for	Be a good listener Do not argue with a guilt-ridden person
	Develops sense of control and serves to explain the unexplainable	Show empathy
Depression	Develops new definition of strength or competency	Show empathy
	Common reaction to loss	Help person development supportive relationships with others
		Foster renewed sense of strength or competence
Anger	Redefines internal sense of fairness or justice	Do not respond in kind with anger
Anxiety	Redefines or prioritizes a person's responsibilities	Make interactions with the person comfortable and welcoming
	Provides energy to seek out necessary information	Encourage the person to strike a balance in addressing responsibilities and needs
		Provide the person with information he or she is seeking

Physical Resources

Cancer not only steals your identity, it transforms your historical perspective on your life and how you measure time. My history is now measured as before cancer (BC) and after diagnosis (AD). My BC life seems like ancient history because it feels as if this cancer has been part of my life for much longer than 8 months. In this cancer fight, I have tried to enhance my coping through reading about the mind-body connection, diet and nutrition, and the body's immune system to help me understand what my body needs to help it resist the growth of cancerous cells.

My colleague Denise Clark gave me the first cancer book that I read AD. Anne and David Frahm (1992) wrote *A Cancer Battle Plan: Six Strategies for Beating Cancer from a Recovered "Hopeless Case."* After an original misdiagnosis of non-cancerous cysts, Anne was diagnosed with advanced breast cancer. Despite 18 months of treatment that involved surgeries, radiation, chemotherapy, and a bone marrow transplant, her doctors predicted an imminent death. Since Anne had exhausted all traditional cancer treatments, she started to explore nutrition and diet. Only 5 weeks after she started a strict regimen of detoxification of her body that included a vegetarian diet and vitamin and mineral supplements, tests revealed that Anne was cancer-free. This was the first time I had ever read the story of a cancer survivor who had beaten such long odds, and Anne's oncologist made a statement that seemed especially inspirational to me: "Anne, I can't cure you with chemotherapy, but perhaps I can keep you alive long enough for you to learn to cure yourself" (p. 129). To provide information and inspiration to other individuals with cancer, Anne and her husband, David, began HealthQuarters Ministries in Colorado.

With my curiosity inspired by the book, I went to the HealthQuarters Web site. The first posting there was a letter from Anne's husband indicating that Anne had recently died. Her cancer had returned to her backbone and pleural lining of her lungs, and fluid had accumulated in the sac around her heart. Reading this letter was a devastating experience, plunging me immediately into a deep despair until I realized that regardless of what had happened, Anne should still be viewed as a survivor because she had defied all medical prognoses of an imminent death by living for several more years. Anne also left a legacy of hope and inspiration for people like me. Her life made a difference in the example she set of fighting a terminal illness against long odds.

Anne Frahm's battle plan included six strategies: (a) know your enemy, (b) cut off enemy supply lines, (c) rebuild your natural defense system, (d) bring in reinforcements, (e) maintain morale, and (f) carefully select your professional help. Most of these cancer-fighting strategies involved the importance of the mind-body connection, good nutrition and diet, vitamin and mineral supplements, and spiritual resources. Efforts to better understand the mind-body connection has spawned a new branch of medicine called psychoneuroimmunology, based upon the interaction of the brain, the endocrine system, and the immune system.

There were two other individuals who were inspirational for me—Dr. Bernie Siegel and Norman Cousins. Both men were pioneers in advancing the belief that your attitudes and emotions have a direct physical impact on your health and on your body's defense mechanisms to ward off disease and illness. Positive emotions and attitudes such as hope, purpose, determination, and a strong will to live are not merely mental states, these feelings have electrochemical connections that impact the body's immune system.

As a child, I would often get anxious about change and novel situations such as starting a new school year with different teachers and classmates. My anxiety would trigger a chain reaction of negative emotions that often led to physical illness. From this experience, it has always been obvious to me that people can make themselves sick by worrying and becoming obsessed with negative emotions, but I did not know that the physical toll on your body and health could be so great. There is a common characteristic that can be observed among those patients who outlive their terminal diagnoses—a refusal to accept the grim inevitability of their medical prognoses.

There is mounting medical research that emotional stress contributes to a higher incidence of cancer by causing abnormal cell development. Chronic stress impairs the immune system by decreasing its capacity to produce killer and helper T-cells, which serve as the body's defense system in destroying and preventing the multiplication of cancerous cells. The immune system is your body's surveillance system, producing antibodies that destroy invading bacteria and viruses. Despair, depression, and fear suppress the immune system, preventing it from functioning properly in guarding the body against invaders. When Anne Frahm's oncologist said he was trying to keep her alive so she could cure herself, he was noting a medical fact that the majority of human illnesses can be healed by the body's immune system.

From my reading about cancer, the immune system, and nutrition and diet, it became clear how lifestyle choices greatly impact our health. There are four methods to enhance your immune system: good nutrition, food supplements, stress reduction, and exercise. The information on good nutrition and eating a balanced diet was not new to me, but until you are faced with a serious health challenge, the tendency is to avoid those lessons and continue your old habits of going to the fast food restaurants and spending an inordinate amount of time in the junk foods aisle at the grocery store. The health crisis facing many Americans these days is directly related to the Standard American Diet (SAD) of fatty foods; fried foods; an excess of meat, dairy products, sugar, and white flour; and an overabundance of processed foods with all kinds of preservatives and additives. The SAD causes an increase in hormones in the body that can trigger the onset of cancer. The best recommended alternative to the SAD is one composed primarily of live foods as opposed to dead foods. Cooking food (dead food) causes a variety of detrimental effects to that food such as enzyme loss, proteins being denatured, heating oils and fats converted to transfatty acids that are carcinogenic, vitamins and minerals are depleted, sugar is increased, and the effectiveness of fiber is reduced. By contrast, a living foods diet involves eating foods in their natural, uncooked state—primarily raw vegetables, fresh fruits, nuts, seeds, and other vegetarian diet staples. One living foods diet advises people to avoid any food that comes from something with a *face*. I assume this means the original source and not the middle merchandiser who has prepared the meal and serves it with a loving and smiling face (i.e., my wife).

At the risk of sounding like the food police, all of the information gathered from my reading about nutrition, diet, the immune system, and cancer has caused me to reconsider the foods in my normal diet. On the positive side, my consumption of red meat has never been conspicuous. When grilling steaks, my wife usually cooks me a chopped sirloin steak (glorified hamburger) as opposed to a filet mignon, T-bone, or top sirloin. My eating sins have largely revolved around junk foods, especially salty snacks such as chips, pretzels, Fritos, and Cheetos. Has my reading caused me to reform these eating habits and shed my former sinful ways? Well, not completely. Although not a vegetarian, I tend to eat primarily pork and chicken instead of red meat and have introduced more fruits and vegetables into my daily diet. In addition, I have started juicing ala Jack LaLanne, who is in his nineties and swears that he owes his good health and fitness to juicing fresh vegetables and fruits. (Editor's note: Jack LaLanne died January 25, 2011.) Ironically, my celiac disease has assisted me by eliminating wheat, barley, and rye from my diet. This has forced me to avoid breads, pizza, pasta, cakes, and many processed foods that are bulwarks of the SAD. My efforts as a "reformed eater"

Craig and his father Russ at the 2008 ARC picnic and award ceremony.

constitute a work in progress, but improving my eating habits is just one more attempt at trying to exert some control over the bully as this life-and-death battle with cancer continues.

Finally, my arsenal of physical resources includes nutritional supplements that are taken regularly in an effort to boost my immune system. My research has uncovered the importance of vitamin and mineral supplements such as zinc, selenium, vitamin E, vitamin C, vitamin A, coenzyme (Q10), glutathione, vitamin B6, magnesium, and dehydroepiandrosterone (DHEA). Without turning this book into a chemistry and biology lecture, suffice it to say that these nutritional supplements have been found to increase the production of T-cells, to function as active antioxidants that increase antibody production and decrease tumor growth, to enhance enzyme production, and in general, to balance the immune system. After discussing these nutritional supplements with my medical team, they approved my proposal to spend a significant amount of time each day in assembling and consuming all of these supplements as well as my prescribed medications. This has resulted in a friendly competition with my 88-year-old father concerning who consumes more pills in a typical day. I think I am leading at the moment.

Emotional Resources

For my most recent book, *Making a Difference: Advocacy Competencies for Special Education Professionals* (2009, 2nd ed.), I conducted a literature review on the topic of emotional resilience. My goal was to identify resources special education professionals relied upon to remain resilient in their advocacy efforts for children with disabilities and their families. Special education advocacy can be stressful, especially if a professional is challenging actions of his or her supervisor or school district. Bobek (2002) defined emotional resilience as "the ability to adjust to varied situations and increase one's competence in the face of adverse conditions" (p. 202). I think of resilience as the capacity to bounce back from challenging circumstances. Remember those inflatable punching bags or figures (like clowns) that many of us had as kids? You punched the inflatable figure and it hit the floor and bounced right back. That's how I think of resilience, especially with regard to my cancer situation. What are the key attributes and characteristics of emotionally resilient individuals? My literature research revealed a number of significant factors.

First, resilient individuals understand the value of collaborative relationships. Since the beginning of my cancer diagnosis, I have tried to develop a partnership with medical personnel by learning as much as possible about lung cancer, treatments, the immune system, alternative therapies, and long-term survival stories. This knowledge influences my interactions with physicians because it enables me to ask a lot of questions and seek more information about specific new treatments described in my reading.

Related to this collaboration characteristic, another resilience factor involves enhancing your competence and skills by becoming a lifelong learner willing to encounter new challenges and unafraid of risks. My cancer diagnosis represents the greatest challenge ever encountered in my life. A cursory review of my past life reveals my commitment to being a lifelong learner, illustrated primarily by those many years of postsecondary education and my choice of a career. Although never anticipating that my learning topics would entail a crash course in lung cancer, radiation, and chemotherapy, it was necessary for me to be focused on these topics to do battle with this cancer bully who threatens my life. When dealing with a serious illness, ignorance is definitely not bliss.

Emotionally resilient individuals assume ownership of their lives—they do not sit back passively and let their lives unfold. Sometimes people with serious illnesses simply resign themselves to their fate, thus ensuring their demise. There are many people in the oncology waiting room who appear to have taken this path. Their demeanor and facial expressions reveal their resignation; they appear to be just going through the motions of doctor appointments, tests, and treatments without any expectation of recovery. There is a critical difference between denying the reality of one's situation as opposed to having a sense of resignation to one's fate. My lung cancer battle involves long odds for my survival, but I am not willing to resign myself to that fate. Not yet at least.

Lance Armstrong (2000) wrote about his competitive spirit and the fact that he never got used to losing. He refused to accept his bleak diagnosis and the odds for long-term survival. He attributed his recovery from a cancer death sentence to this fighting spirit and success orientation. With the help of my family, I was able to pick myself up from the despair and depression of my cancer diagnosis. For 2 weeks after the diagnosis, my only time out of bed was necessitated by trips to the hospital for the radiation and chemo treatments, and even then it was primarily because my wife forced me to fulfill those commitments. She constantly reminded me of all that I had to live for and that quitting was not an option. It took some time, but eventually my competitive juices and success orientation finally kicked in; as my perspective changed, it made a huge difference in my energy and optimism. There are still days when my struggle with despair results in a momentary slip back into being resigned to my cancer fate, but when that happens now, my response is to do something to snap out of that negative thinking. My options include picking up a book to read, calling a friend, playing with my dog in the backyard, planning a trip with my wife, calling my sister or father, checking in with my daughter to find out how she is doing in college, visiting colleagues at the university, or sometimes just simply making a bowl of popcorn.

Another resilience characteristic is to feel productive and useful. After retiring from my faculty position at the university, I felt irrelevant and useless. It was hard seeing any purpose to my life because my career had always been a primary objective and a major source of satisfaction. My cancer and forced retirement created an urgent need to find other purposes and new ways to find satisfaction. Initially my goal was to read at least two books every week, and later I also resolved to write about my cancer experiences. It was important to take satisfaction in simple things such as watching my appetite and my energy slowly return. One measure of my health was to keep track of how long I could mow the lawn before having to rest due to being out of breath. My first attempt at mowing resulted in only 2 minutes of activity before I had to rest. The next time it was 4 minutes; the time after that it was 8 minutes. These goals provided a purpose, a way to feel satisfaction, and a tangible measure of how my body was responding to treatment. This renewed sense of usefulness and purpose fostered a feeling of potency—a recognition of my role and my power in fighting the lung cancer. My feelings shifted from being helpless to a sense of hopefulness and optimism.

As a special education teacher, I knew about the importance of locus of control in one's personality profile. In my work with students who only experienced an external locus of control, it was obvious that they believed they did not have control over what happened to them. This defeatist attitude fostered helplessness and hopelessness. The goal of raising or educating any child should be to instill a strong sense of internal locus of control; the individual needs to believe that he or she has resources to exert power and control over his or her destiny. Although it is not possible to have total control over how cancer responds to treatment, people do have control over their responses to their cancer diagnosis and prognosis. Resilient people refuse to play the victim by engaging in some form of self-pity; instead, they take charge and engage in active problem solving.

Peter Ubel (2006) is a physician and researcher who has studied thousands of people confronted with serious illnesses and terminal diseases. His research has revealed three key traits associated with resilient people confronted with adverse health conditions: an optimistic attitude, a happy disposition, and an interest in serving others. In reflecting on these personal characteristics and my possession of such resilience factors, I had to acknowledge that my natural tendency is not toward optimism; friends have joked that I am more of an Eeyore than a Tigger, in reference to the two characters in the Winnie the Pooh stories. Yet it is clear to me that a positive attitude is essential to my mental state because it impacts on my physical well-being as my cancer battle continues. Although optimism does not come naturally to me, I have consciously worked on developing a more positive attitude through spirituality and meditation.

As for the second trait, if jumping out of bed in the morning and singing in the shower demonstrates happiness, then I can claim to be a very happy person. In addition, part of my daily routine now to strengthen a positive attitude is to count the blessings that have been given to me during my wonderful life and to express gratitude for the experiences that have forged my values and beliefs. With regard to Ubel's final trait, in reflecting on my life, it is clear that what drew me to the legal profession was a desire to work on social justice issues—that was the reason for going to Appalachia to work as a legal services attorney.

Looking back on my career as a professor, one of the activities that has been the most satisfying has been my efforts to assist junior faculty members by collaborating with them on research and writing projects. Service to others has been an important responsibility and a way to demonstrate ethical behavior. It is gratifying to me to read the research reporting on the positive health benefits to be gained by maintaining a life focus outside of oneself; that is, giving back to others.

Several years ago there was a movie starring Kevin Spacey and Helen Hunt called *Pay It Forward,* about a young boy who taught adults in his life the importance of selflessness and giving back to others. Based on the novel by Catherine Ryan Hyde (1999), an 11-year-old boy comes up with a school project for his history class. The boy, played by Haley Joel Osment, proposes that everyone who has benefited from someone's good deeds "pay it forward" by doing a good deed for three other people. The boy sets an example by fulfilling his own admonition, starting with his mother. It was an inspirational film for many people, including me.

Another critical resilience factor is a sense of humor. Most people who have known me throughout my life have appreciated my sense of humor, and people who knew me in junior and senior high school would probably describe me as a bit of a class clown back then. Part of my joy of life has always been to laugh and have others laugh with me, or even at me. Over the past 20 years, considerable medical research has accumulated about the health benefits of humor and laughter. Dr. Bernie Siegel, the noted cancer surgeon and author, has written extensively on the healing powers of laughter. According to Siegel (1986), a hearty laugh, "produces complete, relaxed action of the diaphragm, exercising the lungs, increasing the blood's oxygen level, and gently toning the entire cardiovascular system" (p. 144). Laughter increases the body's production of endorphins, which serve as a natural anesthesia to relax the body and reduce stress.

Norman Cousins was a pioneer in advocating for the benefits of laughter in combating serious illnesses. Cousins was a journalist and for many years served as the editor of the *Saturday Review*. He was diagnosed with the crippling collagen disease ankylosing spondylitis, a disease that causes the connective tissue in the spine to disintegrate. His doctors told him he had a 1 in 500 chance of full recovery. In his groundbreaking book, *Anatomy of an Illness*, Cousins (1981) touted the benefits of laughter for enhancing the body's immune system to resist diseases. Laughter is the mind's way of dealing with life's absurdities. Cousins argued that a hearty laugh gives your internal organs a massage. Cousins overcame his illness and went on to a second distinguished career as a faculty member at the UCLA School of Medicine.

A quotation from 19th-century humorist Josh Billings captures the healing power of humor: "There ain't much fun in medicine, but there's a heck of a lot of medicine in fun." Having lung cancer presented me with an opportunity to personally discover the potential health benefits of laughter. Cancer is no laughing matter, but humor serves an important psychological function to jolt you out of a

Craig's friend Stu Robertshaw, aka Dr. Humor.

negative frame of mind and promote a new perspective. After my cancer treatments began, one of my first visitors was my friend Stu Robertshaw. Stu had retired from the University of Wisconsin-La Crosse and was now a professor emeritus of special education. As mentioned earlier, during that visit he gave me a laughter CD that was very helpful, and it was not just a coincidence that Stu had this tape. Even before he retired from the university, Stu had become a bit of an expert concerning the value of having a good sense of humor.

About 15 years ago, Stu became interested in the health benefits of humor and laughter. He founded the National Association for the Humor Impaired and serves as the organization's CEO. For the past several years, Stu has shared his philosophy and gift of laughter with thousands of organizations across the United States. Under the name of Dr. Humor, he makes humor presentations to schools, universities, governmental agencies, nonprofit organizations, businesses, and other organizations. Stu once gave a humor presentation at the annual convention of the National Embalmer's Association. If only I could have been there to hear that one! Once you have attended Stu's presentation on humor, it becomes obvious that he has a gift for making people laugh, yet at the same time he is promoting a serious message about how we need to laugh more to keep our minds and bodies healthy.

Stu gave me permission to share an instrument he developed called the Quick-Score Test of Humor Impairment. Here it is:

> Rate each item as Not Funny (0), Mildly Amusing (1), Funny (2), or Very Funny (3).
>
> 1. No matter how low your self-esteem, never forget there are others who think less of you.
> 2. I believed Tammy Baker's eyelashes were real.
> 3. I enjoy talking to life insurance sales people.
> 4. I'd give my right arm to be ambidextrous.
> 5. Never mistake asthma for passion or vice versa.
> 6. Death is nature's way of telling you to slow down.
> 7. A single male who leaves a party early is called a premature evacuator.
> 8. Never doubt that people you meet in a bar who tell you they are separated mean they haven't seen their spouse since breakfast.
> 9. Never try to pick up a woman who's wearing a Super Bowl ring.
> 10. Happiness is seeing your boss on a milk carton.
> 11. Never go to bed with a man named "Speed."
> 12. Xerox never comes with anything original.
> 13. It's okay to laugh in the bedroom as long as you don't point.
> 14. You won't hate yourself in the morning if you sleep until noon.
> 15. Always remember that what is sushi to one establishment is bait to another.
> 16. Elective surgery is surgery that doesn't count toward your major.
> 17. Never buy a TV on the sidewalk from a man who's out of breath.
> 18. The closest to perfection that people ever come is when they're creating their own résumé.
> 19. People who eat natural foods will die of natural causes.
> 20. People who lip read get ink on their lips. (Dr. Humor Web site, www.drhumor.com)

Scoring directions for determining your humor quotient: Add up all the points from the 20 items. If your score is 0–20, you are Humor Impaired; 21–24, you are At Risk; 25–32, you have a Healthy Sense of Humor; 33+ Great Sense of Humor. At the Dr. Humor Web site, research reveals that 15% of Americans are humor impaired and another 15% are at risk. Is being humor impaired a real disability? As we learn more about the impact of negative attitudes and emotions on personal health, we may find that a lack of humor is actually detrimental to a person's well-being. Stu is so serious about the benefits of laughter that he has been certified as a laughter leader by the World Laughter Tour.

It would be a delusion, of course, to believe that laughter alone would cure my cancer, but Stu's gift of laughter has lightened my load and brightened my days. I have wept many times since my diagnosis, and no doubt more tears will be shed in the coming weeks and months. Tears and laughter both have their place in human events; they serve as cleansing agents. In coping with my terminal illness, trying to laugh in spite of the grim circumstances is simply a way to restore some needed balance.

With Stu as my source of inspiration, I attempted to enhance my own laughter by developing a comedy piece that parodies comedian Jeff Foxworthy's routine where he delivers a number of one-liners based upon, "You might be a redneck if. . . . " To apply this to my situation, I brainstormed ideas with Stu and with my friend Kent Koppelman. Here are our responses to: "You might be terminal if . . . ":

- you start receiving unsolicited calls from hospice programs.
- you stop buying slightly green bananas.
- you stop worrying about meeting deadlines.
- you fixate on the fact that your investment in life insurance really was a great buy.
- you meet your doctor in the grocery store and he won't make eye contact.
- your friends don't say the word cancer, but instead spell it softly.
- you develop an uncontrollable urge to drive down dead-end roads.
- you lose interest in end-of-season sales.
- you notice a lot of vultures suddenly appearing in your neighborhood.
- friends stop saying to you, "See you later."
- you identify with the disability rights advocacy group called "Not Dead Yet."
- you are uncomfortable using the common expression, "I'm just dying to see you."

In addition to humor and laughter, another emotional resource for me has been to express gratitude each day on a regular basis. Stu encouraged me to keep a gratitude journal by writing out three things I was grateful for each day. Gratitude is defined as a state of thankfulness. When confronted with a life or health crisis, individual reactions seldom include gratitude but more likely feelings of denial, fear, self-pity, and despair. However, the power of positive attitudes and emotions are necessary for restoring balance and health in your life. Since February, every night before going to bed I have written in my gratitude journal. Given my circumstances, I thought it would be difficult to identify three grateful experiences each day, but before long I discovered that it was easy. I could usually identify more than three reasons to be grateful for at the end of the day. Recently reviewing my gratitude journal, there were six themes that emerged in these expressions of gratitude: family and friends, goals, favorite activities, positive distractions, positive emotions, and "stopping to smell the roses." A sampling of my gratitude journal entries for each of the six categories follows:

Family and Friends
Being grateful for

- a loving family.
- the friendship and support of so many people.
- hearing my father's voice.
- a friend's efforts to stay in touch.
- memories of people I haven't thought about in quite some time, such as my grandparents.
- receiving cards from well wishers.
- the remembrances from my colleagues.
- Sheri's loving caregiving.
- restoring contact with long lost friends.
- experiencing another wedding anniversary with Sheri.

Goals
Being grateful for

- purposeful work.
- being able to swallow and eat a little later in the day.
- good health insurance.
- a break from treatments.
- the financial security of a good pension program.
- a clear daily purpose.
- being able to complete a trip without further medical problems.

Favorite Activities
Being grateful for

- reading about baseball.
- listening to music.
- thinking about future trips Sheri and I plan to take.
- being able to do some limited yard work.
- walking in the woods.
- riding my moped on the country roads near our cabin.
- guest lecturing in a university class.
- the time to read and the insights gained in the past 6 months.

Positive Distractions
Being grateful for

- the distraction of reading page proofs of my new book.
- being able to laugh a little.
- the nights I can sleep soundly.
- memories.

Positive Emotions
Being grateful for

- having hope.
- wishing for a better day tomorrow.
- acceptance and resolve.
- relevant information to continue hoping for a recovery.

- knowing the reality of my health situation.
- being able to cry and express my emotions.
- reading about some long-term lung cancer survivors.
- serenity.
- solitude and introspection.
- optimism that my energy will return.
- wisdom and perspective in deciding about future treatments.

Smelling the Roses
Being grateful for

- the experience of simple pleasures.
- seeing new snow in the woods.
- watching Addie (our second English Springer Spaniel) at the dog park.
- the wind whistling through the trees.
- looking up at the sky and trees while lying in a hammock.{/BL}

A final example of emotional resources that combines spirituality with humor is perhaps best illustrated in the daily prayer of Stu Robertshaw's National Association for the Humor Impaired. The prayer serves as a good introduction for discussing the topic of using spiritual resources in coping with cancer:

God, grant me the laughter
to see the past with perspective,
to face the future with hope,
and to celebrate today . . .
without taking myself too seriously.

Spiritual Resources

Although raised and confirmed in a Lutheran church, I am not a traditionally religious person. Throughout my adult life I have not been an active member of any congregation. Like most people, I want to believe that there is an afterlife, that we do not simply end when our bodies give out. It is a natural human longing, perhaps even a need, to have faith in some greater power that offers everlasting peace. Clinging to this belief, I pray to be granted a medical miracle and attempt to seek comfort in my own personal, spiritual faith. In my AD life, my reading choices have included several books on spiritualism and faith that I probably never would have read during my BC life. The spiritual insights and perspectives gained from this reading have come primarily from two authors: Charles Halpern and Eckhart Tolle.

Halpern (2008) wrote about his career as a social activist and his struggle to find inner peace and wisdom in *Making Waves and Riding the Currents: Activism and the Practice of Wisdom*. Halpern has impeccable credentials as a social activist with a commitment to using the legal system to build a just society. An Ivy League graduate, he was educated first at Harvard University and then Yale Law School. His first job after law school was as a law clerk for a federal district court in Washington, DC. His next position was as a junior associate at a prestigious law firm in Washington, DC. During his tenure in this firm, he devoted some of his time and talents to pro bono legal cases.

For many people, there is often a singular event or life experience that has a disproportionate impact on how you think about yourself and your future. For Halpern, that experience came in the late 1960s when he accepted a pro bono case to represent a man involuntarily committed for over 3 years to a state mental hospital. During his confinement, the man never received any active treatment, even though he was found not guilty by reason of insanity for an offense that carried a maximum criminal sentence of 1 year. This case caused Halpern to question his career path, and eventually he resigned from his law firm and founded the first public interest law firm in the United States—the Center for Law and Social Policy in Washington, DC. After several years of significant public interest legal advocacy, Halpern was hired as the founding dean of the City University of New York School of Law—the first law school in the country devoted to public interest law and designed to train advocates for the poor, disadvantaged, and disenfranchised. After establishing this innovative law school, Halpern concluded his formal career by serving as first president of the Nathan Cummings Foundation, a charitable organization supporting social justice causes.

Some people might question how Halpern's career qualifies as a lesson in spirituality, but my definition of spirituality includes activities that serve the needs of others. Reading Halpern's book caused me to reminisce on my first years out of law school, and thinking about those years made it easy for me to identify with Halpern. As a young legal services attorney in Appalachia, I realized that it was not possible for me to be a dispassionate advocate for either side of an issue, especially when the legal issue involved a matter of social justice. In that regard, I was a failure as an attorney and would never have been able to practice in a traditional law firm as a "hired gun."

Two cases in particular stand out during my legal services career in Appalachia. In one case, I represented a functionally illiterate client who was taken advantage of when he signed a loan to purchase and install aluminum siding on his house. He was charged an extremely high interest rate, and he defaulted on his loan after several payments. It was an egregious example of predatory lending practices. Adding further injury was the fact that the siding had been shoddily installed; meanwhile, the lending institution was demanding payment in full on the loan. After investigating this case and the relevant law, it was apparent to me that this loan agreement was clearly illegal according to the federal Truth in Lending Act. I brought this assertion to the attention of the small-town lawyer representing the lending institution. It appeared that he had never heard of the Truth in Lending Act, and I must have sounded like an expert on lending law because the bank's lawyer agreed to rescind the loan agreement and return all payments made by my client. Many of my clients in Appalachia were functionally illiterate, and they would regularly bring me "legal looking documents" to read and explain to them.

In the second case, my colleague Michael Runner and I represented an elderly couple residing across the street from a large coal tipple, a plant where recently mined coal is processed for shipping on trucks or railroad cars. It is a very dirty operation. Our clients purchased their home prior to the establishment of the coal tipple, so the noise and coal dust from this tipple had seriously diminished their use and enjoyment of their property. You could walk into their house with all of the windows shut and still find thick coal dust covering the window sills and furniture, which obviously represented a health hazard for our clients. We sued the largest strip mine company in the county under a legal theory of nuisance. We endured a tough 4-day jury trial against the best private attorney in the county. After delivering the closing argument to the jury, I was so emotionally drained that I went back to my office and wept. The jury deliberated for about 2 hours and returned a verdict for our clients, awarding them some compensation for their losses. Michael and I floated back to our legal services office and celebrated this victory into the early hours of the night. I could never have been an effective advocate for the bank or coal company in these two legal disputes. My advocacy was fueled by a passionate belief in social justice for individuals from poor and disadvantaged backgrounds.

Those 2 years in Appalachia provided an additional experience that served as one of those disproportionate life events that transformed my perception of myself and affected my future goals. That experience involved visiting a client living in the "hollows" of rural Kentucky. The hollows were small valleys surrounded by steep mountainsides. Due to improper surface coal mining and poor and reclamation procedures, many individuals living in these rural hollows experienced flooding and other environmental damage to their properties and to the surrounding countryside. My task was to interview clients as part of the preparation before filing a large lawsuit on behalf of several property owners against some coal companies and the federal Office of Surface Mining for their poor policing of proper land reclamation practices by the coal companies. The interview that disturbed me the most occurred when one client's husband returned from work. This man worked in the best-paying blue-collar job in the area: he was an underground coal miner. As he entered the house, he was clearly exhausted from his day's work. He was covered in black coal dust from head to toe. As I talked to him, it seemed highly likely that in a few years he would probably suffer from black lung disease and die prematurely.

Ever since that time, I have frequently recalled this event, especially during those times when I start complaining about my own job or circumstances. Remembering this grimy, bedraggled, and exhausted coal miner reminded me of what truly hard work was, and that I was privileged to work in a career that paid me to learn and share my knowledge with students every day. That reminder reinforced an appropriate perspective on my life and an appreciation for how fortunate my life was, at least until January 28, 2008. When recalling this incident now, it fosters a sense of irony, since it has become my fate to suffer from a lung disability that will probably cause my premature death.

As for the insights from Halpern's book, he not only chronicled his career, he also described how he began to develop personal insights that led to inner peace. He discussed the growing dissonance between his formal training as a lawyer, which emphasized logical, unemotional advocacy devoid of passion, and his emerging belief that his lawyerly skills and knowledge of legal abstractions such as due process and equal protection of the law were stronger when he maintained a human connection and empathy to his clients and their concerns. He termed this new consciousness as "practicing wisdom." By practicing wisdom, Halpern means living a life of grounded reflection and compassion for others. He tried to practice wisdom by

- aligning his work with his values;
- keeping a proper work/life balance;
- taking time for regular reflection and introspection;
- developing a clear vision of his personal and professional goals; and
- recognizing the impermanence of life—the constancy of change.

Halpern talks about dancing as a useful metaphor for a certain way of living one's life in the moment with grace and pleasure. This metaphor appealed to me and caused me to recall some lyrics from a song written by one of my favorite singer/songwriters, Jackson Browne. I've never been much of a dancer, but now I'm trying to dance with others every day before the time comes when the only thing left for me to do is to dance alone. The song is entitled "For a Dancer."*

I don't know what happens when people die.
Can't seem to grasp it as hard as I try.
It's like a song I can hear playing right in my ear,
that I can't sing.
I can't help listening
and I can't help feeling stupid standing 'round,
crying as they ease you down,
'cause I know that you'd rather we were dancing.
Dancing our sorrow away.
Right on dancing,
no matter what fate chooses to play.
There's nothing you can do about it anyway.
Just do the steps that you've been shown
by everyone you've ever known,
until the dance becomes your very own.
No matter how close to yours
another's steps have grown.
In the end there is one dance you'll do alone.

Halpern's practice of wisdom provided me with several insights that were directly applicable to my cancer battle. First, he advised taking time to reflect on a problem. Such reflection can yield insights that are impossible to recognize when you are immersed in the problem. In the first few weeks after my diagnosis, I was consumed in thinking about my lung cancer. At this time, my "problem" seemed insurmountable and my mood was bleak and pessimistic. Only after consciously stepping back from my situation and taking the time to reflect on my new life did I gain new insights that nurtured hope about my situation. Those reflections became the starting point for writing this book.

Another insight from Halpern was his admonition to avoid using your "ideological filters" when you viewed the world and yourself. The American public is inundated with the results of ideological filters as we watch the talking heads analyzing political races, especially for the presidency. When a conservative television journalist is interviewing a Republican candidate, his or her comments are slanted toward that political perspective and the Republican can do no wrong. The Democratic political pundits engage in a similar ideological filtering in their analytical critiques. The average citizen is left wondering who is right and what are the real facts associated which each candidate's positions or statements. No wonder many people are turned off by the current masters of spin who are either running political campaigns or reporting on them. The voter struggles to determine who is telling the truth; which candidate can be trusted. When faced with a cancer diagnosis, the typical ideological filter spun by oncologists is to quote 5-year survival statistics, and that data have become all-important in doctor-patient interactions. The problem with relying on statistics is that it robs many cancer patients of hope, and thus, a positive attitude. It wasn't long before I learned to stop filtering my thinking through the survival statistics on all of the lung cancer Web sites because it was depressing and it took a toll on my fighting spirit.

A third insight from Halpern's book was to be slow in making judgments of people. He recommended holding your own views less tightly and presenting your ideas in a manner that was more open and inviting to the give and take of real dialogue. What especially struck me was his suggestion about listening "with greater hospitality." As previously noted, I have had a tendency to be terribly judgmental of people. During university faculty meetings, I forcefully presented my views on a regular basis to such an extent that any true debate, especially by junior faculty colleagues, was significantly circumscribed. Unfortunately, this jump to judgment with a forceful presentation of my opinions disrupted some of my interactions and relationships with colleagues, friends, and family members.

I am especially guilty of engaging in this interaction style with my youngest daughter, Lindsay. As she was struggling to adjust to her first year of college and to find her place within this new independent world, my response was to be overly critical of some of her decisions and actions. My judgments of her and recommendations for her were a source of strain in our relationship. My cancer has given me a second opportunity to establish a better, less judgmental relationship with Lindsay. While still offering my opinions, I always conclude by saying that I am simply offering her advice and she does not necessarily have to follow it; she must make her own decisions.

Halpern also addressed the anxiety produced by uncertainty. Living with cancer means living with constant uncertainty, a fear of the unknown that can lead to panic. There have been many such days in my AD life. One of Halpern's friends described the game of Chinese baseball, which is similar to American baseball but with one significant rule change. In Chinese baseball, when the pitcher throws the ball, anyone on the field can move any base so long as the ball is in play. This makes for a radically different game than American baseball since the runner who reaches second base may find that the base has been moved. Similarly, cancer is a radically different existence from what a healthy person experiences. With cancer, you may try to lead your life and strive for goals, but then, without warning, you discover that the bases have changed. With each MRI or CT scan, there is the chance that the bases will change. It will never be possible for me to ever again be certain about where second base is, or any base for that matter. Yet, I have to rely on my competitive nature to continue to motivate me.

Being competitive has been a part of my entire life. Although it has never made sense to me, my wife does not keep score when playing golf. My attitude is that keeping score means you not only know if you've won but if you are getting better, but she has ignored my criticisms and arguments. In my contest with cancer, keeping score means knowing if I am getting better and if, at any point in time, I seem to be winning. In this new game, competing against cancer, players are required to be more nimble, flexible, and adaptable to play the game well. By treating it as a challenge, the ultimate one, my hope largely comes from the ability to rally my competitive instincts and play to win.

Finally, Halpern taught me about establishing a new identity after cancer stripped me of my previous identity and my credentials as a professor. When cancer committed this robbery, it damaged not only my identity but my self-esteem. After Halpern retired from his last position, he struggled with a similar loss of identity and sense of self-importance. His phone stopped ringing, he had no meetings to attend, no decisions to make. He felt lost. Since my forced retirement, I felt lost on many days until realizing the importance of having a purpose and goals in your life to cope with cancer.

What Halpern learned in his retirement was reinforced in my experience—the need to reestablish your identity in new ways in day-to-day interactions with family members and friends. You slowly start to realize that the trappings of your professional position did not truly represent who you are as a person. Cancer can steal those aspects of your professional identity, but it cannot rob you of your true personal essence and humanity. In fact, battling cancer can add to your sense of who you are as you gain new insights and demonstrate new skills that you did not know you had. Such personal transformations often result from other traumatic experiences as well. After my sister's husband tragically committed suicide, she learned a lot about herself, discovering strength and skills that she had never been aware of nor displayed. My responses to cancer seem to be taking me through a similar transformation or metamorphosis. What will I become?

Eckhart Tolle (1999, 2005) is currently one of the most popular spiritual gurus of new-age thinking. He has written two bestselling books: *The Power of Now* and *A New Earth: Awakening to Your Life's Purpose*. As testament to his popularity and influence, his last book was on Oprah's book club list. The new age or inspiration sections of a book store normally have little attraction when making my reading selections, but a university colleague and my sister both recommended Tolle's books. Having lots of time on my hands while receiving chemo infusions, I read his books. Normally, existential writing usually seems excessively esoteric and ephemeral to me, but rereading certain passages several times resulted in discovering several insights from Tolle's books. The following represents my interpretation of his perspective and the spiritual insights that he offers based on my reading of both of his books.

First, Tolle argues that the bane of human existence is the control exerted by our egos. Freud's structure of the human psyche was taught to me in the psychology courses taken during my graduate work, where I learned about the id, ego, and super-ego. Representing that part of a person's personality structure that unconsciously contains basic drives such as food, sex, and aggressive impulses, the id functions on the pleasure principle and is essentially amoral. The super-ego operates as the conscience of a person and seeks to keep the id impulses under control. The ego serves as the person's reason and common sense and functions in a mediating role between the id, super-ego, and the external world. The ego needs to control the primitive drives of the id and will often employ defense mechanisms to handle conflicts between the id, super-ego, and reality.

For Tolle, people experience strife and pain in their lives due to thinking too much with their ego. The ego is never satisfied, always wanting more "things." The ego wants to feel superior, so it is judgmental and blames. The ego distorts our perceptions of events and of other people by personalizing everything and becoming defensive. According to Tolle, the ego is basically the source of many interpersonal difficulties and human pain. Tolle applied basic Freudian psychology to develop insights about how people lose their way in life and experience needless dissatisfaction with their lives.

It wasn't difficult to apply this analysis to my own interpersonal interactions with others. In my career, I have been obsessively preoccupied with my reputation and what others thought of me. This preoccupation kept me from experiencing unpretentious joys that flow naturally from simply performing a job or a task well. Instead, I was never satisfied with my performance and was usually my own harshest critic. This was not conducive to inner peace. Being quick to personalize disagreements with my ideas and becoming overly defensive resulted in a poor leadership style, causing me undue stress and straining some relationships with other people. But cancer effectively strips an individual of all pretensions and arrogance. You realize what is really important and how you have been misled by focusing on superficial symbols of perceived success such as your rank, salary, number of publications, and amount of power and influence you wield. Although guilty of falling into this trap, I would not trade my career for any other, but now a part of me would like to go back and experience that career with this new insight.

Tolle discourages such a yearning to repeat the past. Living in the present is what helps an individual being confined by the ego to develop a state of consciousness or awakening that allows you to experience and appreciate the life you have. Tolle maintains that too many people dwell on the past or the future and forget to enjoy the present moment. We cannot change our past, and the future is unpredictable. Tolle urges people to stop thinking so much and being controlled by that "voice in your head," and instead to focus on the now and on simple day-to-day experiences. Developing a new awareness of your body while living in the present moment can enhance your immune system and the healing powers of your body.

This was a difficult lesson for me because my mind is constantly processing and interpreting events, and my inner voice is always chattering at me. This was the reason I carried around such negative emotions and experiences for unhealthy periods of time. Meditation helps me to focus on simple breathing and clearing my mind of all the clutter. There are some precious times where I have been able to be conscious of the moment and shut down my mind. Watching my English Springer Spaniel running in the woods with unbounded joy has helped me to live in just that moment. Taking a family vacation to the Dominican Republic in August also provided an opportunity to focus on living in the now. It would happen while floating on my back in the pool or in the Caribbean Sea—looking up at the robin's egg blue sky and hearing no sounds because the water filled my ear canals. Sometimes it also happened while lying in my hammock in my own backyard—my mind would simply turn off, allowing me to focus on the simple joy of listening to the birds and looking at the trees blowing in the wind. I am still a work in progress as far as developing this capacity to appreciate simple moments and experiences, but it has become clear to me that each time this state of mind is achieved, it is accompanied by an inner calmness and serenity. This has provided the best escape from my cancer.

Tolle suggests that inner peace comes when you recognize the impermanence of all living forms. In my view, this is what he refers to as "eternal life." A terminal illness can either increase or decrease the control your ego exerts over your thinking and your life. If the illness causes you to complain constantly, feel self-pity and resentment, chances are your ego has taken control and is not allowing you to appreciate the present. On the other hand, if you become more reflective and introspective and gain new insights about who you are as a result of your illness, you have taken an important step toward a heightened awareness and living in the now. Recognizing the transience of life, an ability to focus on the present promotes a feeling of inner peace and a sense of eternal life emerges. This perspective is reflected in the following Tolle quote from *A New Earth*: "So there is no such thing as 'my life,' and I don't *have* a life. I *am* life. I and life are one. It cannot be otherwise. So how could I lose my life? How can I lose something that I don't have in the first place? How can I lose something that I Am? It is impossible" (2005, p. 128).

This spiritual perspective provides me with some measure of acceptance and comfort as I learn to live day-by-day with a terminal illness. The best a person can do in such a situation is to live each day to the fullest and find joy whenever possible, no matter how many days you may have left. Tolle (2005) shares his observations of two ducks fighting. The fight does not last long before the ducks separate and float off in opposite directions. Then each duck flaps its wings frantically to release the surplus energy stored up during the fight. After flapping their wings a few times, the ducks float peacefully as if nothing had ever happened. In my cancer fight, I am trying to learn how to flap my wings periodically to restore some equilibrium.

As part of their engagement in spiritual practices, both Halpern and Tolle extol the benefits of meditation. I have several meditation CDs, but the one I have used most often is called *Scanning Relaxation*. I take about 15–20 minutes for each meditative session. Here is a summary of my meditation process:

Get as comfortable as possible by lying on the couch or bed.
Loosen any tight clothing and close my eyes.
Consciously tell myself to clear my mind of its thoughts and troubles.
Assume a passive attitude to let the relaxation begin.
Open my mouth and slowly move my jaw from side to side.
While moving my jaw, take a deep breath and slowly let it out.
Slowly exhaling, say softly, "Relax and let go."
Breathing normally, feel parts of my body and relax the muscles in each body part.
Becoming more and more relaxed, my breathing slows down.
Think about all tension leaving my body.
A sense of well-being slowly develops and nothing seems to matter.
Experience deep relaxation from head to feet.
Feel the top of my head and forehead.
Take a deep breath and slowly exhale, letting the tensions flow out.
Go through this same process with each area of my body, from head, shoulders and upper back, arms and hands, chest and stomach, hips, legs and ankles, and, finally, my feet and toes.

When the breathing and relaxation has been completed from head to feet, focus on my body for signs of tension.
If tension is felt in any body part, let it out by deep breathing.
Think about the ocean and imagine each wave bringing me massaging relaxation and calmness.

During World War II, the United States rallied incredible resources in a short period of time to fight Hitler, Mussolini, and Hirohito. Our nation was successful in this war because of the bravery of many men and women in the military and the ability of American workers to produce the necessary planes, ships, tanks, guns, bombs, and ammunition to fight this war effectively. My war with cancer requires a similar rally of incredible intellectual, physical, emotional, and spiritual resources in a short period of time to effectively fight this war. Hoping to be as brave as my father's generation, my daily prayer is for a successful outcome as the battle continues.

References

Armstrong, L., & Jenkins, S. (2000). *It's not about the bike: My journey back to life.* New York: Berkley Books.

Bobek, B. L. (2002). Teacher resilience: A key to career longevity. *The Clearing House, 75*(4), 202–205.

Cousins, N. (1981). *Anatomy of an illness as perceived by the patient.* New York: Bantam Books.

Dickinson, E. (1959). Because I could not stop for death. In R. N. Linscott (Ed.), *Selected poems and letters of Emily Dickinson* (p. 151). Garden City, NY: Doubleday/Anchor.

Fiedler, C. R., & Clark, D. (2009). *Making a difference: Advocacy competencies for special education professionals.* Austin, TX: Pro-Ed Publishing.

Fiedler, C. R., Simpson, R. L., & Clark, D. M. (2007). *Parents and families of children with disabilities: Effective school-based support services.* Upper Saddle River, NJ: Merrill/Prentice Hall.

Frahm, A. E., & Frahm, D. J. (1992). *A cancer battle plan: Six strategies for beating cancer, from a recovered "hopeless case."* New York: Penguin Putnam.

Halpern, C. (2008). *Making waves and riding the currents: Activism and the practice of wisdom.* San Francisco, CA: Berrett-Koehler Publishers.

Hyde, C. R. (1999). *Pay it forward: A novel.* New York: Simon & Schuster.

Kūbler-Ross, E. (1969). *On death and dying.* New York: Macmillian Company.

Siegel, B. S. (1986). *Love, medicine, and miracles.* New York: Harper.

Tolle, E. (2005). *A new earth: Awakening to your life's purpose.* New York: Penguin.

Tolle, E. (1999). *The power of now: A guide to spiritual enlightenment.* Novato, CA: New World Library.

Turnbull, A. P. (1988). Accepting the challenge of providing comprehensive support to families. *Education and Training in Mentally Retarded, 23*(4), 261–272.

Turnbull, A. P., & Turnbull, H. R. (1997). *Families, professionals, and exceptionality: A special partnership.* Upper Saddle River, NJ: Merrill/Prentice Hall.

Ubel, P. (2006). *You're stronger than you think: Tapping into the secrets of the emotionally resilient.* New York: McGraw-Hill.

CHAPTER 5

Communicating with Cancer

Being in the field of special education, I am very sensitive to the power of language. Labeling individuals with a disability term results in limited thinking and understanding for those interacting with the disabled. Our society has come a long way from the early 1900s when labels such as moron, idiot, imbecile, and retardate were commonly applied to people with disabilities. Disability advocates have long advocated for "people first" language in an effort to emphasize that a disability is only a part of a person and should not be considered all-defining. The largest self-advocacy group for individuals with disabilities in this country is called People First, and it insists that rather than calling someone retarded, autistic, or disabled, it is more appropriate to refer to a person with mental retardation, a child with autism, or an individual with a disability.

Cancer provided my first personal experience with being labeled by being forced to accept my new identity as a *cancer patient*. Because of the identity theft that inevitably results from having cancer, in the eyes of many people, that label has become my primary characteristic. Some medical personnel can only deal with the cancer part of me, not me as a whole person. Although it is a painful experience, it is important to understand this overriding sense of loss of self and the all-encompassing identity that cancer assumes in the lives of its victims. Cancer does not communicate; it infiltrates and destroys, but those who have cancer need to talk about more than just their disease. It is important that medical personnel, family, friends, and others interact not simply with a *cancer patient,* but with the human being who happens to have cancer.

If we view death as a metaphor for feeling forgotten, I have experienced death even before the formal announcement of my demise. Some people cannot comfortably interact or communicate with a seriously ill or terminal individual. In some respects, America is an immature society, stuck in an adolescent stage of development on many issues. One of these issues is how we react to serious illnesses and talk about terminal diseases such as cancer. An adolescent is self-absorbed and easily embarrassed, and an adolescent is often awkward when confronted with unfamiliar social situations. Most adolescents have an over-inflated sense that everyone is watching and judging them when that is not typically the case. There are friends who have not contacted me since my cancer diagnosis, even though I believe they are concerned and care about me. Their lack of communication makes it seem as if I had already disappeared.

These friends who appear to have abandoned me during my illness are not mean people with negative intentions, but are simply products of this societal immaturity. They seem to be engaging in adolescent behavior by being unable to respond and interact with me simply because of my terminal illness. It reminds me of the Woody Allen short story called "The Shallowest Man." The main character in that story was so afraid of his friend's cancer that he could not even visit him in the hospital. It is important for people to understand how to interact, communicate, and support a friend or loved one who experiences a serious or terminal illness.

Thinking as a researcher, the varied responses to my cancer diagnosis presented me with an interesting empirical question. In my first month AD, 129 cards came in the mail wishing me well and a speedy recovery, and because they meant so much to me, I saved all of those cards. Colleagues, friends, family members, ex-students, current students, and professionals in the schools all sent me cards. Almost all of the cards included brief written comments from the sender. After a while I began to be curious as to how many of the cards included personal comments using the word cancer—the dreaded "c-word." Of those 129 cards, only 17 referred to my cancer in any personal comment. That represents only 7.6% of the cards that I received. Reviewing these personal messages provided me with a list of a variety of euphemisms people used for cancer:

- health problems
- battle
- health crisis
- health issue
- medical challenge
- not feeling well
- sick
- difficult time
- obstacle
- on this journey
- struggle you are going through

Looking at these euphemisms made me think about problems of communication. Why do so many people have a hard time saying the word "cancer" to someone who has it? After all, my prognosis does not hinge upon how many people say the word "cancer" to me, or avoid saying it. Why do we engage in this semantic dance around the actual issue? Again, it seems to stem from this adolescent stage of development in terms of our own fears of mortality and our inevitable death. We all dread the thought of cancer happening to us or a loved one. Knowing someone with cancer is a grim reminder of how fragile and unpredictable life is. In such circumstances, we attempt to deny this reality by not using "that word," or by avoiding the person with cancer altogether. It is as if we think that by these actions (or inaction) we can avoid sharing a similar fate; however, that kind of thinking is a delusion because life is unpredictable, and bad things happen to all kinds of people every minute of every day.

We all want certainty in our lives, and we want to believe that we will be spared catastrophic events. If you know someone with cancer, perhaps it may serve as a painful reminder that it could happen to you as well. Although it is difficult to accept this truth, at some point, all of us must confront our own fears of mortality, and one way to do that is to communicate honestly and openly to the people we care about who have suddenly been diagnosed with a terminal illness like cancer.

In my review of all the cards I received, I also made a second list of the personal comments that were especially meaningful and helpful to me. That list follows:

- thinking of you
- know that I care
- I will stay in touch
- life is precious—friends are like gold
- maintain optimism and hope
- many people are asking about you
- I believe in your ability to fight
- your strength has overcome obstacles in the past
- surround yourself with positive influences
- find doctors you can trust
- ask plenty of questions
- your voice still needs to be heard, your ideas still need to be shared, your vision still needs to be seen
- thanks for all you have done
- you have touched many lives
- your influence has a far reaching impact
- you have inspired me

In rereading these personal comments, five reasons emerged that made them so meaningful for me: they (a) focused on positive feelings, (b) expressed optimism on my strengths to deal with this health crisis, (c) noted my impact on others through my work, (d) suggested helpful ideas to remember, and (e) assured me that they were thinking of me. The simple expression that you are remembered and that people are thinking of you on a regular basis is the most precious gift that can be given to any person, but especially when someone is going through something as devastating as cancer.

The generous spirit and support of many friends and colleagues has been very gratifying. Some of my colleagues in the Department of Special Education have maintained regular contact with me, and I always look forward to hearing from them. Some of these supportive colleagues are Wayne Swanger, Denise

Craig with his childhood friends Bruce Javenkoski and Lou George standing on Granddad's Bluff overlooking La Crosse.

Clark, Billie Jo Rylance, Becky Thorson-Randall, and Bert Chiang. They feel like family to me. Two of my long-time childhood friends, Bruce Javenkoski and Lou George, have shown me unwavering support. It is important for individuals with terminal illnesses to have the anchor of old friends who are able to stir past pleasant memories. John Shaw and Kent and Jan Koppelman continue as a bedrock of support for both Sheri and me. And, of course, family members have constantly provided me with strength and optimism. Cancer can be a lonely and isolating experience unless people close to you reach out and offer their love and support. For the most part, I feel fortunate in that regard.

Reflecting on some of my interactions with friends, family members, and colleagues since my cancer diagnosis, it is easier now to laugh at some of the awkward and socially inept comments people have made to me in their attempts to offer comfort and support. Again, these comments were not mean-spirited, just an indication of our discomfort in dealing with death and dying. For instance, my father called shortly after my sister had told him about my lung cancer. My father has been a loving, supportive person in my life, but he made some comments that night that were not as comforting as he intended. One of his first comments was, "Craig, you have lived a good life." As stated several times in this

John Shaw, a friend and disability activist who worked with Craig for many years presenting Parents in Partnership workshops.

book, my life has been blessed, and I am grateful for all my various opportunities and experiences, but my father's comment seemed to suggest that my status was a "dead man walking" to his execution. He followed that statement with, "Well, I don't expect to live much longer, either." I did not respond, but in my mind, a voice was screaming about the big difference between our two circumstances. My father is 88 years old and I was 55 at the time! Part of my pleasure in my father's longevity was that it helped to strengthen my expectation of living a similarly long and healthy life. Now those hopes and expectations were in doubt. My father meant well, and during my illness he has shown his compassion and support for me in many ways, but these two statements are examples of comments that are made to terminally ill individuals that do not provide either comfort or solace.

On another occasion, a friend visited me shortly after my treatment began. This person is one of the most caring and compassionate individuals I have ever known.

As we talked about my cancer diagnosis and treatment and the poor prognosis for long-term survival, my friend responded, "You know Craig, we are all terminal." Although our discussion continued, including further details of my litany of medical events, I kept thinking that I had already figured out many years ago that all people eventually died. I never assumed that my life would be spared from this universal fate, but given my general good health and family history of longevity, my assumption was that I had many more years of health and would enjoy a comfortable retirement. Learning that my life would probably end in the not-too-distant future was an existential thunderbolt of immense proportions. What was hurtful about my friend's well-intentioned comment was that it seemed to trivialize my fears and apprehension. It was not comforting or supportive of my situation.

Later in this same conversation, my friend suggested that I had an advantage because "At least you know how and approximately when you will die." What he meant by this was having the luxury of time to say goodbye to family and friends and to make any necessary amends in some relationships as compared with someone who suddenly dies in an accident or from a heart attack and is denied that opportunity. However, being aware that my death is coming and that it will be much sooner than expected does not console me nor bring me a feeling of peace and serenity. Suppose you asked a thousand people if they would want to know in advance how and when they were going to die, my bet is that 999 of them would say, "no." There is a mystery to life that we need to maintain.

Despite such problems in my communication with others, it is preferable to deal with that than with the pain caused by those friends who don't communicate at all. When I have complained to some friends about feeling forgotten by a few individuals who have failed to contact me since my cancer diagnosis, they advise me to give those people a call and tell them my feelings and that I want to maintain contact with them. This advice seems good on the surface, but it has not been persuasive to me, primarily because taking such a step seems disingenuous. Regardless of what people might say in response to my call, how could the communication feel genuine and honest if I had to initiate it? It seems too much like fishing for a compliment from someone. These issues and more involved in interactions with seriously or terminally ill people are a troubling and neglected topic of discussion. Fortunately, there is a gem of a resource on these issues that was identified in Charles Halpern's book, discussed previously.

Halpern's wife, Susan, was diagnosed with Non-Hodgkin's Lymphoma in the early 1990s. Her cancer was slow-growing, and her life was not immediately threatened, but it was incurable. As of early 2008, Susan Halpern was still alive and presumably enjoying her life. She has periodically had chemotherapy to control her cancer, and a few years ago she endured a stem cell transplant. Her own stem cells were transfused back into her body to bolster her immune system, which had been ravaged by extensive chemotherapy over the years. Susan had worked as a social worker and therapist for individuals with serious and terminal illnesses. Now she was personally experiencing what many of her clients lived with on a daily basis. Relying upon her personal and professional experiences related to serious and terminal illnesses, Susan wrote a book offering practical advice on how to communicate with and support people you care about who are experiencing a health crisis. Her book, *The Etiquette of Illness: What to Say When You Can't Find the Words*, is a goldmine of helpful information to overcome our adolescent attitudes related to the forbidden and uncomfortable topic of death and dying.

Halpern (2004) maintains that it is the role and responsibility of the "well person" to reach out and make contact with the sick person. In fulfilling this role, she urges people to shed their adolescent awkwardness and step up to the plate (sorry, it's hard for me to avoid using baseball metaphors). The reason people are timid about communicating with a terminally ill individual is because they are worried about what to say, but there are no words to cure cancer. It is not the words employed in these situations that matters; what matters most is the presence of the other person. Just being there for the ill person speaks volumes and sends a clearly understood and powerful message that you are thinking of them and that you care. Halpern offers some practical conversation starters such as

- Do you want me to ask how you are feeling?
- I am so sorry this is happening to you.
- I can't stop thinking about you.
- I keep remembering that time we . . .
- I look forward to seeing you again.

A sense of normalcy is the greatest gift you can offer to a person with cancer. Too often we treat people with cancer as if their cancer now defines them, and we forget that they are still the same person, now afflicted with a serious illness. A major factor in my response to cancer is to refuse to let it become my defining identity; I am more than this disease. My most enjoyable conversations with friends are those where cancer is not the main topic. It is therapeutic to reminisce with old friends about past experiences. They help me to remember my BC life. If people who are ill want to talk about their medical issues, they are likely to raise that topic. As Halpern (2004) suggests, a person can simply ask the individual, "Do you want to talk about your condition?" or "What is this like for you?" And don't try to ignore any physical changes that may have been caused by the cancer treatments such as hair loss and surgical scars. In the United States, the cultural norm is to ignore people who look different. This becomes obvious to anyone who is the parent of a child with severe disabilities. People would go to great lengths to avoid direct eye contact with Jennifer, but turn to sneak a peek at her after they passed by.

Once my treatments began, when people stopped to visit, I usually tried to make the person feel more comfortable by making a joke or a light comment about my changed appearance: "So, do you think a comb over would hide my nearly bald head?" But if you are a friend of a person with cancer, you should feel at ease to say something like, "I see your condition has caused some changes. Do you want to talk about that?" Ignoring the physical changes does not make them magically disappear, and it is unnatural not to recognize changes in our friends. We do this all the time when we meet friends who are not ill. So don't worry about drawing attention to unpleasant aspects of your friend's new appearance. Cancer makes us lose our vanity because, frankly, whether you have hair or not is one of the least troubling issues you face. Beating the odds associated with cancer is by far the greatest issue.

When communicating with someone who has cancer, friends can provide support by engaging that person in conversations about his or her medical condition. The more you talk about your cancer and the fear you feel, the more it loses its power to scare you. President Franklin Roosevelt offered the appropriate reassurance when he tried to comfort the nation during the depression in his famous inaugural speech with his insistence that "the only thing we have to fear is fear itself." When you talk about your health problems with others, there is a release of tension because you no longer have to carry the burden of worry and fear all by yourself.

A friend or family member can assist the person with cancer to discuss their health with a simple question such as, "Do you want me to ask you how you are?" That can serve as a barrier breaker and help the person to open up about his or her cancer. In my case, the most helpful conversations begin on a lighter note, talking about memories or what the other person is doing these days or politics or sports, and then toward the end of the conversation, to give me an opportunity and encouragement to discuss the latest update on my lung cancer and how I am feeling. There is no magic formula, and every person is unique in their preferences, but what is important is to have a balance between helping individuals with cancer get outside of their total focus on themselves and yet also encouraging them at some point of the conversation to talk about their health problem. Achieving this balance will address the most important psychological needs of any person struggling with a terminal diagnosis.

Another cancer communication issue involves the "guilt of the living" phenomenon. Many people who survive plane crashes, wars, or other calamities where others died describe feeling survivor's guilt. Why were they spared and not the person sitting next to them in the car or the soldier walking alongside of them on the road? These are hard existential questions because there are no answers. Some friends are reluctant to talk about their problems with me because in comparison to my lung cancer, their issues seem trivial. But to be involved in a true friendship requires a give and take between the two people where both feel comfortable sharing their problems, concerns, triumphs, doubts, and daily issues. For someone to avoid talking about their problems with a friend who has cancer diminishes that friendship and does not allow the person with cancer a much needed opportunity to give back to another by offering compassion and kind advice or simply by being a good listener.

Another aspect of having cancer is the feeling of being at war with your own body. Most people have a basic psychological need to believe that they can exert a reasonable amount of control over their own lives and destinies, certainly their bodies. It is hard now for me to trust my body because it has betrayed me with this cancer. It is not unusual for people with cancer to lose this trust and their sense of control because of an invading force that often seems to be in total control.

In one of my get-well cards, a friend wrote that her sister always refused to refer to the cancer in her body as "my cancer" because she thought of the cancer inside of her as an unwelcome alien. She did not want to acknowledge this invader as a part of her. It was easy for me to understand her perspective completely. Friends and family members who have interacted with me have helped to restore some sense of control when they remind me of all the things in my life that are still in my control. A good example of this is when Stu Robertshaw encouraged me to practice laughter therapy and to keep a daily gratitude journal. It is also within my power to control my attitude and to enjoy every day to the fullest. It is important to regularly remind those you love who have cancer that they can still control many aspects of their daily lives, no matter how small or insignificant that part of their life may seem. This is one of the best gifts that can be bestowed on someone living with cancer.

Whenever I taught a course on school law for prospective teachers, my students were always amazed at how often the law did not provide clear black and white answers to issues. They had to be repeatedly reminded that in the law there are more shades of gray than definitive black and white responses. Judicial outcomes are affected by slight changes in facts or a judge's judicial philosophy or even a judge's political inclinations. It is similar in cancer world. When you have cancer, you want your doctors to provide definitive answers to allay your fears. You expect black and white answers to your questions about best treatment options, diagnostic test results, and your long-term prognosis. When doctors are unable to provide a clear answer, you feel anxious and uncertain. Doctors are not trying to be evasive; they are simply reflecting the ever-evolving nature of cancer research. Doctors are making educated guesses on what combination of chemo drugs will best attack your cancer. When friends visit and ask well-intentioned questions about how treatments are going or what my overall prognosis is, they need to understand that it is rarely possible for me to provide clear responses to their questions. It is not my intent to hold them in suspense. As a friend, you need to learn to be just as comfortable with the uncertainty surrounding cancer as I have to be.

In his NPR blog, Leroy Sievers said that being a friend of someone with cancer is like being a boxing coach, and the more I thought about this the more it seemed like an apt metaphor for the kind of support that a person with cancer needs. At the end of each round of a boxing match, the fighter returns to his corner and is given encouragement, advice, and attention to his bruises. Having cancer is like a boxing match because you repeatedly experience body blows and often feel like throwing in the towel and giving up. Since my cancer diagnosis, my body has been pricked and poked and prodded in every imaginable way. Sometimes I get tired and want to give up, and that's when all those friends and family members sitting in my corner need to provide the kind of support and encouragement that a boxing coach gives.

My daughter Lindsay is a good coach, constantly encouraging me to fight my cancer and not give up. Also my friend Kent regularly reminds me of what I want to accomplish and that he expects me to be around to complete those goals and projects. We have had a friendly competition on how many books each of us have published. He tells me that he does not want to win this competition by default because of me dying prematurely. My sister has insisted that she expects me to attend her daughter's wedding in October, 2009. There are ample anecdotal examples of terminally ill individuals living long enough so they could be there for an important family event; so I appreciate people who provide me with events or goals that will not occur for 5 or 10 or even 20 years, because I want to be around for that length of time. Since my two favorite baseball teams are from Chicago, my fantasy has always been to witness a Cubs-White Sox World Series. By making that my goal, I may achieve immortality!

A common communication issue faced by individuals with cancer is whether they should tell someone about their cancer. This issue may have to be faced with strangers you are meeting for the first time as well as family members. Does a person with cancer have an obligation to talk about the cancer? Parents of a child with a disability face a similar issue. Total strangers would often ask my wife and me personal questions about Jennifer. We wanted to educate people about mental retardation, but sometimes we lacked the emotional or physical strength to address that subject once again. Someone told me about a parent of a child with autism who dealt with this issue by having business-sized cards printed that briefly and simply described autism. When asked by a stranger about her son's autism, the mother handed out one of her "autism business cards."

ABC television journalist Diane Sawyer interviewed Randy Pausch after he had gained notoriety with *The Last Lecture* (2008) concerning his battle with pancreatic cancer. In the interview, Sawyer asked whether Randy's children knew about his cancer and his approaching death. All of Randy's three children were very young, under 5 years old. Randy and his wife decided not to tell their children about his cancer, and given their ages, this is a completely understandable decision. But my situation was much different with a 22-year-old daughter. For the most, part I have been very open with my daughter about my cancer. For example, Lindsay was told about my lung cancer the same day Sheri and I received that diagnosis. Lindsay was in her senior year of college, and she deserved to be treated like the adult she is. We have regularly informed her on my health condition. Susan Halpern (2004) encourages open communication between parents and their children when one parent has a serious or terminal disease. She argues that keeping a parent's terminal illness a secret from their children is more detrimental to the family's well-being than the illness itself. Halpern maintains that this kind of family secrecy sends a counterproductive message that we do not talk about problems in this family. She also believes that a child can be empowered when a parent is seriously ill because the family needs more assistance from the child now.

As for informing strangers of my cancer, that is more problematic. In March, Sheri and I took a vacation at our house south of Tucson, Arizona. One night we went to a dinner theater mystery production. We sat at a large round table with four other couples. Having just finished with radiation and being in the middle of my chemotherapy, I was bald and haggard looking. Being self-conscious of my appearance, throughout that evening I felt a need to tell these strangers sitting at the table, "This is not really me. I was just diagnosed with lung cancer in January. Normally I have long, thick salt and pepper hair and look like Richard Gere." However, timing is everything and I resisted this urge, thinking it might put a damper on an evening that was supposed to be festive. It became especially hard to exercise self-restraint when Sheri asked the man sitting next to her about his occupation, and he revealed that he was only working part-time right now due to his recent diagnosis of multiple sclerosis. I bit my tongue to stop from saying, "Oh, you think that's bad. I was just diagnosed with terminal lung cancer." It was a good thing to refrain from this morbid kind of competition; you know, "my disease can beat your disease." Instead, from my arrival to my departure from this dinner theater, the other guest probably viewed me simply as the "bald guy." I've been called worse epithets.

In the summer of 2008, my lung cancer had metastasized and my condition was downgraded to stage IV cancer. During that summer, Lindsay was taking 11 credits at summer school and working nearly 40 hours per week, so she was under a lot of stress. For the first time, Sheri and I decided not to tell her about my changed diagnosis until after the summer. We debated whether this was the right decision, but that's what we did. It seemed the right decision at the time and it still does. As the fall semester started, we did tell Lindsay that my condition had now reached stage IV. At first she was upset and even angry that we kept this information from her for more than 2 months, but in time I believe she will understand that we did it out of concern for her.

There are moments when it is hard to remember what my life was like before cancer. Sometimes it feels like it was "In a galaxy far, far away . . ." as in the famous opening of the first *Star Wars* movie. Like the movie, cancer world often seems like living in a parallel universe with all kinds of alien situations. When you get cancer, it is easy to become self-centered. It is difficult for me to avoid this because I think about my cancer 24/7. This "all about me" phenomenon is another example of typical adolescent behavior, but it is also easy to observe this self-centered behavior in many elderly individuals as their lives become more

Craig and Sheri delayed telling Lindsay that his health status had been downgraded to Stage IV so that she could focus on her college classes; he would have been proud to see her graduate.

limited and they are beset with medical problems. My father will talk at such length about his medical problems that he often fails to ask about the lives of his grandchildren or about what's going on in my life. There is no question that he cares about us all, but over time he has developed tunnel vision and has become focused on his own situation. Although this is natural, it is not healthy. We all need to get outside of ourselves and experience the full expanse of the world, a world that entails more than cancer or other medical concerns.

My passion for baseball is shared by one of my colleagues, Wayne Swanger. One day when he came to visit, Wayne brought his old baseball cards from the early 1960s. It was such a great time looking at those cards and talking baseball. Furthermore, it was a wonderful distraction from my 24/7 cancer obsession. When friends visit, it is important for me to remember to ask them questions about how they are doing or what is going on in their lives. At times, I suspect that I have failed to do this, but it is my hope that my friends will break the barrier and start talking about issues other than my cancer.

Well-meaning people sometimes want to shower a terminally ill person with pity and sympathy. This response infuriates me because, like most people, I do not want to be turned into an object of pity. My sensitivity to this issue is due in part to my parenting experience of a child with a disability. My wife and I can always tell when someone is displaying pity or sympathy about the fact our daughter is disabled because they usually get a "deer in the headlights" look on their face. Pity and sympathy can be helpful in certain situations, but they can also be debilitating emotions that turn individuals into victims by assuming that you passively accept your circumstances and are not a fighter. Although it has gotten better over the years, it is still not possible for me to watch the Jerry Lewis Muscular Dystrophy (MD) Telethon without cringing because of how individuals, especially the children with MD, are exploited to play on people's sympathies in order to get them to reach deeper into their pockets.

Instead of pity and sympathy, people should give terminally ill individuals something far more helpful—empathy. In the dictionary, empathy is defined as "the action of understanding, being aware of, being sensitive to, and vicariously experiencing the feelings, thoughts, and experiences of another." Empathy shows understanding and concern, and it is an empowering emotion because the sick person feels a little less lonely and isolated. Friends can also empower people with cancer by sharing stories of other individuals who have experienced miraculous recoveries. A card received from one of my friends mentioned that her sister had beaten stage IV cancer and encouraged me to believe that this was just as possible for me as well. It is so important to hear about such stories; they help me believe in miracles and fuel my optimism and hope.

In my AD life, I have become a reformed hugger. Prior to my cancer, I was the type of person who scoffed at "touchy, feely" workshops. These experiences made me feel quite uncomfortable, in part because of my lack of interest in hearing about the feelings of a complete stranger. Although appreciating the underlying message, I always felt uneasy seeing Dr. Leo Buscaglia (aka Dr. Love), who has a background in special education, going through his "hugfest" after his lectures. Now I am an unabashed advocate of hugging people as a most basic sign of support and concern. A hug or a simple touch on the arm can convey more caring than words. This is the most basic way to be physically present for another. People should not worry so much about saying exactly the right word or making a perfect speech to their terminally ill friend or loved one. I'm not expecting the eloquence of an Abraham Lincoln when a person visits me; the physical presence of a friend is enough. So for those of you who tend not to be physically demonstrative in your interactions with friends and family, my advice to you is simple: "Get over it."

My struggle with cancer has involved many episodes of anger, and unfortunately, my anger has sometimes spilled over onto my wife. When I get angry at Sheri, it normally has nothing to do with her; I am simply angry that this cancer has chosen my body. As psychologists tell us, anger is frequently displaced on another person, and caregivers are inevitably going to bear the brunt of the anger. In moments of anger, I have commonly complained to Sheri that she does

Craig with Sheri, his caregiver and life-giver.

not know what it is like to live with a terminal illness. To these tirades she often replies, “No, I don’t know what it feels like to have cancer, but if I was in your situation, I would be living my life to the fullest and doing my best to make pleasant memories in whatever time I have left.” With this response she is usually able to snap me out of my depressed mood, and it has often led to making plans for our next bucket list experience to change my focus to a positive activity. Sheri is helping me to find daily joy in my life and to work on repairing and reestablishing lost relationships with some old friends.

Sheri is more than a caregiver; she is my life giver. My cancer has greatly added to her already busy and stressful life. She has assumed more of the household chores such as grocery shopping and cooking (OK, she did those two before my cancer), and now she has to do the lawn chores as well as tasks related to my cancer, such as keeping track of all medical appointments, updating friends on my medical condition, driving me to the hospital and oncology clinic, bolstering my spirits, and much more. Despite these added burdens and stressors, she has managed to do them all with grace and a smile.

In the past several months while Sheri has been carrying these added burdens, I have sometimes forgotten a basic tenet of the family systems theory that I had taught to my students—in a family, what affects one individual affects all family members. In many real respects, Sheri has lung cancer as well. Caregivers often experience depression and anxiety as a result of a loved one’s illness. Caregivers want to fix the problem and make their loved one well again. It is important for me to remember to show my appreciation for Sheri’s loving support and to ask her on a regular basis how she is doing. It is critical for me to remember to encourage her to take breaks from the demands of taking care of me and to take care of her own needs, if only for a short time.

When someone is caring for a person with cancer, it is normal for that person to go through many of the same feelings and fears as the person with the disease. People with cancer or another serious disease need consider the impact of their illness on their caregivers. With this thought in mind, I asked my wife to write down her thoughts on what frustrates her and what advice she could give me for making my cancer experience easier on her. Sheri made this point when she wrote the following in response to my request for honest feedback about her feelings and frustrations:

> Dreams lost for parents of children with disabilities are similar to the dreams lost when your husband has lung cancer. My world is upside down, too. Life is no longer predictable. I am no longer able to confidently plan for our future, plan travel and visits with friends, time together. Craig is sometimes so withdrawn he can go all day without saying more than two or three words. He often gives me only one word responses to my questions. He does not see tasks that need to be done around the house or he simply chooses to ignore them. Instead, he leaves these chores for me and I feel so overburdened. I really get upset when Craig uses his cancer as an excuse

> not to do something or to take advantage of me and all I do for him. I get angry and resentful as to how his moods have damaged our relationship. I would like him to plan dates for the two of us so that we can enjoy each other and whatever remaining time we have together.

Sheri's blunt honestly was like a knife cutting through me. It was a much needed reality check and magnified some of the issues we faced in our marriage before my cancer. It has always been easy for me to be overly consumed with my career and, thus, exceedingly self-absorbed. Further, my personality tends toward moodiness, and I treated my home as a refuge from having to talk since that was part of my responsibilities all day long at work. Consequently, I was not a fully engaged partner with my wife. There is no excuse or defense to offer in response to Sheri's indictment of my behavior and of my temperament either BC or AD. The key question is how to make amends and move forward to best enjoy our remaining time together.

Recently it occurred to me that my struggle with cancer for the past several months has meant waging two battles at the same time—one with cancer and the other with my emotions. Although the odds of winning the first battle may not be very good, the chances for winning the battle on the second front are within my grasp. Further, it seems clear to me that if I don't win that battle, cancer will claim my life earlier than expected. This has fueled my efforts to engage even more vigorously in the battle with my attitude and emotions. Some days I slide backward and regress to self-pity. On those days, Sheri and Lindsay remind me of my promise shortly after the cancer diagnosis: to live each day to the fullest, to laugh, and to make pleasant memories for all of us. This bears repeating on a daily basis; indeed, it must become my mantra.

Another way of supporting individuals with cancer that needs to be emphasized is to contribute to and promote funding for research on lung cancer prevention and treatment. Compared with research on other forms of cancer, lung cancer is seriously underfunded. According to a report broadcast on the CBS Sunday Morning News (August 31, 2008), in 2006, funding per lung cancer death was $1,638 compared with funding of $13,519 per breast cancer death and $11,298 per prostate cancer death. The report noted significant progress in the treatment and 5-year survival rates for some cancers such as breast, prostate, and colon, but from 1975 to 2004, the 5-year survival rate for individuals with lung cancer increased by only 3% (13% to 16%). Each year in the United States there are approximately 213,000 newly diagnosed cases of lung cancer, and there are over 160,000 lung cancer deaths in the U.S. each year. Having cited this data, the report noted that lung cancer claims more lives than any other cancer, accounting for one-third of all cancer deaths in the United States. More people die from lung cancer than breast, colon, and prostate cancers combined. Although smoking is the leading cause of lung cancer, there are increasing numbers of nonsmoking-related lung cancer cases. Like me, 15% of lung cancer patients have never smoked.

What explains this lack of funding for lung cancer given the fact that it is the number one cancer killer in the United States? Because of the stigma associated with it, lung cancer is considered to be the invisible cancer. The prevailing attitude is that lung cancer is self-induced by smoking; most Americans tend to believe that people with lung cancer have caused their illness through their own negative behaviors. In the United States, researchers have identified a historic pattern of blaming others for one problem after another, especially for their own problem. Poor people are blamed for their poverty; rape victims have been blamed for being raped; people of color are called troublemakers when they complain about racism. Even in cases where people may have made some bad choices or exercised poor judgment, pointing an accusatory finger at people as a way of dismissing their problems is a punitive response, and not a helpful one. At times, all of us could be accused of engaging in one kind of egregious behavior or another, but we need to stop this adolescent tendency of blaming others. Compassion and commitment to solving our social and medical problems are the better responses.

This stigma against lung cancer patients translates to less attention, advocacy, and funding than other serious diseases. Perhaps funding will increase when the general public starts to realize that more and more individuals stricken with lung cancer have never smoked in their lives. However, even if a person is diagnosed with smoking-related lung cancer, why do we single out that particular unhealthy behavior by not committing sufficient research funding to enhance prevention, early detection, and treatment? Should people who increase their risk for heart attacks by overeating and not regularly exercising face similar reduced funding for heart disease research? Of course not. Any significant public health crisis deserves our attention and funding support to eliminate or reduce the effects of that medical problem. We should encourage people to be more prevention oriented by practicing a healthy lifestyle, but for those who don't because they smoke or eat too much or drink alcohol excessively, they are still human beings who are deserving of our compassion and medical resources to treat their afflictions. There should not be a moral litmus test for deciding how to spend medical resources.

In June, when Sheri and I were on the Alaska cruise, we had an experience that can serve to summarize the issues related to communicating with individuals experiencing serious or terminal illnesses. Having just completed my fourth chemotherapy cycle a little more than a month earlier, I boarded the ship as a bald man with a pale complexion and fatigue written all over my face. Sheri and I went to dinner at a Chinese restaurant on the cruise ship. Deciding to spare the waitress the story about my lung cancer, I mentioned only my allergy to wheat products due to my celiac disease. After she took my order for dinner, she went to check with the chef to make sure the dish was gluten free. After two or three back-and-forth conversations between the waitress, the chef, and me, my order was finally determined and we waited for our food. For the rest of the dinner, the waitress only talked to Sheri, even when the waitress was discussing my food order. The waitress was so oblivious to my presence at the table it was as if I had ceased to exist in the world, as if my body, mind, and personality had suddenly disappeared.

I have seen this same behavior when people ignore a person with a disability and instead talk only to the person's companion, as if they assume that the disabled person is unable to communicate or understand. Despite my previous communication with this waitress, she seemed uncomfortable in continuing to interact with me. It was probably not a consequence of my dietary issues, but of the poor health reflected in my rather sickly looking appearance. The waitress had obviously chosen to deal with the more normal looking person—my wife.

People who care about individuals with serious or terminal illnesses must be sensitive about how best to communicate with and support people in such stressful situations. Otherwise, it is possible that their medical condition may be exacerbated by a daily existence that is made to seem less than what it should be. This is especially critical for friends and family members because they are the links to a life before cancer. It is vital that those links be maintained.

REFERENCES

Halpern, S. P. (2004). *The etiquette of illness: What to say when you can't find the words.* New York: Bloomsburg.

Pausch, R., & Zaslow, J. (2008). *The last lecture.* New York: Hyperion.

CHAPTER 6

Trying To Be An "Exceptional Patient"

As a profession, special education requires collaborative partnerships between many people—special education teachers, parents, general education teachers, therapists, school administrators, community human services personnel, doctors, and many more. In the 1960s and 1970s, William Morse was one of the pioneers of special education. To note how this professional collaboration can be difficult, frustrating, and unfamiliar work for many, Morse (1994) stated, "A wry observer of the current scene is reported to have said, 'Collaboration is an unnatural act between two non-consenting adults" (p. 532).

Because of my professional commitment to collaboration, my goal shortly after the cancer diagnosis was to work hard on fostering a partnership with the physicians on my medical team. Cancer patients demonstrating the characteristics of what Dr. Bernie Siegel refers to as "an exceptional patient" tend to experience better treatment outcomes and survival rates. Having a collaborative relationship with my doctors seemed to be the way for me to become that exceptional patient who tended to develop effective partnerships with their physicians. I knew it would not be easy, but it was important to me to resist playing the role of a passive recipient of medical advice. No matter how daunting it might be to establish a collaborative partnership, I wanted a more active, decision-making role because, after all, this was my life we were talking about. This chapter describes what I have learned from the past 8 months about doctor-patient relationships based on my own observations, personal experiences, and reading, and that includes communication issues, factors affecting the quality of a doctor-patient relationship, characteristics of exceptional patients, stressors on both doctors and patients, and some of the important topics that must be addressed in medical partnerships.

The skill with which a doctor communicates a devastating diagnosis to a patient can make a big difference in that patient's level of optimism and fighting spirit. As discussed previously, one's attitude is a major determinant of healing. Of course, it is imperative that doctors should be truthful about any diagnosis, however dire, but that information can be couched in words of hope. Physicians do not know enough about cancer to deny hope to a patient. After the initial shock of my cancer diagnosis, it was essential for me to know more about what I was facing and my prospects for long-term survival, but without the doom and gloom of those dreadful 5-year statistics. Yet this information often had to be drawn out of my physicians instead of being volunteered by them.

During an early appointment with my pulmonologist, Dr. Avery, I asked if he had known any patients with lung cancer similar to mine who had beaten the odds and made it past the 5-year survival mark. Dr. Avery thought for a moment; then he stated that he had treated at least two patients with lung cancer comparable to mine who had beaten the odds. Even though one of those patients continued to smoke, he was still living more than 8 years after his cancer diagnosis. My first reaction was that perhaps at the advanced age of 56, I should take up smoking—strictly for therapeutic reasons, mind you!

None of my other treating physicians ever mentioned patients in circumstances similar to mine who had experienced miraculous recoveries. Although doctors must honor the confidentiality rights of their patients, I was not looking for names, just some information about people in similar circumstances, people who had survived with cancer. Perhaps doctors are concerned about fostering "false hope" in the mind of a terminally ill patient, but my belief is that fostering hope of any kind is exactly what doctors should be doing with their seriously ill or terminal patients. They should regularly share stories of miraculous recoveries, even when they can't explain why the individual recovered, rather than forcing their patients to drag this kind of information out of them. Doctors must learn how to present a grave prognosis with mediating words of comfort, and the words of comfort should focus on the fact that you still have a life to live and that doctors can not always accurately predict survival rates.

It is part of their professional obligation for doctors, oncologists in particular, to be scientifically grounded in the knowledge provided by current research statistics on treatment options and long-term survival rates, but an overreliance on statistics can distort a doctor's thinking and lead to an excessive predilection to offer only pessimistic predictions of how long a patient has to live. In our conversations, I told my doctors that I did not want them making those kinds of predictions. Each patient should be perceived as an individual, and my preference was that my doctors not put me into a research category with other cancer patients. As scientists, doctors must rely upon group statistics, but as a cancer patient, my focus needs to be on my individual case and on those cases of medical miracles that cannot be explained by current medical knowledge. Doctors usually tend to discredit single, anecdotal experiences and gravitate to studies with large numbers. As a researcher myself, I understand this tendency, but when a person has a terminal illness, those individual anecdotes are essential to give a patient inspiration and hope. Believing in these mysteries encourages me to muster the strength and courage to get up each day and lead a meaningful life. Doctors who work with me must be capable of maintaining optimism and hope just as I do, even in the face of seemingly insurmountable odds.

For a cancer patient, there's no point in denying a terminal diagnosis, but you need to defy the corresponding verdict. This perspective is best demonstrated in an article by Dr. William Bucholz, first published in the *Western Journal of Medicine*; the following excerpt from his article appeared in *Head First* by Norman Cousins (1989):

> As I was eating breakfast one morning I overheard two oncologists discussing the papers they were to present at the national meeting of the American Society of Clinical Oncology. One was complaining bitterly:
>
> "You know, Bob, I just don't understand it. We used the same drugs, the same dosage, the same schedule, and the same entry criteria. Yet I got a 22 percent response rate and you got a 74 percent. That's unheard of for metastatic lung cancer. How do you do it?"
>
> "We're both using Etoposide, Platinol, Oncovin, and Hydroxyurea. You call yours EPOH. I tell my patients I'm giving them HOPE. Sure, I tell them this is experimental, and we go over the long list of side effects together. But I emphasize that we have a chance. As dismal as the statistics are for non-small cell, there are always a few percent who do really well." (p. 99)

If a terminal diagnosis is presented in a manner devoid of comfort and hope, a patient's response will likely be a combination of panic, helplessness, and depression. These emotions can contribute to a suppressed immune system, exacerbating the disease. The words used to communicate medical information are critical and can contribute to further illness or promote recovery.

In addition to language, tone and sensitivity are important components in every doctor-patient communication. After my early-August CT scan, Sheri and I had made appointments to meet with Dr. Avery and Dr. Cooper later that day to discuss the results. We met with Dr. Avery first. As we were waiting anxiously for him in the examination room, he entered full of enthusiasm with a big smile on his face and immediately said he wanted to share some good news. He said my cancer had not spread and what we thought were four new tumors in my right lung looked to him like they were now calcified and not cancerous. My diagnosis was still the same, but having rarely received any good medical news in the past 8 months, this felt like something to celebrate.

In comparison, we met later with Dr. Cooper. Although he is always pleasant, he tends to be much more subdued during patient interactions than Dr. Avery. Like everyone else, doctors have different personalities, but the personality, tone, and demeanor of a doctor have significant implications on his or her patients' attitudes. Dr. Cooper reviewed the same CT scan information that we heard from Dr. Avery in the morning, but his tone was not celebratory in any manner. At the end of our appointment, I finally asked if he would say there was any reason for me to find some comfort or optimism from these latest CT scan results, and he responded, "Yes, I would." Although his response reinforced what we heard from Dr. Avery, a patient should not have to plead for that information; the doctor should provide it with an appropriate amount of hope and optimism.

When patients complain about doctors, the majority of these complaints relate to their perception of not being treated with sensitivity and respect. Reporting on a study of why patients changed physicians, Cousins (1989) revealed that patients sought new doctors not because their old doctor was incompetent but because of their doctor's interpersonal communication style and lack of sensitivity to them as individuals. Too many doctors fixate on cases, charts, diseases, treatments, and prognoses instead of concentrating on the patient as an *individual*. Although making money is essential to hospitals and clinics, medicine should not simply be a business driven by the profit motive. Doctors provide the most personal kinds of services imaginable to human beings. People don't tend to demand personal responses from our butcher, baker, or candlestick maker, but when it comes to our own body, most individuals want and expect to be treated not just as a collection of symptoms, but as a whole person.

Physicians need to understand what a disease means to the person who has it. Doctors need to ask their patients on a regular basis how they are dealing with bad news. A doctor doesn't have to be a psychiatrist to be concerned about the person's emotional state as well as physical health, but many doctors are emotionally unavailable to their patients. Being a compassionate listener is a good start for addressing a patient's emotional issues while they are living with a terminal diagnosis.

Perhaps this emotional detachment is the result of medical school training and its emphasis on not becoming overly involved with any patient. The same lesson tends to be taught in law school, but in my experience, maintaining an emotional noninvolvement with my clients and their cases was simply not rewarding. The clarion call that told me to leave the legal profession occurred as a result of reflecting on my interactions with clients during my second legal services job in my hometown of La Crosse. Because of my increasing tendency to be annoyed and even angry at the crazy circumstances my clients "had allowed themselves" to be placed in, I began to engage in classic victim blaming reactions, and that prevented me from feeling empathy for my clients. Having come to this realization, I had the good sense and courage to leave the practice of law and find a new career that inspired passion and renewed my sense of compassion and dedication. Even more than lawyers, doctors must feel compassion and empathy for the people they are trying to help. In an effort to foster greater sensitivity for their patients, Susan Halpern (2004) suggests that doctors ask themselves these questions:

- Think about a time in their lives when they were hurting. What was helpful?
- What did people do that was helpful to them during these troubled times?
- What did they not like in terms of how people treated or interacted with them?
- How did it feel to be on the receiving end of assistance?
- What was healing for them in those troubled times?

Going through this mental activity could enhance a doctor's empathy toward his or her patients. This perspective is beautifully captured by Norman Cousins (1989) in the physician's credo he delivered as part of his commencement address to graduates of the UCLA School of Medicine. Parts of his address follows:

> There are qualities beyond pure medical competence that patients need and look for in doctors. They want reassurance. They want to be looked after and not just looked over. They want to be listened to. They want to feel that it makes a difference to the physician, a very big difference, whether they live or die. They want to feel that they are in the doctor's thoughts. The physician holds the lifeline. The physician's words and not just his prescriptions are attached to that lifeline . . .
>
> I pray that you will never allow your knowledge to get in the way of your relationship with your patients. I pray that all the technological marvels at your command will not prevent you from practicing medicine out of a little black bag. I pray that when you go into a patient's room you will recognize that the main distance is not from the door to the bed but from the patient's eyes to your own—and that the shortest distance between those two points is a horizontal line—the kind of straight line that works best when the physician bends low to the patient's loneliness and fear and pain and the overwhelming sense of mortality that comes flooding up out of the unknown, and when the physician's hand on the patient's shoulder or arm is a shelter against the darkness.
>
> I pray that, even as you attach the highest value to your science, you will never forget that it works best when combined with your art, and, indeed, that your art is what is most enduring in your profession. For, ultimately, it is the physician's respect for the human soul that determines the worth of his science. (pp. 308–309)

Since my cancer diagnosis, my fascination with the word *iatrogenic* has increased. According to Cousins (1989), iatrogenic means "any adverse condition brought about as a result of any aspect of medical treatment, including hospital care" (p. 317). Cousins believed that iatrogenic problems in medicine were primarily due to physician errors in the diagnosis or treatment of patients. After his own personal health crisis, and based upon research he was involved with at UCLA School of Medicine, it became apparent to him that "errors or failures in communication can be equally iatrogenic" (p. 268). These communication failures are especially an issue when a doctor delivers terminal diagnostic information to patients or predicts terminal dates. Some doctors refuse to make such negative predictions regardless of how dire the medical condition. Cousins describes what such doctors communicate: "They tell the patient that no one knows enough to make a precise forecast, that remissions continue to be reported that were not considered possible, and that the doctor should be concerned not with prophecy but with heroic and compassionate treatment" (p. 269). I concur completely and wish more of this sentiment had been expressed in my physicians' communications with me. The point is not that doctors should foster "false hope" in their patients, but that encouraging a hopeful frame of mind enhances the desire to fight the cancer. After all, how can there be such a thing as false hope when there are reported cases where a person with a similar disease survived? Hope does not rely upon statistics; hope is dependent upon faith and optimism.

There are several key factors affecting the quality of doctor-patient relationships. Bernie Siegel (1986) maintained that a patient's active participation in the decision-making process is fundamental in determining the quality of the doctor-patient relationship. Shared responsibility enhances a patient's healing and recovery. A more active patient role fosters a greater sense of control over illness. One way to assume an active role in treatment is by reading as much as possible about lung cancer, traditional treatment plans, and alternative treatments. With this knowledge in mind, the patient can ask questions about the treatment and raise issues about other approaches.

Sheri usually comes to my doctors' appointments because it is helpful to have a second person listening to the same information, especially since the terminal patient is understandably quite emotional during many of these doctor visits. Before a doctor's appointment, Sheri and I make a list of questions we want to ask. We are insistent that the doctor takes ample time in responding to our questions without rushing us, and we have been fortunate because all of my doctors practice patience with their patient (me). I ask for copies of my MRI and CT reports from the radiologist so that I may study them in greater detail and perhaps prepare follow-up questions. Sometimes the doctor has had to take an emergency call or is called out of the examination room during my appointment. When the doctor returns, I always pretend to be crushed to discover that I am not his only patient. Although it is just my attempt at a joke, it is no joke to say that all patients need to feel that they are special to their doctor, and that their doctor will not rush through the appointment as if the patient is on an assembly line.

A second factor enhancing doctor-patient partnerships is empowering the patient to draw upon his or her strengths. One of the biggest stumbling blocks is the orientation underlying medical preparation that views patients largely from a deficit (i.e., collection of symptoms) or a pathological perspective. Of course, physicians are in the business of diagnosing their patients' symptoms to develop treatment plans, but this medical approach too often intrudes into how doctors communicate and interact with their patients. Doctors could learn from a significant change in the disability field over the past decade—the emergence of family-centered support services. These services are based on several fundamental principles, including professionals respecting and acknowledging family expertise and strengths. Again, this special kind of empathy allows doctors to gain respect for a patient's situation. Without this level of respect, it is unlikely that a doctor will value the input of his or her patient.

Patients experiencing a health crisis are typically unaware at that moment of their personal strengths; in fact, they are likely to be feeling quite vulnerable and

Mixing business with pleasure, Craig and Sheri have a glass of wine while thinking of questions to ask his physicians.

powerless. With that in mind, I made a conscious effort to tell my doctors about my career as a university professor and that my publications included several special education books. The purpose was not to bolster my ego but to let my doctors know that one of my strengths as a patient was being an individual who was likely to do his homework and research his medical condition. This was the initial signal to my doctors of my intent to take an active role in my treatment plan. By acknowledging the strengths a patient possesses, doctors can activate that patient's determination and fighting spirit. On several occasions, Dr. Cooper has reminded me of my strengths to help me focus on and rally my resources to weather the emotional storms of my terminal disease. Pointing out these strengths was invaluable to me because there have been plenty of times that I have been consumed by feelings of vulnerability and by an overwhelming sense of inability to cope with and fight my cancer.

In any partnership, you should normally expect to establish some sort of personal relationship with the other party. This does not mean becoming best friends with your doctors, but most people want and deserve a doctor-patent relationship that extends beyond mere patient files and diagnostic results. In my life-and-death struggle, I need a personal relationship at some level with my treating physicians. Dr. Bernie Siegel, the cancer surgeon previously mentioned, always encouraged his patients to call him Bernie. Siegel (1986) said he would regularly give his patients a hug, recognizing that there were times when this type of interaction might be more beneficial than his prescription pad.

In my relationship-building efforts, I have always shown respect and a certain amount of deference to my doctors by addressing them formally as Dr. Cooper, Dr. Dalton, and Dr. Avery. Sometimes it makes me laugh to think that by having accumulated my four degrees, I probably have more years of formal education than my physicians. As a private joke with my wife, I have proposed insisting that my doctors call me "Dr. Dr. Fiedler" to appropriately acknowledge my two doctoral degrees—Juris Doctor (JD) and Doctor of Philosophy (PhD). Given the amount of status and respect generally enjoyed by most physicians in our society, many doctors seem to be more comfortable in a hierarchically arranged relationship with their patients, exerting a "power over" approach, but my goal has been to promote a true partnership reflecting a "power with" perspective. Frankly, I would prefer to call my doctors by their first names as Bernie Siegel did with his patients; however, I have not yet reached that point in any of my physician relationships.

As we were leaving from an appointment with Dr. Cooper, it dawned on me that he had never used my name. I asked Sheri if she recalled any time when he called me by name, any name such as Mr. Fiedler, Dr. Fiedler, or Craig. For about 8 months now Dr. Cooper has been my medical oncologist, and neither Sheri nor I could remember a time when he referred to me by name. He says hello upon entering the examination room and asks how I am doing. He is always pleasant in his interactions, but distant. The result is that it feels like I am just another "cancer case" to him instead of a human being who is fighting for his life. In waging this struggle, it seems appropriate for my physicians to give me at least the minimal recognition of calling me by my name. Referring to patients by name is not a minor issue—it goes to the heart of establishing a true partnership.

Finally, in reviewing medical research, it was interesting to note that a significantly lower percentage of primary-care physicians are involved in malpractice lawsuits. Perhaps one reason for this finding is that primary-care physicians are more likely to have established a longer and more trusting relationship with their patients than specialists. People are going to feel less inclined to sue someone with whom they have a close relationship. That made sense to me because trust is another critical element in any partnership; little is accomplished in the absence of trust. Emotional and psychological assistance, collaboration, and partnerships are dependent upon trust-based relationships and interactions.

A salient element of trust is dependability, the belief that an individual will conscientiously and reliably perform in accordance with standard expectations. In my case, one of my major motivations for researching lung cancer and treatments is to engage my doctors in conversations about cutting-edge treatment options. For example, after reading that avastin had demonstrated some success in enhancing survival time for patients with lung cancer, I asked Dr. Cooper if he ever considered using avastin as one of my chemotherapy drugs. Dr. Cooper immediately responded that he was considering prescribing avastin, and that if I went on another chemo cycle, he would recommend that as one of my new drugs.

After that, further reading provided information about the use of radiofrequency ablation, a minimally invasive cancer treatment using imaging techniques such as ultrasound and computed tomography (CT) to guide a needle electrode into a cancerous tumor. This procedure heats and destroys cancer cells. In response to my inquiry about the possible use of radiofrequency ablation (RFA) to treat my cancerous tumors, Dr. Cooper said he was quite familiar with this treatment procedure but felt that I was not a good candidate for RFA. A host of factors entered into this treatment decision including size of the tumors and location. His conclusion seemed reasonable for the moment, but it is likely that at some time in the future I will ask Dr. Cooper if my situation has changed so that RFA is now a viable option. These examples illustrate why my trust in Dr. Cooper has grown. By demonstrating that he has kept up on new cancer research and treatments, he persuaded me that he was dependable to perform his duties as my medical oncologist.

Trusting relationships are predicated upon creating an atmosphere of safety and confidence that doctors will do what they say they will do, that the best interests of the patient governs a physician's decisions, and that confidentiality will be maintained at all times. The following recommendations of ways to establish trust in doctor-patient relationships are derived from my reading and my experiences:

- Maintain a positive and sincere demeanor with patients.
- Strive to be sensitive and accepting of the emotional and psychological needs of patients.
- Be willing to acknowledge your limitations in addressing the medical conditions of your patients.
- Avoid making hasty judgments about your patients.
- Avoid making promises that you may not be able to keep.
- Actively involve your patients in treatment decisions.
- Attempt to understand the patient's personal and family circumstances to provide maximum support.

In education, we have long known that relationships with students are strengthened when teachers disclose personal information. In my college courses, I have encouraged special education teachers to divulge some personal information about themselves to the parents of their students because this fosters a more personal connection between people. The same outcome can occur when a physician willingly discloses personal information with his or her patients. This is not to suggest that teachers or doctors must disclose their religious or political affiliations or intimate aspects of their private lives, just simple glimpses into their identity as a human being. They need to be able to share something about the person inside the standard white doctor's coat. During one of my appointments, Dr. Avery was typing some information about my condition and his recommendations into the computer. Watching him use the "hunt and peck" method of typing, I could not help laughing and asked how he ever completed college and medical school typing the way he did. He stopped hunting and pecking and laughed with me. He admitted that he always had to date a woman with good typing skills. The humor of this interaction provided us with a light moment during an ominous time.

On another occasion, an appointment with Dr. Cooper was scheduled shortly after Sheri and I returned from Arizona, where I got to see three spring training baseball games. Upon mentioning this to Dr. Cooper, he talked about being a baseball fan and that he even played baseball in college. Apparently, he was a pitcher with a decent fastball in the upper 80s. He also revealed that his son was a Milwaukee Brewers baseball fan, and that reminded me that someone had given me a Brewers bobble-head doll a few months earlier. At my next appointment, I handed the bobble head doll to Dr. Cooper and told him to give it to his son. He gratefully accepted my gift. It is such simple moments during doctor-patient interactions that turn a patient from a medical case into a human being. That is my goal in working with any physician on my medical team.

Dr. Siegel (1986) argues that physicians should be "privileged listeners" of their patients. What this means is the responsibility for physicians to take adequate time to address their patients' emotional states, to allay fears, and to find out their patients' strengths, coping mechanisms, and resilience in the face of living with a terminal disease. If my doctors have been adequately attentive, they have learned from our interactions that I have a very supportive spouse and family, a strong network of friends, a sense of humor, the ability to search for cancer information, an interest in reading books for enjoyment and distraction, and a capacity to reflect upon my condition and prognosis. They should have noticed my strong will to live, but also my tendency to get very emotional about my situation and require emotional assurance at regular intervals. Doctors are primarily used to being in the role of delivering information, and for that reason, all doctors should pay special attention to their listening skills. For the most part, my doctors are good listeners. I have been lucky in that regard.

A good doctor-patient partnership is based upon patients demonstrating appropriate assertiveness by regularly asking their doctors questions, by demanding they be allowed an active decision-making role, by asserting their desire to be treated with dignity and respect, and by displaying a tenacity for life. Yet doctors may not always appreciate these assertive behaviors. According to Bernie Siegel (1986), patients that some physicians consider to be "difficult" or uncooperative are the ones most likely to get well. Medical researchers maintain that these so-called difficult patients may have more killer T-cells than docile "good patients." In my role as a cancer patient, my intent is to be pleasant, but it is important for me to remember that this is not a popularity contest. If some degree of belligerence is required to have my input considered and my questions addressed, then I am willing to display such behaviors.

An effective doctor-patient partnership is stimulated by the physician helping the patient to set goals. Establishing regular goals is an integral part of cancer treatment because it can be such a long, exhausting ordeal. Once goals have been established, however small, accomplishing them gives a patient a sense of pride and a desire to celebrate those achievements. Patients need encouragement and support to climb that next mountain. My main goal right now is to have a moratorium from treatment for as long as possible. My last chemo cycle ended in late April of 2008, and since then, my energy and appetite have slowly returned. This has restored me to some sense of my former life, and that has been a true gift over the summer months. During those months, an additional goal was to travel without experiencing any medical setbacks. At the time of this writing, that goal has been successfully achieved.

Since all of my doctors have encouraged me to exercise by walking on a regular basis, this activity became part of my daily routine during our summer travels, but I need to incorporate more exercise into my daily routine at home.

Craig and Sheri on vacation in San Francisco, walking along the bay.

Although Sheri and I tend to celebrate the achievement of a particular goal, doctors also need to celebrate any of the goals their patients accomplish. Such celebrations enhance a patient's persistence and determination, which are critical attitudinal components in cancer recovery.

In an interesting survey of over 600 oncologists, Cousins (1989) reported on their opinions regarding the importance of various psychosocial factors, such as the will to live, being hopeful, and a patient's coping ability. According to this survey, most of the oncologists overwhelmingly agreed that three factors were critical: "a strong will to live, confidence in the physician, and emotional support from family and friends created an atmosphere conducive to effective treatment" (pp. 217–218). In that survey, the following psychosocial factors elicited a response of "very important or moderately important" in treatment efficacy by over 60% of the oncologists:

- Seeking medical treatment at an early stage in the disease process
- The patient's determination to comply with doctor recommendations
- The patient's willingness to assume a proper share of responsibility for his or her own health and recovery
- A positive approach to the challenge of the illness
- Strong will to live
- Confidence in their physician
- Emotional support from friends and family members
- The patient's ability to cope with stress
- The patient's hopefulness concerning treatment outcome
- The patient's willingness to communicate and share concerns with the physician
- The patient's involvement in creative and meaningful activities

It was in the 1970s that Bernie Siegel founded Exceptional Cancer Patients (ECaP) to empower cancer patients. He has written extensively about his observations of people he has called "exceptional patients" and his beliefs concerning why their treatment outcomes were more successful and their survival longer than predicted. Siegel (1986) described three kinds of patients he has encountered in his medical practice: First are those patients who consciously or unconsciously prefer to die as a way of escaping life's travails—this constitutes about 15%–20% of all patients. Second are the majority (60%–70%) of patients who are primarily concerned about pleasing their doctors, so they are passive participants in their treatment plans. Finally, there is the group that Siegel refers to as exceptional patients (15%–20%), refusing to play the victim, fighting for survival. Since I have worked with exceptional children (another term used for children with disabilities), perhaps now I can aspire to my own category of exceptionality. I want to be an exceptional survivor.

According to Siegel (1986), it all starts with the outlook of exceptional patients. He regularly asks his patients if they want to live to be a 100 years old. Without hesitation, those patients who are exceptional respond with an enthusiastic "yes." Reading this reminded me of one of the most positive, upbeat, and inspirational people I have ever worked with. Before he recently retired, Ted Balser was a Career Services Director at the University of Wisconsin-Oshkosh. Ted's long-stated goal was to live to be 100 years old, and with his attitude, it would not be smart to bet against him. Although my answer to Siegel's question would be affirmative, a cancer patient needs more than that. You need Ted's confidence that this goal can be achieved.

Exceptional patients want their doctors to serve as their advisors and teachers, not as a dictator. Siegel (1986) described a patient who walked into a doctor's office and found a sign on the desk that said, "Compromise means doing it my way." If any cancer patient were to see a sign like that, Siegel's advice is to turn right around and walk out the door. Siegel disparages typical medical school education because this concept of exceptional patients is not taught to future physicians; there are no courses on healing and love, or how to talk with patients, or reasons for becoming a doctor. The courses focus on human anatomy, symptoms of various diseases, diagnostic techniques, treatment protocols, and such. It has to be hard for a doctor to practice holistic, integrative medicine when your educational background does not advance that perspective.

To ascertain the emotional health and background of his patients, Siegel (1986) asks them three questions in addition to the question about wanting to live to be 100 years old. Those questions are: (a) What happened to you in the year or two before your illness? (b) What does this illness mean to you? and (c) Why did you need this illness (pp. 106–108)? Siegel is not trying to play an amateur psychiatrist here; his goal is to assist his patients in better understanding and thus articulating their emotional needs associated with whatever physical affliction they are suffering from. With this kind of personal insight, patients can develop more effective attitudes, affording them a better chance of survival. As William James asserted in his well-known quotation: "The greatest discovery of my generation is that a human being can alter his life by altering his attitude."

Siegel (1986) advises his patients to insist on the following Patient's Bill of Rights by sending an open letter to their physicians. A portion of that letter follows below:

> Dear Doctor:
>
> Do not tell me how long I have to live! I alone can decide how long I will live. It is my desires, my goals, my values, my strengths, and my will to live that will make the decision.
>
> Teach me and my family about how and why my illness happened to me. Help me and my family to live now. Tell me about nutrition and my body's needs. Tell me how to handle the knowledge and how my mind and body can work together. Healing comes from within, but I want to combine my strength with yours. If you and I are a team, I will live a longer and better life.

> Doctor, don't let your negative beliefs, your fears, and your prejudices affect my health. Don't stand in the way of my getting well and exceeding your expectations. Give me the chance to be the exception to your statistics. . . .
>
> You must learn what my disease means to me—death, pain, or fear of the unknown. . . .
>
> Doctor, teach me and my family to live with my problem when I am not with you. Take time for our questions and give us your attention when we need it. It is important that I feel free to talk with you and question you. I will live a longer and more meaningful life if you and I can develop a significant relationship. (pp. 127–128)

Siegel (1986) describes exceptional patients as complex, often contradictory people. He writes: "They are both serious and playful, tough and gentle, logical and intuitive, hard-working and lazy, shy and aggressive, introspective and outgoing. . . . They are paradoxical people who don't fit neatly into the usual psychological categories. This makes them more flexible than most people, with a wider array of resources to draw upon" (p. 161). It is probably because

I want to see myself in these characteristics, but it does seem to me (and to others) that my personality includes many of these apparent opposites. Other notable characteristics of exceptional patients include

- Successful at careers they enjoy
- Receptive and creative, but sometimes hostile, having strong egos and a sense of their own adequacy
- High degree of self-esteem
- Rarely docile
- Strong sense of reality
- Self-reliant
- Tolerant and concerned about others
- Nonconformists who appreciate diversity among other people
- Child-like appreciation of life; innocent curiosity
- Observant, nonjudgmental style
- Willingness to laugh at self
- Comfortable in complex and confusing situations
- Positive outlook and confidence in adversity
- Ability to absorb new and unexpected circumstances and be changed by them
- Active imagination

Perhaps Sheri and other people who know me best could review these characteristics and tell me if I should be worried when looking at the above list.

Finally, Siegel (1986) cites the research of Dr. Kenneth Pelletier's psychological study of patients who recovered despite great odds. His research identified five common characteristics in those patients. First, they all experienced profound intrapersonal change through meditation, prayer, or other types of spiritual practice. Second, they developed closer relations with other people as a result of their illness. Third, these patients altered their diets, choosing food with better nutritional value. Fourth, these survivors had a deep sense of the spiritual aspects of life. Fifth, they believed their recovery was not a gift but the result of a long, hard struggle that they had won for themselves (pp. 184–185).

In any quality relationship or partnership, each party must be sensitive to some of the stressors impacting the other, and there are some key stressors that patients and doctors must overcome. Of course, being diagnosed with a terminal illness and having that death sentence hanging over your head every day is unimaginable stress. It has been a struggle for me to adequately describe my feelings at different points during the day to my loved ones and friends. The best analogy occurred during an event that happened when Sheri and I were vacationing in Maui several years ago. We took a snorkeling trip on a boat and went out fairly far into the ocean. As we were enjoying snorkeling, I was caught unaware by a wave that washed over my snorkeling tube, causing me to swallow a lot of water. Although an adequate but by no means a strong swimmer, a sense of panic overwhelmed me. I tried to catch my breath and started swimming frantically to reach the side of the boat. Trying to live with a terminal illness has caused this same sensation of panic, even gasping for air on occasion, similar to that day off the coast of Maui. Each and every day now seems like that struggle to reach the safety of the boat.

My life now largely revolves around waiting for the latest MRI and CT scan results. It is pure agony, and it's easy to play all sorts of mind games with myself. Do I dare hope that the tumor has disappeared, even though Dr. Cooper has said that is highly unlikely? How will I handle any news involving the cancer spreading to other parts of my body? As Sheri and I sit in the examination room waiting for the doctor to review the test results with us, we can barely speak to each other. It is part of my routine to stare into space and become lost in thought. When the doctor enters the room, my immediate reaction is to try to read his body language. Waiting for those few minutes for the verdict from the scans is to experience the very meaning of anxiety, knowing that my life is literally hanging in the balance.

Experiencing this anxiety reminds me of my first year in law school and the anxiety that affected all students during final exam week. In law school, an entire course grade was based upon a 3 to 4 hour essay exam where you analyzed and critiqued legal theory, issues, and cases. This illustrates the concept of "high stakes testing." This was no time to develop a brain freeze or to panic, yet during that first year, several of my fellow students cracked under the pressure and left midway through the final exam. Those students were not sitting in my classes the following semester. One of my goals now is to overcome this anxiety just as I did back then, and to be around for the next semester, and for several years to come.

In his NPR blog, Leroy Sievers talked about "waiting for the cavalry" to arrive. He was referring to the hope offered by continued research advances in the treatment of cancer. That research represents the cavalry that cancer patients hope will arrive in time to save them from a potentially deadly fate. Some of my doctors say that every year cancer treatment becomes so much more targeted and sophisticated that in 10–15 years, most cancers will be viewed as a disease that is largely managed much like current chronic conditions such as diabetes and arthritis. Hearing this, my first thought is to be frustrated at my bad timing—I got this damn disease too early! It should have attacked me when I was much closer to the fort and the cavalry could then have been quickly dispatched to save me. My second reaction is to wonder if my survival will last long enough to give the cavalry sufficient time to reach me.

Having cancer is a full-time job. It is overwhelming and stressful to try to keep up with all the research information related to this illness. Well-meaning family members and friends often besiege cancer patients with information and encourage them to check out some well-known research and medical center in the United States or in another country. People send me articles about studies concerning new drugs or therapies to combat cancer. It would be easy to spend all of my days researching this information or traveling from one medical center to another or one presumed miracle cure after another. The questions every cancer patient must face are these: Is that the best investment of your time? Will that bring you enjoyment or will you just become an experimental gerbil constantly spinning on a wheel in a cage? Investigating experimental trials for which I might be qualified has not produced any viable options, so my goal has been to make sure that this activity does not consume me. It does not help to read all day about only cancer. Any person, but especially a cancer patient, needs distractions and other entertainment, just to relax and enjoy very simple daily pleasures. This is not possible if I must remain constantly vigilant about cancer treatments or programs. This is the point where trust must play a major role in my medical treatment as illustrated by my delegation of these responsibilities to my medical team.

I have great respect for doctors such as oncologists who spend most of their days facing death and dying situations. Perhaps that explains the emotional detachment of many physicians treating seriously ill or terminal patients. They cannot afford to get too close emotionally to their patients. This has to be stressful, and every doctor must have to develop his own coping devices. The stress in the medical profession is borne out by studies showing that physicians have high rates of alcohol abuse, suicide rates, and premature death. Although one can speculate about the stress facing doctors who work with terminal patients, it is not an adequate excuse to justify emotional noninvolvement in the treatment of patients. Perhaps for medical students desiring careers as oncologists, better screening is needed to determine their psychological disposition to handle the emotional roller coaster of such a medical practice. They have to understand that an emotional element is part of the territory that comes with the job of being an oncologist, and if a physician cannot handle that burden he or she should choose another field.

Medicine is not always the exact science that lay people think it is. As with the law, there are a lot of gray areas where current medical knowledge is incomplete, or at least evolving. The early detection and treatment of cancer is this kind of gray area. Physicians treating cancer patients are often only able to give educated guesses to questions that the patient would like more definitive responses. Cancer is highly unpredictable, and that is the mystery and frustration of this disease. Patients quite naturally want to believe their doctors have all of the answers, and that belief places an awesome responsibility and a burden on the shoulders of physicians. Given the prestige and status heaped upon doctors, it must be difficult for them to admit they do not know or that they only think a particular treatment might work. They cannot guarantee success. It is called "medical practice" because there is a certain amount of trial and error involved in treating complicated diseases like cancer. Doctors probably feel the stress of always being expected to have a definitive answer to any patient questions. It is not only cancer patients who need to learn to live with uncertainty in their lives; so must physicians.

As a parent of a child with a disability, I have often observed that some doctors were uncomfortable in treating Jennifer, perhaps because her disability was not a condition that could be "cured." Doctors are in the healing business, and when they encounter a patient whose condition they cannot cure, their professional psyche is at stake. What do you do if you are a healer who cannot cure a patient's cancer? Do you define your professional success by other measures such as alleviation of pain? Prolonging a person's life by a few months? Easing an individual's acceptance of death? All of this must be very stressful for doctors treating terminally ill patients.

There is one last issue that is difficult for me to address: terminal patients eventually have to face the issue of quality versus quantity of life. Each person wrestles with this tough issue in his or her own way. Sheri and I have only broached this subject tentatively so far because of my need to remain as optimistic as possible, but there is no alternative to planning for the future, and unfortunately, my future will probably force me to address this issue. It seems strange to think about this topic, as if such thoughts have nothing to do with reality but should be relegated to college philosophy or ethics courses.

In my professional life, this topic has come up in respect to disability issues, especially in the early 1980s with the so-called Baby Doe intensive neonatal care unit cases. At that time, there were a few highly publicized cases involving a parental decision to withhold treatment from their severely disabled infant, resulting in the infant's eventual death. In some cases, medical personnel acquiesced in the parents' wishes to withhold treatment; in others, the hospital challenged the parents' decision. A few years ago, *The Journal of Disability Policy Studies* that I co-edited with my colleague Dr. Billie Jo Rylance, published an entire special issue on end-of-life issues for people with disabilities. Now this topic is no longer simply an intellectual pursuit; it is real and personal.

The conversations Sheri and I have just started to have with my doctors seem surreal to me as they revolve around the goal of maintenance instead of curative intent. By maintenance, the medical goal is to slow the spread and growth of my cancerous tumors. It was an emotional blow when the focus of our medical discussions switched from cure to maintenance. The doctors now couch their recommendations for further treatment in statements such as: "We think this therapy can give you three or four months more of life." My feelings vacillate from one day to the next on whether I will decline further chemotherapy or radiation treatment if it is recommended for me.

In talking to my doctors about whether to submit to the preventive brain radiation therapy, one doctor stated that he has used this procedure with several patients and in his own words: "It is not like those patients are walking around like zombies or anything." It is hard to get excited and appreciative when having such a conversation. There was little comfort to be taken from the "zombie standard" of quality of life as employed by this doctor. On the other hand, it did make me look forward to the possibility of appearing as an extra on the upcoming remake of the film classic, *Night of the Living Dead.*

My goals used to involve thinking in terms of living 3 or 4 more decades; when my cancer treatment began it was years, now it is months. Although it is now only 8 months after my cancer diagnosis, there are still days when it seems hard to believe that I am facing these issues. But I am. If further treatment erodes my energy and appetite to the level it was during February, March, and April, it is difficult for me to call that "living." I was sleepwalking through my days, and just walking from the bedroom to the living room was like wading through chest-deep water. More time to spend with family and friends is valuable, and that's my highest priority, but not if I cannot be fully or reasonably able to engage in those interactions. So now my task is to weigh quantity and quality of life issues and prepare to make a decision at some point in the future. It is my best hope now—my only hope—that as a result of my relations and partnership with my medical team, wisdom will come to my aid.

References

Cousins, N. (1989). *Head first: The biology of hope and the healing power of the human spirit*. New York: Penguin Books.

Halpern, S. P. (2004). *The etiquette of illness: What to say when you can't find the words.* New York: Bloomsburg.

Morse, W. (1994, January). Comments from a biased viewpoint. *The Journal of Special Education, 27*(4), 531–542.

Siegel, B. S. (1986). *Love, medicine, and miracles*. New York: Harper.

CHAPTER 7

A Cancer Apprentice: Lessons in Redemption

An apprentice is variously defined as "one who is learning by practical experience under skilled workers, a trade, art, or calling; an inexperienced person; a novice." For me, the past 8 months have been an apprenticeship with cancer as my teacher. Prior to that time I certainly was a novice and inexperienced on the subject. Unfortunately, one result of the master teacher's influence is that I have become too skilled in the ways of cancer. Sometimes I wonder if cancer was my true calling?

Redemption comes from the root word redeem, which means "to free from what distresses or harms; to extricate from or help to overcome something detrimental; to release from blame or debt; to change for the better; to exchange for something of value; to atone for." All of these definitions apply to my cancer experience. In many respects, cancer has taught me many lessons, and it would be ungrateful of me not to appreciate them. Unfortunately, there was a severe price to be paid for these lessons. In this final chapter, it seems appropriate to share some of the lessons I have learned because they also provide insights on my changed life and circumstances. There is no particular order of importance to this list of lessons in redemption.

Living in Cancer World

In 1983, the first *Vacation* movie starring Chevy Chase as the father of the Griswold family featured Wally World, the name of an amusement park. In the movie, the family decides to drive from the midwest to California to see the wonders of Wally World. After a very eventful cross-country trip with numerous misfortunes, the Griswolds finally arrive at Wally World only to discover that it is closed for 2 weeks for repair and cleaning. Mr. Griswold goes berserk at this information and forces his way into the amusement park by threatening the security guard with a BB gun.

For some odd reason, several weeks into my cancer treatment I began thinking about this silly movie. Perhaps these first few weeks dealing with my disease reminded me of the movie because my life now felt like riding on a roller coaster at an amusement park, but my amusement park is called Cancer World and it's not amusing because the rides are really scary. Unfortunately for me, Cancer World is always open so the Fiedler family is riding the roller coaster each and every day. But as a well-known quote (adapted for the title of a movie with Nick Nolte) from the journalist Hunter Thompson reminds us: "You buy the ticket, you take the ride."

Why Me?

Initially after my cancer diagnosis, "Why me" was a question I often asked, but there was never a clear answer. During my work with parents of children with disabilities, they often asked this question. Some resorted to their religion for answers, believing that God only gives burdens to those who can handle them. I prefer not to think of individuals with disabilities as burdens, but if a person's religious beliefs help him or her cope with their reality, who am I to judge? After spending some time trying to answer that question, it struck me that dwelling on it would only lead to self-pity, and that was not the path toward healing. Instead, it made more sense to me to turn the question around and ask, "Why not me?" Catastrophic events happen to people every day. Nobody is immune from this chain of events. Contracting this disease simply meant that I was one of the unlucky ones, and the past is irrelevant to the cancer that is part of my new reality. Rather than ask "Why" questions, it seemed more useful to focus on "How" questions. How can I change my diet to improve my immune system? How can I best partner with the doctors on my medical team? How can I be a more supportive husband for my spouse? How can I be a better father? How can I be a better friend? How can I enjoy each day? These are far more important questions when you are living in Cancer World.

Appreciating Life Even When Feeling Miserable

In my first several weeks of treatment, it was an exaggeration to say that I was truly living. Most of my time was spent sleeping, and I did not read much because it was hard to focus. This raised the quality-versus-quantity of life issue that was discussed earlier. Yet, there is still something to be said on behalf of life, even when you are struggling to appreciate it. In my conscious moments during those bleak days, I could still dream, think about comforting memories of people and places, hope for a better day tomorrow, look at my wife through bleary eyes, and have my dog lick my face. On some of my more exhausting days, the dog licking constituted my shower. I guess as long as you are alive, conscious, and not in agonizing pain, there is always, however slight, a burning hope for improvement, for a miraculous intervention, for inner peace and comfort.

One of Craig's simple pleasures, out on a boat with his dog licking his face.

Inevitable Change

When you have a terminal illness, you go through unavoidable changes, not just physically, but emotionally and spiritually. I am not the same person I was before cancer, and this has nothing to do with the addition of tumors in my body. When you are healthy, the prevalent attitude is often procrastination as you promise yourself to do something tomorrow, or next month, or next year. But it is not possible to know how many of these tomorrows will be allotted to me, so there is a certain urgency to my life. This does not mean that my life is a frantic existence, but it has become necessary for me to embrace the perspective that life is to be lived right now. Why put things off any longer?

I see life differently now and experience simple daily events in a much different manner. Each day offers an opportunity to take some time to examine and contemplate what is going on around me. A colleague at the university, Becky, used to tease me about being oblivious to my environment. She was right because my focus was always on what was necessary for my teaching, research, and writing. That meant missing out on a lot of simple pleasures around me. It should not take a crisis to awaken us from our slumber, but most of us try to forget that we are not immortal. We believe there will be plenty of time to say "I love you" to someone, or to thank somebody for a particular kindness. I would urge every person and every family to make their new motto the one that now guides my life: "There is no time like the present."

Preparing for the Worst

Many terminally ill people prepare themselves for the worst every time they have a doctor's appointment and new test results are reviewed. This is a defense mechanism they employ so that they do not feel blindsided by the latest diagnostic results. Because I was blindsided back on January 28, I have tried to avoid having that happen again. This may seem like a reasonable approach to a grim set of circumstances, but I now realize that you can never be adequately prepared for bad news. It still strikes you like a thunderbolt, and life goes into slow motion for awhile. The problem with preparing for the worst is that such a focus may result in failing to appreciate life and those around you.

Unfortunately, people are not constitutionally wired to be hypervigilant all of the time. Studies of abused children reveal that they suffer in a multitude of ways and the effects are lingering, often lifelong. When you suffer an abused childhood, the body's defense mechanism becomes hypervigilant about your environment and the people in it. This not only creates incredible stress for your body, but it leads to significant trust issues in your relationships with others. This is another way that cancer acts as a thief; it can steal your enjoyment of day-to-day experiences because you cannot stop thinking about your cancer. Instead of always focusing on cancer, consider some alternatives that have worked for me. When laughing, I'm not thinking about my cancer. When engaged in a lively conversation with a friend, I'm not focused on my cancer. When hugging my wife, I am not consumed with my cancer. Cancer might take away your future, but you can make sure that it doesn't rob you of the joy in the present.

Courage and Cancer

It is hard for me to feel courageous in this cancer battle. Given the situation, I am just trying to do the best I can. Books about American history have often included stories of courage, and reading about the Civil War and World War II has always fascinated me. It has also often caused me to wonder what it takes to be a soldier on the front lines of a battle knowing that your life could end at any moment. What was going through the minds of those young boys who stormed the beaches on D-Day or at Iwo Jima? What was it like for the soldiers during the final day's conflict known as Pickett's Charge at the pivotal Civil War battle of Gettysburg? My suspicion is that when someone is faced with a potentially imminent death situation, that person doesn't think but simply reacts as the adrenaline kicks in. My death is not imminent, so there is ample time to think about it, but it's not clear to me which situation is better. On some days, the "frontlines" adrenaline approach seems like it would be the best way to go. As for the courage required to battle cancer, it is measured by getting up every day and putting one foot in front of the other. It does not feel heroic; it is simply my life at this moment.

Moral Authority

Some cancer patients appear to claim a level of moral authority that permits them to judge the behavior of others. Perhaps they think their terrible disease gives them this divine right because they believe that from great suffering comes insight and wisdom. A human trait that has always been repugnant to me is arrogance. Exercising moral superiority over others or judging their behaviors is the height of arrogance. I have gained some wisdom since my cancer, but it has primarily had to do with learning more about myself, a full-time job in and of itself, and not about judging others.

One day while making an appointment to see my pulmonologist, there was a woman in the waiting room, perhaps in her 60s, who was wheezing and gasping for air. Every breath seemed to be a great struggle. She was talking to her respiratory therapist in a tone of voice that made it impossible not to hear the conversation if you were in the waiting room. She was apparently a heavy smoker, and despite her respiratory problems, she did not want to give up smoking. She asked the therapist if it was permissible to smoke at night right before going to sleep because she heard that the effects on her body would be less harmful. Perhaps she found that absurd information in one of those grocery store tabloids, right next to the story that someone's baby was fathered by an alien from space. She asked if it would benefit her health if she could cut back to one pack of cigarettes per day. She kept pressing the smoking issue until finally the respiratory therapist said, "With your breathing difficulties you should not smoke at all, period. You need to talk to the doctor if you feel you cannot quit."

It seemed surreal to be listening to this conversation, knowing I was the one with lung cancer even though I had never smoked. If there was ever a time for me to feel morally superior and justifiably outraged toward anyone, it was now. And to be honest, for a time those old judgmental feelings returned, but on my arrival back home and giving more thought to this scene, my sense of moral superiority subsided. As I kept thinking about this woman, I could not help but feel compassion for someone engaged in such a struggle with such an obviously severe addiction. Although she had clearly made and was still making some bad choices, it was not my place to judge her any more than judging other cancer patients if I disagreed with their treatment decisions or if I viewed them as not fighting the disease sufficiently. For many years now, this strong sense of moral righteousness has been pervasive among Americans, and it seems to have intensified in recent years, but it leads to intolerance and lack of compassion toward others. This is not the sign of a healthy society.

Humility

Part of my previous judgmental attitude toward others stemmed from thinking that some people did not live up to my standards or expectations. Even though I despise arrogance, it was now clear to me that I have practiced it myself. Cancer is a humbling experience. It strips away the illusion of our own invincibility. It robs us of our vanity. With cancer, you stop worrying about your foolish pride and ask for help. It is this uncertainty that accompanies cancer that should make you humble; it's another lesson that cancer teaches. I have been more sincere and honest in my interpersonal interactions without worrying about my reputation or if someone likes me. Cancer has given me a more pressing issue to contemplate.

The Meaning of Cancer

In his NPR blog, when Leroy Sievers asked people to finish this sentence, "My cancer . . . ," he was flooded with responses. Here are some that I found compelling.

- My cancer reminds me that no one is permanent and I will not be the exception to this.
- My cancer has made me more compassionate and more appreciative of the time I have left.
- My cancer has helped me realize what is truly important.
- My cancer makes me try harder.
- My cancer made me stop taking myself so seriously.
- My cancer introduced me to a whole new world, where complete strangers truly care for each other.
- My cancer stopped the life I was living in its tracks.
- My cancer has taught me valuable lessons about living, loving, and dealing with things, all of which I would have been happy to have learned from a book instead.
- My cancer today is only a small part of my identity.
- My cancer taught me to recognize parts of myself that I had denied.
- My cancer grounded me in reality; made me more empathetic and compassionate for the suffering of others.
- My cancer taught me that I was stronger than I ever knew.
- My cancer made me take a new look at life, my family and friends, the sunshine, a snowfall, a flower in my garden.
- My cancer has given me FREEDOM I never had.
- My cancer made me so aware.

Some of these statements are more compelling for me than others, but there is a wisdom in all of these blog postings that anyone with cancer understands.

What If?

I have always liked to play historical "what if" games. What if Abraham Lincoln had not been assassinated in 1865? Would reconstruction and reconciliation with the South have been better? What would race relations be like today? What if Robert Kennedy had lived and won the presidency in 1968? Would he have been the great reformer and champion for civil rights that many of us thought? With cancer, you can play a lot of "what if" mind games. What if I had gone to the Mayo Clinic for my treatment? What if I had never agreed to be interim college dean and instead reduced the stress in my work life? What if I had been a lifelong vegetarian? Although interesting diversions, these what if games tend to stimulate regret and an unhealthy obsession with the past. It is more helpful for me to focus on today and on how to spend each day as my cancer battle continues. What if I could be successful in making that my focus?

Continuing to Fight a Losing Battle

Cancer is relentless. It works 24/7 and never takes a vacation. Talk about a workaholic! One of my new habits is to constantly poke and prod my chest to see if I can feel any new tumors. Hopefully this action does not stir up my cancer cells into more feverish activity. I like to visualize my T-cells rushing into battle with *Star Trek* phasers and blasting the cancer cells to smithereens based on the assumption that my T-cells have turned their phasers from "stun" to "kill." Or I think about the old familiar video game and imagine my T-cells as a hungry Pac Man gobbling up my cancer cells. Leroy Sievers talked about the old western movies where the cowboy or soldier would invariably say as they were awaiting another attack, "It's too quiet. I don't like it." And sure enough, the next scene would have an arrow piercing the heart of that soldier. My cancer works in a quiet manner. It does not cause any physical pain, and the only rumblings to be heard are from my stomach telling me it is time to eat. My MRI and CT scans are the advance scouts that tell me where the enemy is presently located and how large a force it has. This lets me know what the odds are for winning this conflict. If it looks like a losing battle, I think about heroic figures like Spartacus, William Wallace, and Davy Crockett fighting an insurmountable foe. It just occurred to me that it might be better to think of some other role models since all of these heroic figures just mentioned died! It has never been my aspiration to be a heroic figure; I would be content just to go on living.

Loss of Innocence

One of my favorite musicians is Don Henley. He was one of the founding members of the band the Eagles, and he has had a successful solo career. One of my favorite Henley songs is *The End of the Innocence*,* especially this verse:

Remember when the days were long
And rolled beneath a deep blue sky
Didn't have a care in the world
With mommy and daddy standin' by
But happily ever after fails
And we've been poisoned by these fairy tales
The lawyers dwell on small details
Since daddy had to fly
But I know a place where we can go
That's still untouched by men
We'll sit and watch the clouds roll by
And the tall grass wave in the wind
You can lay your head back on the ground
And let your hair fall all around me
Offer up your best defense
But this is the end
This is the end of the innocence.

Cancer is a thief by robbing you of your innocence. I innocently thought my future included a long and healthy retirement. I innocently planned my future research and writing projects to work on during the remaining years of my career. I innocently pondered growing old with Sheri and seeing our daughters mature and thrive. My innocence is gone. Cancer has stripped that away with its brain and body scans, radiation, and poisons dripping into my body. Apparently it was time for me to grow up. And yet I still want to find the place Henley describes with the tall grass and the clouds overhead; I still want a measure of peace and serenity. We yearn for what we don't have or can't have, but that doesn't stop us. It reminds us that we are human.

Second Chances

It seems strange that a terminal illness can provide you with a second chance, but that is exactly what cancer has given me. Being self-absorbed is a common affliction affecting many of us in the late 20th and early 21st centuries. Like many people, I have been excessively preoccupied with my career and other adult responsibilities, and in doing so, allowed some long-term friendships to slip away. Cancer has reunited me with some old friends that I had lost touch with over the past several years. Old friends are the ones who really know you best because we were all going through new experiences in our young lives together. These friendships are primarily formed during the high school and college years, but also during the transition from adolescence to young adulthood. Although I have made some good friends in my adult years, I tend to be more hesitant to make the necessary effort. Making friends as an adult often seems largely about putting on a façade so that we don't offend the other or in an effort to maintain a certain image. For me, it has been far more difficult to bring to later life friendships the same honesty, intensity, and curiosity that were part of my high school and college relationships. Specifically, three old friends who have now reentered my life and enriched it by their loving connections are Jack Bortz, Steve Kern, and Michael Runner. Better late than never.

Jack Bortz and I shared a common love of music, sports, and an iconoclastic perspective on society. We became good friends in our last year of high school and early college years. There are many vivid memories of sitting for hours in Jack's bedroom at his parents' house listening to the musical icons of the 1960s: Joni Mitchell, the Beatles, Led Zeppelin, the Doors, Neil Young, and many others. Jack had the most extensive album collection of any of my friends, and his stereo system was top-notch. Jack, Bruce Javenkoski, and I would talk for hours about adolescent issues and our dreams as we listened to our favorite

Craig demonstrating his newfound desire to hug people as he greets his old friend Jack Bortz.

music. Despite the closeness of our friendship, Jack and I would gradually fall out of touch as we progressed through college and our careers. The last time we met was in April of 1987. Sheri and I went to New York City for a conference where I was presenting a paper with some of my colleagues from the University of New Hampshire. This was the beginning of my career in special education, and Jack and his wife, Lisa, were wonderful hosts for our 2 days in New York City. Walking with them through Central Park is an especially vivid memory.

By the following summer, I had accepted a new faculty position at the University of Wisconsin-Oshkosh. Sheri and I invited Jack and Lisa up to our house in New Hampshire for a weekend before we left for Wisconsin. We were looking forward to their visit, buying lots of food, and making plans concerning the places we wanted to show them. On the Saturday when Jack and Lisa were supposed to arrive, we got a late morning call. Jack had overslept, so he and Lisa decided not to come to New Hampshire for the weekend. After hanging up the phone, I fumed to Sheri that they were not coming and added that "This is typical irresponsible Bortz behavior." Did I mention that I could be judgmental? That was the last time I had any correspondence with Jack until he heard about my lung cancer and sent me an e-mail in September of 2008. I held a grudge against Jack for his social slight that lasted over 21 years. What a waste! After being diagnosed with cancer, I have gained a new appreciation of how precious life is and how important are your family and friends. I am grateful that Jack reached out to me, and for our regular e-mail correspondence since then. My hope is to see him while my health holds out.

Steve Kern is another high school and college friend and one of the most unforgettable characters you could ever meet. His pranks and wild sense of humor are legendary among the group we hung around with in those years. In the mid-to-late 1970s, we often went to football games at the University of Wisconsin, even though Wisconsin always had terrible teams. After the game, lots of students went to Union South to party with a polka band. The party atmosphere did not really depend upon whether the Wisconsin Badgers won the football game or not. There was always alcohol to help bolster everyone's spirits. During a break by the polka band, Steve would often commandeer the microphone and lead the assembled throng in a stirring rendition of the Eddy Arnold classic, "Cattle Call." Steve had a gift in his ability to make people laugh.

Steve eventually ended up in Seattle and has been working for a company that makes electronic systems for the aerospace industry. Over the past 2 decades I had periodic contact with Steve, and in the mid-1990s Sheri and I visited him in Seattle when I was presenting at a conference there. As is often the case with old friends, we picked up our relationship as if we had been seeing each other every day for the past 20 years, but since then there has been very little contact with Steve. He heard about my lung cancer through the grapevine, and after a few months of being in denial about my condition and not knowing what to say to me, he sent a warm and heartfelt e-mail in September. It was welcome medicine to me.

My third reunited old friend is Michael Runner. He was my closest friend during those early law school days at Drake University. We both transferred from Drake and finished our law degrees at the Universities of Wisconsin and Kentucky, respectively. Michael graduated from Kentucky a semester before me, and he landed a legal services job with Appalachian Research and Defense Fund of Kentucky (ARDF) in Barbourville. Michael wrote to encourage me to apply for some attorney positions at his legal services office. And so my career began in August of 1977 as a legal services attorney in southeastern Kentucky. Michael and I lived together during my first year in Kentucky, but as with my other old friends, we lost touch with each other several years ago. In February, Sheri called Michael to tell him about my lung cancer, and then he asked to speak to me and we talked. We have spoken several times since then, and Sheri and I started planning a trip to San Francisco where Michael now lives. After that first trip, Sheri and I visited Michael on two more occasions. Having these old friends back in my life was like stepping into an old pair of favorite slippers. It feels so naturally comfortable.

Craig's friend from law school and his colleague during the Appalachian experience, Michael Runner.

My Legacy

How do I want to be remembered by family and friends? As people approach their death, this question probably runs through everyone's mind, and lately I have given it a lot of thought. A few months ago there was a poignant article in the bulletin published by the American Association for Retired Persons (AARP). (Does it show how much I have aged to note that I have gone from subscribing to *Rolling Stone* magazine to being a member of AARP?) The author of the article was a woman who was watching her father die from a terminal illness. As she visited him in the hospital at the very end of his life, he whispered in her ear, "Please don't forget me." That's my greatest fear in facing my own death—that I will be forgotten. Like the dinosaurs, all traces of my existence and my footprints in life will disappear except for my journal articles and books, sitting like fossils on library shelves, waiting to be discovered.

It is a natural human psychological need to feel our life meant something, that we made a difference in the lives of others. In my profession, I was driven to be successful as measured by the typical higher education standards: good student evaluations of my teaching, numerous professional publications and presentations, productive community involvement, and leadership activities. Even though my entire 23-year higher education career was spent at universities that were not top-tier research institutions, I was proud of my scholarship record that included five books and numerous professional journal articles and research grants. The purpose for being engaged in those activities was not for any fame and certainly not for fortune (my books are not bestsellers), but for personal satisfaction. Much of my writing was focused on providing pragmatic strategies and resources for family members, friends, educators and others who want to be an effective advocate for a person with a disability. I will not be remembered for any seminal, groundbreaking research in my publications, but that is fine with me.

In terms of my professional legacy, I received a letter from a former colleague who had just learned of my cancer. She honored me with this wonderful gift when she wrote:

> I want you to know how much you've impacted my professional and personal journey. . . . I have multiple memories of your influence . . . your encouragement to stretch myself and grow the early childhood program, your support in connecting with other professionals on campus, . . . your sporadic stops into my office down at the end of the hall to check in with me and ask how things were going. My mom once told me that our first experiences in a new career or challenge are the most memorable. I think she was right. I have many memories of you as my mentor and department chair, making me feel that my work was valued and important to the future. Your commitment to professionalism and advocacy has stayed with me. I thank you for all that you did to assist in my launching.

She is too kind in her praise, but I will gladly accept her words as a description of what may be viewed as part of my professional legacy.

In terms of my legacy for family and friends, in a recent e-mail from my reunited friend, Jack Bortz, he shared a story that our mutual friend, Steve Kern, told him about my last trip to Seattle to visit him. Sheri and I had taken a ferry ride across Puget Sound to one of the islands with Steve and one of his friends. On the ride back, I was acting juvenile and silly and began chasing Steve around the deck of the ferry, for no particular reason I might add. Apparently Steve told Jack: "Envision two grown men, one a leader in his field (I guess he meant me), chasing the other around a crowded ferry boat . . . Well, his national reputation (another exaggeration) hadn't changed him much." Jack wrote, "Craig, I would want that as my epitaph." I'll take remembrances like that from family and friends. Ultimately, it is my fervent hope that people who know me can every so often think of some interaction they had with me, however long ago, and that memory can bring a broad smile across their face. I can think of no better legacy.

Luxury of Reflection and Introspection

My professional work life was very busy and chaotic. Some days it felt like being on the proverbial treadmill, and I came home exhausted far too many nights. Life is busy and stressful for most of us, but that's why it is critical to take time for personal reflection, whether that is through meditation, visual imagery, or another spiritual practice. The gift of retirement for me is the additional time and luxury to read, write, reflect, and learn more about myself. There is no more rushing out to teach a class or go to a meeting. I can sit and stare out at the backyard for as long as I like, or at least until the neighbors call the police. I read somewhere that you never truly know yourself until you are faced with a crisis. My personal Waterloo was instigated by my cancer diagnosis on January 28, 2008. What has been my response? What have I learned about myself?

Most surprisingly, I've responded with more peace and calm than I would have predicted. That is certainly a testament to the love from Sheri, my daughters, extended family, and friends. Yet, I also realize that my relative calm could all come crashing down around me with the results of the next MRI or CT scan. One of the most important lessons learned is that my life has been even better than I had thought a year ago. It has been my privilege to work in a profession that I loved, and to have great colleagues and students to work with. Another important lesson is learning that I am not as bad a person as I thought I was on some days, and conversely, that I am not as good a person as I had believed on other days. The truth usually falls somewhere in between.

Time Passes Quickly

Since my cancer diagnosis, I have noticed that when you are told that your life is now limited and time is short, the time seems to fly past even faster. I may be reading on the couch and think that 20 minutes has passed only to discover that 2 hours have gone by. A nap that was supposed to take half an hour turns into a 3-hour slumber. It feels like vacation time, which always seems to go faster than time spent at work. As a university administrator spending an inordinate amount of my workday in meetings, the minutes and hours seemed to crawl by or at times to stand still completely. I believe that formal work meetings prove there is a Supreme Being because they are God's way of telling us we have been too productive and we need to slow down and not be so work oriented. If I were ever to return to a university administrator's role, I would ban all formal meetings in favor of informal, ad hoc gatherings of people where actual problem solving could take place rather than the pontificating and subtle or blatant advocacy for hidden agendas that predominate most university formal meetings in my experience.

New Normal

The tragic events of September 11, 2001, created a "new normal" in this country that included the constant fear of terrorism. Think of all the changes in our lives since 9/11. Airline travel is a radically different and much less pleasant experience. A new federal department was created, the Department of Homeland Security, as billions of taxpayer dollars are spent in waging this war on terrorism. The federal government created a new color-coded threat warning that goes to more or less heightened alert every day. My body is also usually on heightened alert these days. This state has become a new normal in the struggle with my own Osama Bin Laden. Cancer is a terrorist. It strikes and kills innocent people all the time. Lots of people argue that the United States is losing its battle against terror. Lots of medical research suggests that my battle against cancer is hopeless. Even though it may be too early to tell what the final outcome will be for Uncle Sam, I am very confident that our nation will prevail, and my hope for myself is grounded in my desire to defy these predictions and prevail in my battle against terror.

Maintaining Hope

Never underestimate the importance of hope. I really believe that hope offers me the best chance for a recovery, or at least outliving the survival statistics. Hope determines your daily attitude and disposition, and that impacts your immune system. During my BC life, my approach was typically to see the glass as perpetually half empty. Perhaps this pessimism was a primary defense mechanism for me, because if life does not go your way, you have the satisfaction of saying, "I told you so." On the other hand, if something good happens to you, it is unexpected, and that makes the experience even more of a joyous occasion. My pessimistic attitude was why so many friends accused me of being like Eeyore in Winnie the Pooh books. Today, much of my hope springs from my competitive nature. Cancer has picked a fight with me, and for once I want to fight back against this bully, one of several metaphors that I have used to describe my opponent. My hope is to beat cancer into submission, or in this case, remission.

In high school, there were not many people, either teachers or friends, who would have predicted that I would become a lawyer, earn a PhD, and teach at the university level; and for me it has been an immensely satisfying experience to become an exception, one of the statistical outliers. For that reason, survival statistics and negative odds have now become another challenge to me, and it is my goal to prove that those statistics, and especially this bully called cancer, have greatly underestimated me. No matter what the outcome, I will be fighting back for as long as there is breath left in my body.

Loss of Independence

As a parent of a child with a severe disability, I often wondered what life was like for Jennifer. What is it like to be dependent upon another person to feed you? To change a dirty diaper? To transport you from one room to another room in the house? In an introductory special education course required of all education majors, I conducted a number of disability simulations. The students had to watch a TV program with the sound turned off and report on their experience; they also were asked to write a paragraph using their nondominant hand. In another lesson, I taught students how to read from a script that contained fake symbols representing each letter of the alphabet. These simulations were designed to spark these able-bodied individuals into thinking about what losing their independence might be like.

As I write this, my 88-year-old father still drives his own car, even though he is blind in one eye. Although worried about his driving, I resist advising him to give up his driver's license because, like most Americans, the automobile is his ultimate symbol of independence. Before taking this independence away from him, I would need some evidence that my father has become a hazard to himself or others on the road.

In my case, cancer threatens my independence. In my daily life I have become much more dependent upon Sheri's assistance. We recently reviewed our long-term health care insurance policy to find out what services are covered in case I require a higher level of assistance in the coming months. Losing your independence is frightening and a constant reminder that your life is waning. Yet experiencing this loss represents the full circle of life. We come into this world in a dependent condition and many of us leave this world in a similar state. Even so, recognizing this symmetry of life does not make me any more comfortable with the inevitable loss of my independence.

Need for Patience

Anybody who knows me realizes that patience is not a characteristic that has defined my personality. I was notoriously impatient at work, at home, and even at play, and this has been a lifelong trait. As a child, I remember sitting at the kitchen table trying to assemble a model airplane with my father helping me. I would get so impatient at this process that I would sometimes stomp out of the room. One of my greatest frustrations of working at a university is the glacial pace of decision making and change. University faculty members prefer talking and philosophizing as opposed to taking action. Perhaps experiencing this at work has made me even more impatient with my family and friends. Unfortunately, my daughter Lindsay seems to share this trait with me. Perhaps by reading this book and my reflections, she will realize more deeply (and sooner) than her father managed to do that life requires great patience.

Cancer requires great patience as well. I want total remission of my cancer and I want it to happen right now! However, cancer has its own agenda, and it is extremely patient as it systematically engages in destruction. Meanwhile, the pace of cancer research seems to be agonizingly slow. There are studies upon studies before any new treatments or drugs are approved. As a researcher, I understand this process and why it is necessary to have these scientific safeguards, but what a cancer patient hears is the clock ticking, and it is hard not to be impatient.

Moving Past Fear

Fear can be paralyzing and demoralizing. Religion for many people offers relief from fear as they think about death. My barber happens to be a recovering alcoholic and a born-again Christian, and he is certain that when he dies he will be going to a better place. Such beliefs provide him with tremendous comfort. In many ways, I envy him because I am not as certain about eternal life. Since most human beings love life, we fear death. My fear of death also includes the pain that may precede my death. When my fears become too overwhelming, I try to think of those old Buck Rogers space adventures and imagine death as a great adventure, rocketing me into space, and following the advice of Star Trek's Captain Kirk by "boldly going where no person has gone before."

My friend Kent Koppelman is a great collector of quotations, and he shared some with me that reflected on death and dying. As an empirical scientist, Francis Bacon (1985) compared the two significant human experiences of birth and death:

"It is as natural to die as to be born, and to a little infant, perhaps, the one is as painful as the other." Georges Simenon (1984) provided a completely different perspective: "I adore life but I don't fear death. I just prefer to die as late as possible." Finally, Woody Allen (1988) has had a lot to say on the topic of death, including: "I'm not afraid to die. I just don't want to be there when it happens." Reading such thoughts remind me that we all share the same fate and the same fears, but succumbing to fear is not the best way to meet that fate.

Living Life to the Fullest

Everyone in my situation is advised to spend however much time you have left by living life to the fullest. Living with a terminal illness is like being given a consumer product code that says, "Best if used by . . ." with a stamped expiration date. Despite my predicted expiration date, I want to stay as fresh as possible for as long as possible. But how are we supposed to live life to the fullest? That becomes an individual and personal issue. This is what it means to me: not taking loved ones or friends for granted, breathing deeply, reading about and contemplating complex and important issues of the day, sitting around doing nothing, watching a baseball game, traveling to a new place, walking in the woods, hugging family members and friends, watching my dog play in the backyard, drinking a piña colada, writing, appreciating the change of seasons, smelling a campfire, and much more. From my perspective, the way to live your life to the fullest may not necessarily require living your life differently from what you have done before, but it is primarily about being more engaged and alert to your everyday existence. It is about making no assumptions of the future. It is about living in a particular moment.

My Funeral

I know some people who have obsessed about their own funeral to the point they have scripted it out. Although not wanting to dwell to such a degree on my funeral, I provided Sheri and some close friends with a general outline of how to conduct my funeral. For me, it would be hypocritical to have an overly religious ceremony. Instead, I only want four things: (a) three songs from the '60s/early '70s to be played, (b) a few selected people to make some comments in my memory without gilding the lily, (c) an open-mike time to allow anyone to say whatever they want, and (d) a celebration of life where people feel free to laugh and enjoy themselves.

The first song is "You Can't Always Get What You Want" by the Rolling Stones. The most poignant part of the lyrics for me is when they say that even when you can't get what you want, just by trying you may end up getting "what you need." Getting what you need rather than what you want is a thought that appeals to me.

Craig with his wife Sheri and daughter Lindsay a few months before he died.

The second song is Bob Dylan's "Knockin' on Heaven's Door." The first verse is the most compelling one for me. The speaker is a sheriff or a police officer, someone in a position of power and authority, and in the first verse he says to take his badge away because as death approaches such symbols from our daily lives are no longer meaningful. And as it says in this verse of the song, when my life is ending and it begins to get dark, "too dark to see," it is also my hope to perhaps find myself at the threshold of an afterlife, knocking on heaven's door.

Although it was made popular by the band Blood, Sweat and Tears, Laura Nyro wrote the third song to be played at my funeral: "And When I Die." I take some comfort in the song's refrain that reminds all of us that when we die, there is a child being born out there somewhere "to carry on" with this great gift that we call a human life. Once my life has run its course, there is one last thing that I want. I must rely on others to satisfy this final request. I hope my family and friends will continue to carry a loving memory of me, and of what we've meant to each other. If this is the only kind of afterlife we are granted, then that would be enough for me.

References

Bacon, F. (1985). Of discourse. In J. Pitcher (Ed.), *The essays*. London: Penguin Books.

Sievers, L. My Cancer (now Our Cancer) www.npr.org/blogs/mycancer (Since LeRoy Siever's death Laurie Singer has taken over this blog).

Simenon, G. (1984). *Intimate memoirs.* (H. J. Salemson, Trans.) San Diego, CA: Harcourt Brace Jovanovich.

Woody, A. (1988). Quotation found in R. Byne (Ed.), *Best things anybody ever said* (p. 12). New York: Fawcett Columbine.

EPILOGUE
Remembering Craig

Craig Fiedler died on Sunday, January 4, 2009.

There are few sentences that can afflict me with more profound sorrow than this one. It hardly seems possible that Craig's death occurred less than a year after his cancer diagnosis. His AD life was supposed to last longer than that. As soon as my wife and I heard that the surgery to remove the cancer had failed, we made immediate plans to drive across the state to see him. Sheri and Lindsay stood near his bed as we entered his hospital room. After greeting them, Jan walked over and kissed Craig while I stood dumbfounded at the sight of my friend, still looking healthy despite the seeds of death scattered inside his body. Perhaps guessing my thoughts, Craig looked up at the ceiling and, as if speaking to unseen spirits in the room, he cried out, "I don't want to die." The anguished tone of his voice struck me like a hammer, and tears filled my eyes. I felt a compulsion to do something and yet there was nothing to be done.

My first encounter with Craig occurred when he was the coordinator for the Citizen Advocacy program in La Crosse, Wisconsin. He made a good first impression because of his lively intellect and his obvious commitment to people who had disabilities, but it didn't take long before I was enjoying his sense of humor as well. He would quickly perceive the absurdity in a situation and portray it in a way that made you laugh; you couldn't help yourself. He also loved to tease people, but he laughed at himself just as easily, and much of his humor was self-deprecating. Yet behind the joking and teasing was a passion to right wrongs, to defend the underdog, to take on the powerful bullies who had an unfair advantage and used it against their victims. It did not surprise me when he left La Crosse to pursue a doctorate in special education at the University of Kansas, but I assured him that our friendship would continue.

The Craig that Jan and I came to know well in what he has called his BC years was not a perfect human being, and he would have been the first to admit it, but you had to admire his tireless efforts in teaching and writing about disability. He frequently taught additional classes at night and during the summer, and he

The BC version of Professor Craig Fiedler, PhD, JD.

conducted weekend workshops to give parents the knowledge and tools to use in advocating for their children. And later he took on thankless administrative positions when few other faculty members were willing to do these jobs. Because of his commitment and activities, he set high standards for his colleagues, his students, even his daughter, and his humor at times would take on a bitter tone when they fell short of his expectations. Was he judgmental? Yes, but it was judgment based on idealism and disappointment, not stemming from any sense of moral superiority or arrogance, and he never stopped trying to encourage people, including his daughter, to use their abilities to the fullest.

After Craig's diagnosis, his AD life forced him to change, and my perceptions of that are consistent with what he described in his book. He was clinging to the essential part of his personality while jettisoning the parts that he viewed as unnecessary baggage. At the awards ceremony adding him to the Hall of Excellence at La Crosse Central High School, he described how important his wife Sheri was in his life, and that she deserved some of the credit for his

The AD version of Craig Fiedler as he enjoys being near the ocean.

achievements. He also praised his daughter Lindsay for being a good, decent human being, and he said he was proud of her. His standards were still high, but the measuring stick was now focused on the ability to love and forgive.

Jan and I made frequent trips to the Fiedler home and to their cabin, and traveled with them to San Francisco and Cooperstown. On Labor Day weekend of 2008, we visited them at the cabin, and I shared the news about my recent invitation to be the Academic Director for the coming spring semester at a study abroad program near Edinburgh, Scotland. In my enthusiasm, I only heard Craig's verbal congratulations, but later that night, Jan told me there were tears in his eyes as I was talking. She said, "He doesn't think he will live until we get back." My initial response was shame at having been so insensitive to his emotional response, but then shame turned to anger—not at him but at the thought that he might die in a few months rather than a few years from now. If he thought that, he had to be wrong; he had to have more time left than that.

Craig and Sheri were intending to leave for Arizona well before Christmas, and Jan and I planned to spend Christmas and New Years in San Diego, then rent a car and drive to their home south of Tucson. A few days before leaving for

California, I called Craig to see how he was feeling. After we talked for a few minutes, he stunned me when he said, "Well, it's no longer an abstraction." We both knew that "it" meant death. Yet he still sounded clear and coherent, and I could not believe that his death was imminent. I was wrong. On New Years Eve, Sheri called to say that Craig was fading fast, and when she put him on the phone, the effort it took to breathe did not allow him to talk. I told Sheri that Jan and I would leave as soon as possible. We arrived the next afternoon.

By the time we arrived, Sheri had called the local hospice and they had set up a hospital bed in the living room. Craig could not walk or talk and could barely eat. He spent most of his energy just breathing. Lindsay was there with Colin, her boyfriend, and all five of us took turns talking to Craig while holding his hand or stroking his head. Since Craig had brought some books he had not finished, Sheri suggested that I read to him. While I was reading or just talking to Craig, he would be alert at times, but then his eyes would seem to glaze over. And of course, he slept a lot.

The weather had been beautiful, so on the third afternoon I encouraged everyone to get out of the house, get some fresh air and enjoy the sunshine while I stayed with Craig. After they left, I read aloud for about half an hour even though Craig's eyes were closed; then he suddenly opened his eyes and looked at me directly in a way that suggested a conscious and coherent state of mind. I set the book down and talked about how much our friendship meant to me over the years. Although neither of us was religious, I shared my belief that some part of us survives death, even though I couldn't say exactly what it was or how it happened. I don't know if my words were comforting or not because he still had no strength to respond. Eventually he shut his eyes and slept.

As we left that night, Jan worried that Craig would not last much longer, and in the morning, Sheri called to say that Craig had died during the night. Jan and I came to see him one last time before his body was taken away to be cremated. There is no more helpless feeling than standing over the body of a loved one who has died. You touch and stroke and hold a hand but there is no life left to animate that cold flesh. When the man from the funeral home came, he was careful and efficient, but it felt like a horrible mistake to see him cover Craig's body in a sheet. The man asked Sheri if she wanted his face covered, and irrationally I thought of Craig's claustrophobia and hoped she would not do this. Sheri said to leave his face uncovered. In a few minutes, the vehicle pulled away and it was over. The next task was to prepare for a Memorial Service in Wisconsin based on Craig's instructions for his funeral.

Craig had asked that his family and friends share humorous stories during this Memorial Service, but that was difficult to do. No one felt like laughing until an event occurred that could have been interpreted as Craig's spirit trying to provoke some laughter to remind us all that this was what he wanted. John Shaw opened the service, and then we listened to the Rolling Stones singing, "You Can't Always Get What You Want." After the song, John shared some of his memories about Craig before asking that the second song be played—Bob Dylan's "Knockin' on Heaven's Door." The funeral home director pressed "play" and we heard Mick Jagger's voice once again singing "You Can't Always Get What You Want." People at the service began to chuckle, and the solemnity was momentarily shattered. Even so, the sense of loss was so great that few of us could muster a lighter tone. Craig's sister Candy made an attempt during her speech when she said, "Craig is my kid brother. Growing up, he was my playmate and ally, a pest and a nuisance, a partner in crime and a tattletale. In other words, a pretty typical little brother. But even then there was a compassion for the underdog, a gentleness not common to most boys."

When Bruce Javenkoski stood up to speak, he came closer to satisfying Craig's request for humor than anyone else as he shared stories from their childhood and adolescence, including the following example:

> In ninth grade biology, Mr. Lindner assigned a very sophisticated project. We were to assemble an insect collection. So, it involved group work, blended theory and lab experience, and was an active project. In many ways it was an assignment way ahead of its day. Well, the deadline was fast approaching and Craig's collection consisted of one mangled butterfly he had found on the grill of his parent's Buick Skylark. In the genius born from desperation, Craig dug around his closet and found his old Creepy Crawler set. Yes, he manufactured fake bugs. He even conned some other kids into trading him real bugs for some Creepy Crawlers.

The poet Wordsworth (1936) said, "The child is father to the man," and that was true for Craig. He kept this youthful spirit and irreverent sense of humor in his adult life, and this was what I wanted to say at the Memorial Service by introducing my comments with the lines from the great Irish poet W. B. Yeats (2002, p. 69):

> I see a schoolboy when I think of him,
> With face and nose pressed to a sweet-shop window,
> For certainly he sank into his grave
> His senses and his heart unsatisfied.

> Even when Craig began to get gray hair and had back problems and suffered other burdens associated with aging, he always seemed young to me. I think it was because of his ever-youthful sense of humor, and the boyish grin that accompanied his humorous comments, and the love for life that beamed out of every pore of his body. You saw that schoolboy in him when he talked of sports, especially the White Sox, or showed you his classic collection of statues of some of the great baseball players. So even though he was 56 years old, he was still that schoolboy, face pressed to the window of the world, looking at all the sweet possibilities life has to offer that he had not yet tasted.

It was because Craig loved laughter and fun so much that he had specifically asked the people attending the service to remember those good times, but I'm afraid he would have been disappointed by the seriousness and sorrow of most of the remarks. For that reason, I was grateful to Bruce Javenkoski for being there, and for his willingness to share many humorous anecdotes from his experiences with Craig. It couldn't have been easy for him. My favorite story was the one about Craig moving to Kentucky after graduating from law school, because it demonstrated how a humorous story can capture someone's personality better than any of the serious comments made at this Memorial Service:

> Following law school, Craig decided to make the world a better place. He elected to join Mike Runner, his former law school buddy, in Barbourville, Kentucky, to work in a public legal aid office. So, we loaded up both of Craig's possessions in my car and with the cassette deck blasting, headed south. . . . We met Mike in Barbourville and had an adrenalin-filled reunion. Spirits ran high. Finally, exhaustion took its toll and we went to bed. However, Craig was Craig. I fell sound asleep but the young, legal, humanitarian took this opportunity to slowly, quietly, stealthily crawl into Mike's bedroom. When he got to the edge of Mike's bed, Craig jumped up and grabbed a totally asleep Mike Runner by the throat. Mike let out a piercing scream that vaulted me off the couch and I could see the neighbors' lights come on. Then Craig let loose with a sustained version of "the laugh." It was a loud, hearty "gotcha" kind of laugh. I hated that laugh! I believe, to this day, Mike still sleeps with a baseball bat clutched in his hands.

This story characterized much of Craig's life—being in Kentucky to pursue a serious purpose that he was passionate about, and yet never missing an opportunity to have some fun. Although humor was a major aspect of Craig's personality, my suspicion is that his family and friends are more likely to remember him for what he did for others, especially people with disabilities. He influenced many people directly with his teaching and his community service, and many more indirectly through his journal articles and books. Ultimately, he will be remembered for the quality of his relationships with a broad spectrum of people. Near the end of her remarks, Candy told a story that perhaps best illustrates this. She talked about her daughter Beth being diagnosed with special needs, and that it was ironic that Craig was her godfather: "His relationship with her was unique. . . . He was always kind, gentle, and respectful—never condescending. My daughter probably said it best when she told me, 'Uncle Craig understands me.'"

It is hard to let go of such a person. For all of us who knew Craig, there is less laughter in our lives and a sense of loss that lingers. Craig asked that we remember him, and that is easily done, almost too easy. I wish he had given us a harder task, something that would have required great effort to achieve, but in the achieving of it, we could have taken a sense of satisfaction in honoring his memory. And yet, he has given all of us who loved him a hard task that will last a lifetime. We have to live in the shadow of his absence, no longer nourished by his energy, his passion, his laughter, his love. That task is enough of a burden, but it is a burden of love.

Kent Koppelman
August 22, 2010

Beth and Katie, the daughters of Craig's sister, Candy.

Editor's Note

Craig's colleagues, friends, and family have used the donations received and a fundraiser to establish a scholarship fund in Craig's memory. The fund will provide support to those students majoring in Special Education since they will "carry on" the work to which Craig devoted his life. For those interested in contributing to this fund, please go to the UW-Oshkosh Web site: http://www.uwosh.edu/foundation/how-to-give/give-online.php

After indicating the amount of the gift, choose the College of Education and Human Services box and in the Gift Allocation Notes section type Dr. Craig Fiedler Special Education Fund # 8436.

Note: All dictionary definitions come from Merriam-Webster's online dictionary at www.merriam-webster.com

References

Armstrong, L., & Jenkins, S. (2000). *It's not about the bike: My journey back to life.* New York: Berkley Books.

Bobek, B. L. (2002). Teacher resilience: A key to career longevity. *The Clearing House, 75*(4), 202–205.

Cousins, N. (1981). *Anatomy of an illness as perceived by the patient.* New York: Bantam Books.

Cousins. N. (1989). *Head first: The biology of hope and the healing power of the human spirit.* New York: Penguin Books.

Fiedler, C. R., & Clark, D. (2009). *Making a difference: Advocacy competencies for special education professionals.* Austin, TX: Pro-Ed Publishing.

Fiedler, C. R., Simpson, R. L., & Clark, D. M. (2007). *Parents and families of children with disabilities: Effective school-based support services.* Upper Saddle River, NJ: Merrill/Prentice Hall.

Frahm, A. E., & Frahm, D. J. (1992). *A cancer battle plan: Six strategies for beating cancer, from a recovered "hopeless case."* New York: Penguin Putnam.

Halpern, S. P. (2004). *The etiquette of illness: What to say when you can't find the words.* New York: Bloomsburg.

Halpern, C. (2008). *Making waves and riding the currents: Activism and the practice of wisdom.* San Francisco, CA: Berrett-Koehler Publishers.

McKeith, G. (2005). *You are what you eat: The plan that will change your life.* New York: A Plume Book.

Pausch, R., & Zaslow, J. (2008). *The last lecture.* New York: Hyperion.

Servan-Schreiber, D. (2007). *Anticancer: A new way of life.* New York: Viking.

Siegel, B. S. (1986). *Love, medicine, and miracles.* New York: Harper.

Tolle, E. (1999). *The power of now: A guide to spiritual enlightenment.* Novato, CA: New World Library.

Tolle, E. (2005). *A new earth: Awakening to your life's purpose.* New York: Penguin.

Turnbull, A. P. (1988). Accepting the challenge of providing comprehensive support to families. *Education and Training in Mentally Retarded, 23*(4), 261-272.

Turnbull, A. P., & Turnbull, H. R. (1997). *Families, professionals, and exceptionality: A special partnership.* Upper Saddle River, NJ: Merrill/Prentice Hall.

Vanderhaeghe, L. R., & Bouic, P. J. D. (1999). *The immune system cure: Nature's way to super-powered health.* Upper Saddle River, NJ: Prentice-Hall

Wordsworth, W. (1936). My heart leaps up. In *Complete poetical works.* Oxford: Oxford University Press.

Yeats, W. B., (2002). Ego Dominus Tuus. In R. Finneran (Ed.), *The Yeats reader: A portable compendium of poetry, drama and prose* (p. 69). New York: Scribner Poetry.

Index